POLICY

FOR WASHINGTON STATE | 3rd Edition

Edited by Paul Guppy

POLICY GUIDE

FOR WASHINGTON STATE | 3rd Edition

Edited by Paul Guppy

Table of Contents

POLICY GUIDE

FOR WASHINGTON STATE | 3rd Edition

Foreword

by Daniel Mead Smith, President

"Every day in Olympia people come to my office and talk about their problems. But you (Washington Policy Center) come here and talk about solutions and a vision for moving Washington forward." That ringing endorsement from a legislator is the basis for this third edition of our *Policy Guide for Washington State*. It also tells us we are doing our job—offering lawmakers positive solutions to the policy challenges facing our state.

Washington Policy Center is a think tank, not a trade association or lobbying organization. We testify before committees when invited and work with legislators at their request. We do, however, measure the impact of our ideas. It is one thing to publish studies and hold events, and another to have our ideas and analysis influence the public debate.

We continue to increase our impact by opening new research centers, working with policymakers and reporters, opening a new office just two blocks from the state Capitol, and tracking our ideas that become official policy in our state.

Our mission is to improve the lives of our state's citizens through market-based solutions. That is what this new book offers in its ten comprehensive chapters and over 300 pages. We offer practical recommendations, for example, to improve our state's business climate, schools, environment and traffic congestion.

This book is a revised edition and is presented in the same format as our previous policy guide books. Our state continues to rank high in the wrong categories when it comes to education, congestion, taxes and our business climate. By adopting the policy recommendations that follow, state policymakers can make our state a better place for all citizens.

Our *Policy Guide for Washington State* offers innovative ideas, ranging from incremental to sweeping, for reforming and improving government performance. Each of the ten chapters is divided into a number of topical subsections for easy reference. Each subsection includes background on the issue, policy analysis and specific policy recommendations, as well as listing additional resources for further information on each issue.

I encourage you to contact us at (206) 937-9691 or wpc@washingtonpolicy.org with your comments, to order additional copies of this book, or any of our individual studies. These provide additional research and information on the issues presented here.

I also encourage you to use our legislative website, WashingtonVotes.org as a resource during the legislative session and also as you vote. This free website summarizes all legislation and allows users to search by issue, track legislation during the legislative session and keep track of how legislators vote on the issues, all in an easy to use, plain-English format.

To policymakers, we thank you for your service to our state and hope you will continue to find this guide a useful resource. To citizens, we encourage you to keep our recommendations in mind as policymakers address the major issues facing our state.

Our special thanks go to our supporters, their loyal support of our organization is greatly appreciated. I also want to recognize two private foundations that provided funding for our first two editions: M.J. Murdock Charitable Trust in Vancouver, Washington and The JM Foundation in New York. This book project, which started in 2004, would not have been a reality without their early support.

On behalf of our board of directors, advisory boards and staff (all of whom are listed at the end of the book), thank you for your interest in our work and improving lives through market solutions.

POLICY GUIDE

FOR WASHINGTON STATE | 3rd Edition

Five Principles of Responsible Government

by Paul Guppy
Vice President for Research, Washington Policy Center

Our democratic system is founded on the principle that people have certain fundamental rights, and that the purpose of government is to protect these rights, so people can live peacefully together within a system of ordered liberty.

The Washington constitution makes this point clearly in Article One, Section One:

> "All political power is inherent in the people, and governments derive their just powers from the consent of the governed, and are established to protect and maintain individual rights."

Government provides certain basic services that enable citizens to enjoy the benefits of modern society. To do its work of protecting citizens' rights and providing basic services, government requires tax revenue, rules, enforcement and all the bureaucratic apparatus of large regulatory agencies.

The problem of government

There is a persistent concern, however, that government itself poses a threat to people's rights. In Washington, this threat does not take the form of a direct assault, but occurs subtly, through the continuous expansion of state regulations and programs, and the incremental rise in taxes, restrictions and penalties that goes with it.

In its effort to upgrade public programs, or to expand their reach, government tends to impose increasing taxation and broader regulations that gradually erode basic freedoms.

This tendency is encouraged by a variety of special interests that benefit from rising government spending. These interests are always ready to argue for new taxes, larger budgets and expanded programs, while downplaying the higher cost and added constraints imposed on ordinary citizens.

Limiting the scope and power of government is not just about saving money; it is about protecting people's rights. Since most of the people employed by government and the interests that benefit from public spending have little incentive to restrain the reach of the state, this task falls to the people and their elected representatives.

The purpose of this Policy Guide is to help state and local elected officials preserve the people's freedom as they do the daily work of government. It is also designed to serve as a ready reference for citizens, so they can better understand public issues, and judge the laws and regulations government officials adopt in their name.

Five principles of responsible government

Washington Policy Center advocates five principles that should guide government officials in doing their work effectively, and in a way that respects the trust the public places in them. These ideas are not original to the Washington Policy Center; they are commonly cited as essential elements of good governing.

Here are short descriptions of these principles and why they are important to achieving effective and limited government in our state. They are in no particular order – in fact, they are interrelated; adhering to one makes it easier to implement the others.

1. Exercise budget discipline

It is in the nature of government to expand. Government has no competitors and cannot be put out of business, so it operates without the natural constraints that bring financial discipline to private organizations. Instead, policymakers are under constant pressure to channel public money to this or that cause, or toward advancing a particular group or special interest.

The gain from funding requests is usually specific and easily seen, while the cost is diffused and barely perceptible. Lawmakers usually find it easy to be generous with other people's money – especially when most people tend not to notice.

Lack of budget discipline causes governments to become overextended and unable to meet its commitments. This produces a pervading sense of financial crisis, joined with recurring calls for tax increases.

Adopting a protected reserve fund, setting expiration dates for tax increases, canceling failed programs and establishing clear funding priorities are some examples of how policymakers can make sure government lives within its means. The problem of bringing budget discipline to public spending is discussed in Chapter 1 of this book.

2. Focus on core functions

There will always be people who feel government needs to do more, regardless of the added cost to society. In addition, people in government, just like those in other parts of the economy, want to work in a growth sector, so they tend to benefit when government takes on more tasks.

That is why it is so important for policymakers to keep government focused on its core functions. Expending time and finite resources attempting to tackle new missions means that other public services suffer as a result. Government can only do so much, and public agencies are most effective when they strive for excellence by doing a few things well.

Another reason to focus on core functions is that many times government's efforts to help end up doing more harm than good. New laws and programs are launched with high enthusiasm and the best intentions, and often end up having unforeseen consequences that are worse than the original problem. A focus on core functions provides government with fewer opportunities to harm citizens and their interests.

A clear focus on core functions also enables policymakers to resist calls for ever higher levels of spending. Not trying to do too much allows agency managers to improve the quality of the services they provide, and it enhances the public's confidence in government's ability to act effectively and positively.

When public officials tap the benefits of competition, contracting out and performance audits, they keep government focused on core functions, to the benefit of taxpayers and the public interest.

3. Respect property as a basic civil right

Private property – meaning land, a home, a business, savings and investments, and intellectual and artistic creations – is the foundation of a free society. Property rights are civil rights that give citizens the means to defend all their other rights, whether from the encroachments of government or the incursions of other people.

Property gives people the means to pursue their dreams and live their lives the way they choose. Private property also provides people with the ability to help others, through their time and voluntary giving. When government takes property in the form of taxes, or reduces its value through regulation, it makes it harder for citizens to defend their rights, pursue their dreams or help others.

Most people gain their property through hard work, long hours, patience and careful planning. When government officials respect property, they respect the people who earn or create it.

Government must often tax and regulate the use of property in its various forms, but lawmakers should keep taxation and regulation to the minimum needed to carry out essential public functions. Sound policy recommendations, like those presented in this book, provide examples of how policymakers can keep the tax and regulatory burden at reasonable levels.

4. Use voluntary incentives, not coercion, whenever possible

Many people have strong views about what they think society should look like. They are often tempted to use the power of government in an effort to make their social vision a reality.

Proponents of social change should work in the marketplace of ideas to persuade others to share their vision and work towards it.

They should not use the power of government to force through their own ideas, but should seek to change policy, if that is needed, once reform is broadly supported by the public.

Similarly, policymakers should favor voluntary incentives to encourage positive change, so citizens do not feel they are the passive objects of social engineering imposed from above.

Washington lawmakers have enacted radical changes in the past, only to see them fail or be repealed once the temporary political conditions that made them possible have passed. In contrast, persuasion and voluntary action ensure that the reforms that are adopted will be popularly supported and enduring.

Public policy built on market incentives and individual choice avoids the problems created by involuntary, top-down dictates.

5. Resist political pressure from public sector unions

Public sector unions occupy a unique position within our governing system. They represent one part of government (public employees) which is organized to lobby another part of government (the legislature).

Employers and unions in the private sector operate under the unyielding discipline of the market. Union leaders know that if their demands cause the company to go under, everybody loses. Government, however, cannot go out of business. There is no natural limit to the demands that public union leaders can make on the treasury, especially since each expansion of government spending generally increases the amount of monthly dues paid to the union.

In the private sector, unions negotiate directly with the owners and managers of a company. If company stockholders are unhappy, they can take their investment elsewhere. In government, the "owners" are the taxpayers. They have no involvement in negotiating with public sector unions, and they also have no choice about paying for whatever conditions, salary or benefits the legislature has agreed to provide.

Public employees should receive fair compensation for the work they do, and it is in the public interest to attract hard working, talented people to public service. But government is about more than providing high paying jobs and generous benefits. If a government program or service no longer makes sense, policymakers who respect taxpayers should end it, and devote the savings to effective programs, or to reducing the tax burden on citizens.

Ten questions to ask about every new bill and regulation

It is difficult to know how to implement the principles of responsible government. A good place to start is with a practical and objective way of judging the thousands of new bills and regulations proposed every year. Following are ten questions lawmakers and citizens should ask when reviewing any new legislative proposal:

1. Will it expand or restrict people's freedom?
2. Does it respect people's work, property and earnings?
3. Does it serve the general good, or only advance a narrow interest?
4. Does it increase or reduce the tax burden government officials place on citizens?
5. Does it provide a needed service that the private sector cannot do better?
6. Does it duplicate something the government is already doing?
7. Does it create a policy or program that has failed in the past?
8. Is it ineffectual – a costly program with a nice sounding title but no chance of actually helping people?
9. Does it accomplish very little today in exchange for great cost tomorrow?
10. Will it automatically expire on a certain date if it does not work?

If the supporters of a new bill or regulation cannot provide satisfactory answers to these questions, it should not be adopted.

Conclusion

The purpose of government is to serve the people, not the other way around. The principles described here will produce government that serves the people of Washington. Government actions should be authorized in law, adequately funded and limited in scope.

The pages that follow present dozens of specific recommendations for carrying out the five principles of responsible government.

CHAPTER I

1. Structural Budget Reform

Recommendations

1. Adopt performance-based, Priorities of Government budgeting to slow the rate of spending growth and end the chronic sense of crisis in state finances.

2. Place performance outcomes directly into the budget.

3. Adopt a 72-hour budget timeout.

4. Require updated six-year budget forecasts be tied to quarterly revenue forecasts or adoption of new budgets.

5. Require completed fiscal notes before bills can be acted on.

6. Sell non-essential real estate holdings.

7. Begin a "base closing" process for state programs and agencies to determine which ones can be consolidated or eliminated.

Background

Washington's two-year general fund budget spends more today than at any point in state history, about $33 billion. Much of government spending growth is set on auto-pilot by entitlement policies. The total state budget every two years is over $61 billion when entitlements and federal grant funds are included.[1]

Failure to set clear priorities has created a structural deficit by locking in past spending, regardless of importance, while leaving more urgent needs unmet. This results from the legislature's habit of practicing reverse budgeting, in which routine government activities are funded first while high priority needs are left in fiscal crisis.

This occurred recently when legislators and the governor, despite facing a projected deficit, permanently increased spending in 2008 by $306 million. In 2005, the legislature and the governor enacted a permanent tax increase of $450 million. The sharp increase in spending only exacerbates the budget deficit and created permanent taxpayer obligations in the future.

Illustrating the unsustainable nature of these spending increases, despite an increase in forecasted revenue, the nonpartisan Senate Ways and Means Committee in April 2008 forecast a $2.5 billion deficit for 2009-11. Committee staff estimated the rapid rise in spending will cause the deficit to grow to $5.3 billion by the 2011-13 biennium.

Setting the stage for unnecessary tax increases

Although the amount of money the state collects from citizens continues to increase, lawmakers regularly boost state spending by an even faster rate. The legislature's failure to set priorities and fund urgent needs first creates a false sense that the tax burden government places on citizens must be increased, when new taxes revenues are actually not needed. The result is a structural deficit created by the gap between the increased level of planned spending and the actual increase in tax revenues.

Spending rising faster than revenue causes structural deficit

To understand the structural deficit, it helps to look at the budget in a broader context. Citizens tend to forget that state government is constantly growing. The only fiscal issue the legislature debates every year is how fast spending should rise.

When lawmakers discuss "cuts," they are referring to reductions in the *rate* of spending increase. When tax revenues rise more slowly than *planned* spending, the difference is called a "deficit." When revenue rises faster than the rate of spending increase, the result is a surplus. Either way, except in very rare cases, overall public spending is constantly rising.

Between 1960 and 2005, the state's population grew 120 percent, while general fund revenue grew in inflation-adjusted terms by more than 400 percent. During the 1990s, a time of unprecedented economic prosperity, when there was less pressure on social services, state government spending still rose at a rapid pace.

Instead of controlling spending and preparing for the downturn that was certain to come, state policymakers sharply increased financial commitments and left the treasury with few reserves to maintain services during difficult economic times. Even in today's economy, lawmakers are continuing their habit of overspending.

State government is badly overextended

Lawmakers' instinctive attraction to new spending, while satisfying in the short run, makes it harder for them to meet their obligations in the long term. State government is badly overextended because it tries to do too much. The legislature and the governor make permanent promises but only provide temporary funding. When money inevitably runs short, elected officials seek more revenue from the public, leaving citizens with less of their own earnings to meet life's daily needs.

The result of this approach is an ongoing financial crisis in which recurring deficits are an endemic part of the budget process.

Policy Analysis

An effort to rationalize Washington's budget structure was initiated by former Governor Gary Locke in 2002 when he established his Priorities of Government process.[2] The process requires each agency to rank program activities in order of their importance to the public.

The Priorities of Government process is centered on three strategies.

1. View state government as a single enterprise;

2. Achieve results, at less cost, through creative budget solutions;

3. Reprioritize spending, eliminating programs or consolidating similar activities in different agencies.[3]

Governor Locke described Priorities of Government as "focusing on results that people want and need, prioritizing those results, and funding those results with the money we have."[4]

Measuring government performance

The natural next step in the Priorities of Government budgeting process is to identify measurable performance outcomes for those programs funded in the budget. By having detailed performance information, better prioritization can occur by funding strategies that deliver the best results.

Providing adequate time to review spending proposals

The state's combined budget (operating, capital and transportation) is hundreds of pages long. Despite the length and complexity of these documents, however, hearings are usually held the same day the budget bill is introduced, and it is amended and enacted with inadequate time for meaningful public input.

The opportunity for a detailed review by the public before legislative hearings or votes on budget bills would increase public trust in government and enhance accountability for the spending decisions lawmakers make on the people's behalf.

Know full impact of spending proposals before making decisions

One of the most recognizable measurements of the state's fiscal health is the regular six-year budget outlook. These updates, however, are not done on a regular basis. To provide updated information throughout the year on the state's fiscal outlook, the legislature should issue an updated six-year budget outlook each time the official revenue forecast is released, or when a new appropriation bill is adopted.

Along with the budget outlook, another tool used to make spending decisions is the legislative fiscal note. These analyses provide information on the added cost a spending proposal will impose on taxpayers. Unfortunately, bills are sometime acted on before these estimates are completed, thus robbing the public and lawmakers of the information they need to make informed decisions.

Selling non-essential real estate

State government owns approximately eleven percent of the land in the state, or about five million of Washington's 42.5 million acres. Much of it consists of essential lands that serve the public interest: forest trusts, state parks, and hundreds of important public buildings.

Since 1889, however, the state has acquired properties that never did or no longer serve a public purpose, or which could be leased at much lower cost. In an example from the private sector, ZymoGenetics, a Seattle-based biotechnology company, sold its headquarters building in 2002, and then leased it back for a term of 15 years. The move allowed the company to get out of a business – real estate – that is not its core competency, and at the same time raise $52 million in cash. Through a simple leaseback arrangement the company made money, saved itself the headache of owning and managing a large corporate campus, and retained use of the building for its own needs.[5]

Set up a land review commission

Lawmakers can help reduce the structural deficit by initiating a thorough review of the state's real estate holdings, perhaps through a special temporary body like the federal Base Closure and Realignment Commission (BRAC). Such a review body would recommend properties that could be sold to the public. This policy would show respect for taxpayers, would increase opportunities for private land ownership and would partly relieve the state of an activity that is not a core government function – managing real estate.

"Base closing" review process for state programs

Currently there are more than 550 agencies, boards and commissions in Washington state government, administering hundreds of programs and funds that serve a wide array of purposes.[6] As the business of government grows over time, programs become unnecessary or redundant. Yet management will always insist that their programs remain in place and even grow regardless of whether they are needed.

Comparing private industry with government shows that private industries innovate and improve services ending old practices and developing new ones. In contrast, government stagnates as entrenched interests such as management and labor unions fight within the status quo. Lawmakers should, from time to time, evaluate the purpose and function of state programs and improve services by consolidating, eliminating, or privatizing operations. This "base closing" process should be as independent of the legislative branch as possible.

Ending the sense of crisis in state finances

Reducing the long-term structural costs of government will ease the burden on taxpayers and ensure that future economic slowdowns do not force the state into yet another financial emergency. Structural budget reforms would promote efficiency, improve the quality of services to the public, and resolve the constant sense of crisis that pervades the state's public finances.

Recommendations

1) Adopt performance-based, Priorities of Government budgeting to slow the rate of spending growth and end the chronic sense of crisis in state finances. The Priorities of Government standard has proved successful in the past. The legislature and executive agencies should adopt it as a permanent part of the budget process by requiring all budgets be adopted based on this sensible review process, so essential public services are funded first.

Priorities of Government brings discipline to public spending, slows the growth of the tax burden government places on its citizens, and directs limited government funding to where it is most needed.

2) Place performance outcomes directly into the budget. To improve budget accountability, high level performance outcome measures should be placed directly into the budget so lawmakers and citizens can quickly see whether past goals have been met before each new increase in spending is considered.

3) Adopt a 72-hour budget timeout. To facilitate public involvement, the legislature should adopt a 72-hour timeout period in the legislative process once a budget, tax or spending bill is introduced or amended. This would allow lawmakers and the public a three-day period to calmly consider the two-year budget, new taxes or new spending before legislative hearings or final voting occurs.

4) Require updated six-year budget forecasts be tied to quarterly revenue forecasts or adoption of new budgets. To provide updated information throughout the year on the state's fiscal outlook, an updated six-year budget outlook should be issued each time the official revenue forecast is released, or a new appropriation bill is adopted.

5) Require completed fiscal notes before bills can be acted on. Lawmakers and the public should know the full impact of a spending bill before final legislative action is taken. Bills proposing increased spending should not receive hearings or votes until a thorough fiscal analysis is completed and released to the public.

6) Sell non-essential real estate holdings. Policymakers should evaluate the real estate holdings of each state agency to determine whether taxpayers would be better served by selling a particular property. Properties that do not benefit the public should be sold to raise revenue and to reduce costs to the state. In other cases, the state may be better off leasing facilities, rather than owning them outright.

7) Begin a "base closing" process for state programs and agencies to determine which ones can be consolidated or eliminated. This review process would help optimize state spending by eliminating state programs that are unnecessary, wasteful or have fulfilled their purpose. The money saved could be devoted to higher-priority programs that provide valuable services to the public.

2. State Spending Limit

Recommendation

1. Adopt a constitutional amendment to limit the growth of spending to inflation and population growth.

Background

In 1993, Washington voters passed Initiative 601 to limit the annual growth of state spending to inflation plus population growth.[7] The limit worked for a time. In the decade before Initiative 601, state spending increased on average by 17.3 percent per biennium. Since Initiative 601 became law, state spending increases have averaged 8.9 percent, almost half the previous rate of spending increases. But over the years legislators gradually suspended those restrictions and the rate of annual spending growth again is in the double digits.

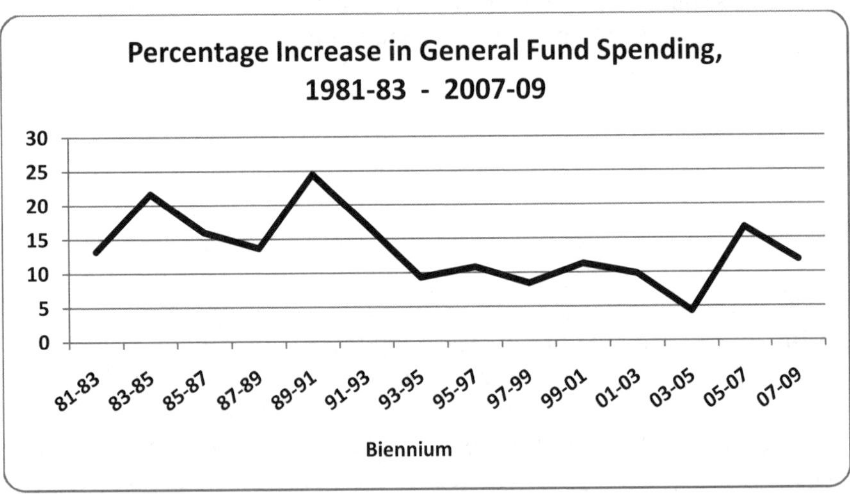

The graph above shows a major drop in the percentage increase in state spending when Initiative 601 took effect during the 1993-95 biennium. Until the major changes to the law by the legislature in 2005, these percentage increases were relatively stable.

What the people intended to be a firm but reasonable check on the growth of state spending has been reduced almost to zero by the legislature, as lawmakers seek to accommodate their desire for spending increases. Today it is a meaningless cap that is bypassed regularly by lawmakers intent on boosting spending.

Initiative 601 was not made part of the Washington constitution, and it was easily overturned by a simple majority vote in the legislature. Colorado's spending limit, in contrast, was enacted as part of the constitution and has proved much more effective at protecting citizens from aggressive state spending.

Passed by the people in 1992, Colorado's Taxpayers' Bill of Rights (TABOR) limits the amount of tax revenue the state can keep each year to the sum of inflation plus population growth. Any taxes collected above this amount must be returned to taxpayers in the form of rebates.[8]

The table below shows how TABOR succeeded in restraining the growth of government and allowed the people of Colorado to keep more of their own money. Over the ten years after the state implemented TABOR, non-government job growth in the state increased dramatically, as did per-capita personal income.[9]

Colorado: Comparison of economic growth and state spending before and after passage of Taxpayer Bill of Rights (TABOR)

	1983-1992 Growth Rates (pre-TABOR)	1993-2002 Growth Rates (post-TABOR)
Population	10.4%	25.3%
Inflation	29.7%	37.3%
TOTAL	40.1%	62.6%
State Revenues (Taxes)	104.7%	61.3%
State Spending	89.8%	63.8%
Per Capita Personal Income	59.2% (+$7,810)	65.3% (+$14,437)
All Job Growth	18.1% (248,000)	34.6% (586,000)
Govt. Employment	21.1% (50,000)	20.0% (59,600)
Non-Govt. Employment	17.5% (198,000)	37.3% (526,400)

As a constitutional protection against government overspending, TABOR cannot be weakened through the ordinary budget process. Colorado lawmakers do not harbor unrealistic expectations about how much tax money they will be collecting in the years ahead. This in turn serves to keep unsustainable government spending in check.

In 2005, Colorado voters approved Referendum C, which provides for a temporary increase in TABOR spending limits. After five years, the original limits will be applied to future spending growth.[10]

Policy Analysis

Thirty states have some form of spending limit to protect their citizens from overtaxation.[11] More than half of these spending limits are part of the state's constitution.[12]

Research shows that the most effective spending limits are constitutional instead of statutory.[13] Constitutional spending limits are insulated from attempts by narrow legislative majorities to open loopholes that allow higher spending increases. Research also shows that tying the growth of government spending to inflation plus population increases a limit's effectiveness, compared to other methods of measuring economic activity.[14]

Originally, Initiative 601 pegged government growth to a combination of inflation and population growth, but in 2005 the legislature and governor changed the fiscal growth factor to a ten-year average of state personal income growth.[15] This allows spending to increase at a much faster rate.

Tying increases in public spending to the growth in the average of personal incomes artificially exaggerates the impact of wealthy people's incomes on state spending. Under this budget rule, state spending and taxation go up for everyone, even though not everyone's income has increased to keep pace.

Washington's economy and its citizens would benefit from a state spending limit that is both constitutional and tied to a growth in inflation and population.

Recommendation

1. Adopt a constitutional amendment to limit the growth of spending to inflation and population growth. Reasonable budget limits similar to those of Initiative 601, but as part of the state constitution, would protect taxpayers and bring greater discipline to public finances.

3. Public Workforce Policy

Recommendations

1. Restore the legislature's authority over state collective bargaining agreements.

2. Adopt collective bargaining transparency.

3. Eliminate positions vacant more than six months.

4. Bring state employee health care premium contributions more in line with the private sector.

5. End automatic deduction of compulsory monthly union dues from public employee paychecks.

6. Phase in a defined-contribution retirement plan that gives state workers benefits that can never be taken away.

Background

Since 1995, state public employment has grown by over 19,000 people, reaching nearly 112,000 FTEs (full-time equivalent positions) in 2008.[16] The largest employer in Washington is state government. State public employment grew 20 percent in a little over ten years. In fact, government is the only sector of the economy that consistently grows year by year, even during recessions. The rapid rise in state public employment in recent years is shown below.

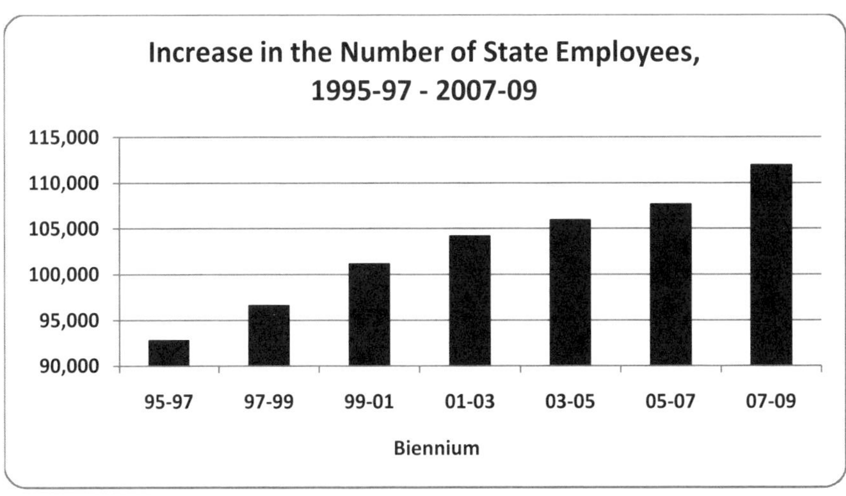

Average annual compensation for full-time state employees tops $66,000. This includes a salary of more than $53,000, plus a generous $13,000 benefit package including medical coverage, free dental care, a comfortable 401(k) retirement plan, a minimum of 12 days paid vacation, 10 paid holidays each year, and protective union rules that virtually guarantee lifelong employment. [17]

The average annual salary for a typical Washington state resident is about $40,414. [18] During an economic downturn many people in the private sector face a reduction in pay or the loss of their jobs, while government workers are generally assured employment with regular raises.

Policy Analysis

Maintaining the present growth rate in the state workforce will eventually push the cost of government beyond what taxpayers can reasonably support. A change in workforce policy is needed to reduce the pressure a rising permanent payroll places on public budgets. A number of ideas for achieving this goal are presented here.

Improve collective bargaining transparency and oversight

State collective bargaining law prevents the legislature, and the public, from knowing the process that determines employment contract details. The current system undermines transparency and public accountability for the tax dollars being spent through the state payroll. Under the 2002 Civil Service Reform Act, the legislature can only vote "yes" or "no," with no amendments or other changes, to a contract negotiated secretly by the governor and union officials.

The legislature should reassert its authority over state employment policy to ensure greater public accountability and transparency. This would help advance improvements that reduce costs while rewarding the excellent work of state employees.

Eliminate positions vacant for six months

A major cost in state government are the number of people on the public payroll. These are desirable, good-paying jobs with excellent benefits. But taxpayers expect government to be about more than providing good jobs to people fortunate enough to be in the state workforce. A starting point in reducing built-in personnel costs would be to eliminate all positions that have been vacant for six months or more.

State employee medical coverage

State employees receive generous health care benefits from an array of eleven plan choices (though not all choices are available in every county). Public employees receive well above the average wage in the state, and a generous benefits package makes up more than 20 percent of their total compensation.[19]

In 2008, state employees will pay, on average, just $64 per month, or $187 for a family plan, well below the typical employee cost of private sector plans.[20] Taxpayers will pick up the rest. In addition, taxpayers pay 100 percent of the cost for employee and family dental coverage. More than 330,000 pubic employees and families members are enrolled.[21]

In addition to current costs, the legislature is adding to the financial burden of the program by expanding its generous coverage to more groups. In 2007, lawmakers passed five bills allowing groups such as same-sex domestic partners, part-time university employees and employees of tribal government to buy coverage under the state program.[22]

As health care costs continue to climb, the current arrangement will place a growing strain on the state budget. In order to make their employees better stewards of health care dollars, private sector employers have increased the share of premiums contributed by employees. This has the effect of making the cost of health care as a portion of overall compensation more visible. Washington would do well to follow this example.

Lawmakers should also allow state employees to receive their benefits in the form of personal Health Savings Accounts. HSAs give workers tax-free cash to pay their medical expenses, and give them direct control over their health care dollars. The legislature has authorized HSAs for public employees, but the governor's office has yet to set up the program so workers can actually sign up.

Compulsory union deductions from employee paychecks

Currently, the Washington state workforce is mostly a closed shop. Most state employees must belong to an approved union as a condition of employment. Failure to join a union is cause for dismissal.

Union dues are automatically deducted from workers' paychecks. State law provides for mandatory union dues to be set through talks between union leaders and the governor.[23] Currently, monthly dues average around $45 a month. Typically, government unions collect some $2 million a month, or about $24 million a year from workers. Part of this money is used to pay administrative costs and handle workplace issues, while some is devoted to lobbying, candidate campaigns and other political activities.

Washington's "union security" clause

In 2007, the Washington legislature approved a new contract negotiated by unions and the governor behind closed doors, in which union representatives insisted on a "union security" clause requiring mandatory paycheck deductions. Any employee who does not want to join the union or pay mandatory dues can be fired.

The text of a typical "union security" clause is shown below (emphasis added).[24]

Article 36.3 Union Security

All employees covered by this Agreement will, as a condition of employment either become members of the Union and pay membership dues or, as nonmembers, pay a fee as described in A, B, and C below, no later than the 30th day following the effective date of this Agreement or the beginning of their employment. If an employee fails to meet the conditions outlined below, the Union will notify the Employer and inform the employee that his or her employment **may be terminated**.

Despite the mandatory requirement for most state workers to join and pay a union, the unions are not public entities but instead are private organizations. This scheme shields the unions from the accountability and transparency requirements mandated under state law for public entities.

As an employer, the state should not be forcing individuals to join selected private organizations. However, if such a requirement does exist, the unions should be treated as public entities and be subject to all applicable laws and disclosure requirements. State workers and the public should be fully informed about union activity.

Pension reform

State and local government employees in Washington are required to participate in pension plans administered by the Washington State Department of Retirement Systems. The system pays benefits to more than 590,000 current and retired employees through 15 different plans, and pays out about $2.5 billion in benefits each year.[25] The state's plans are mostly defined-benefit plans, meaning they pay a pre-calculated set of benefits based on number of years worked and salary earned.

Lawmakers often criticize private companies for raiding employee pensions, yet this is exactly what the legislature has done by skipping payments into the state pension fund. The state pension plans have assets of $47 billion, but face liabilities of more than $52 billion.[26] That means the legislature has under-funded the state pension plan by at least $5 billion, creating a potentially crushing financial burden for future taxpayers.

Defined contribution plans

Because they operate under the discipline of the marketplace, private companies have developed a smarter approach. They have moved away from old-style defined-benefit plans to defined-contribution plans and 401(k) accounts. Defined-contribution plans give employees their retirement money upfront, in the form of tax-free contributions to their personal retirement accounts. Employees can contribute to the account as well, also tax-free.

The great advantage of defined-contribution plans is that they give workers direct ownership of their own retirement money. As investment strategies and risk levels change with age, defined-contribution plans give workers the freedom and flexibility that one-size-fits-all government pensions do not. Employees in such plans are not forced to rely on promises that might be broken in the future.

As an additional benefit, defined-contribution plans protect future taxpayers from massive unfunded liability, such as the one state plans carry today.

Recommendations

1) Restore the legislature's authority over state collective bargaining agreements. The legislature should reassert its authority over state employment policy to ensure greater accountability and transparency, and it should advance improvements that reduce costs while rewarding the excellent work of state employees.

2) Adopt collective bargaining transparency. State employment contracts should not be negotiated in secret. Taxpayers are ultimately responsible for funding these agreements. They should be allowed to monitor the negotiation process and to hold state officials accountable for their actions.

3) Eliminate positions vacant more than six months. If a position remains open for more than six months, it is reasonable to assume the agency can do its work without an employee in that position. By eliminating these vacant positions, the state can cut payroll in areas that are not critical to public safety or the basic functioning of state government. This policy would provide more accurate budget information for the legislature and would lower costs to taxpayers.

4) Bring state employee health care premium contributions more in line with the private sector. In order to make their employees better stewards of health care dollars, the state should increase the share of health insurance premiums contributed by employees. Policymakers should also promote the option of Health Savings Accounts, so workers can have direct control over their health care benefits.

5) End compulsory monthly union dues from public employee paychecks. If government union leaders collected voluntary dues from their members, instead of resorting to mandatory automatic payroll deductions, they would be more responsive to their members' needs and views. It would also encourage union officials to be more transparent and accountable for how they spend their members' money.

6) Phase in a defined-contribution retirement plan that gives workers benefits that can never be taken away. Personal retirement accounts with tax-free defined-contributions would end the financial crisis in the state retirement system. Lawmakers can best keep their promises to retirees by creating a pension system that is personal, flexible and financially sustainable.

4. Competitive Bidding

Recommendations

1. Encourage state agencies to save money and improve service to the public by using competitive bidding authority.

2. Protect competitive bidding authority from being restricted or bargained away during mandatory collective bargaining negotiations.

Background

The state's tight financial situation lends fresh urgency to the use of competitive bidding as a long-term way to bring rising spending under control. Competitive bidding allows state agencies to open work normally performed by in-house employees to bids from a variety of sources. Public employees are allowed to bid for contracts along with contractors from the private sector. Competition allows government managers to provide improved services at lower cost to taxpayers.

Until recently, state law based on a court ruling in the 1978 Spokane Community College case that was later codified by the legislature, held that any work historically performed by state workers had to always be performed by state workers.[27] Private companies were not allowed to submit bids to see if the same amount and quality of work could be done at lower cost.

In 2002, the legislature, as part of a larger collective bargaining and civil service reform measure, enacted a law which gave state agencies the authority to open work contracts to competitive bidding.[28] The new rule went into effect in July 2005.

Unfortunately the state has done little to pursue savings from competitive bidding with the private sector. This is due in part to the current political climate in Olympia and the fact that the 2002 reforms created an overly-complicated process for pursuing bidding. Currently, opposition from government unions and a burdensome process prevent the state from realizing the full benefits of competitive bidding.

A performance audit conducted by the Joint Legislative Audit and Review Committee (JLARC) in January 2007 found:

> "...few agencies have competitively contracted for services in the 16 months since receiving authorization to do so.
>
> Agency managers reported two main reasons for not competitively contracting. First, managers perceive the process itself to be complicated and confusing, providing a disincentive to pursue competitive contracting. Second, competitive contracting is a subject of collective bargaining, which creates additional challenges by requiring labor negotiations. Managers must bargain, at a minimum, the impacts of competitive contracting.
>
> Additionally, some agency collective bargaining agreements include provisions which prohibit agencies from competitively contracting."

Policy Analysis

There are four key benefits of competitive bidding that show how competition successfully improves quality and eases the budget strain of core government programs. These are presented below.

Four benefits of competitive bidding

1) **Lower cost.** Private companies are disciplined to seek efficiencies through the need to operate at a profit while providing superior service at a competitive price. By employing the techniques of competition, public managers find efficiencies within their operations and lower the cost of performing a service.

2) **Higher service levels.** Monopolies, whether public or private, frequently lack the stimulus to innovate and improve service delivery. By opening services to competition governments can upgrade services and achieve cost savings.

3) **Better management**. Government can streamline its operations by using the same accounting procedures and productivity measures that the private sector uses, which are more accurate and comprehensive than traditional government methods.

4) **Changed government culture**. When a government seeks dynamic competition over a monopoly status quo its culture changes. Instead of performing many functions with limited expertise, governments that are open to competition liberate themselves to perform a smaller set of core functions better than ever before, while leaving much of the routine work to contractors.

Across the country, state, county and city governments are opening services to competitive bidding that were once performed exclusively by government agencies. These competitions are often won by government workers themselves, showing that efficiencies can be found even when public employees continue to do the work. For public leaders, tapping the benefits of competition is a better alternative than pushing for ever-rising levels of taxation.[29]

Recommendations

1) Encourage state agencies to save money and improve service to the public by using competitive bidding authority. Many opportunities for competitive contracting exist throughout state government. Experience from other states shows typical cost savings of 10 to 25 percent when agency managers introduce open competition for government work.

2) Protect competitive bidding authority from being restricted or bargained away during mandatory collective bargaining negotiations. Washington policymakers should simplify the bidding process to make it easier for agencies to use competition to improve services. Lawmakers should shield contracting out from union and political influence by removing it from the collective bargaining process. Improving service to the public is too important to be a bargaining chip in government labor negotiations.

Additional Resources from Washington Policy Center

"Look Beyond the Numbers of State Budgeting," by John Barnes, March 2008.

"The Washington State Piglet Book: Connecting the Dots on How Government Wastes Your Money," by Paul Guppy, January 2008.

"Citizens Guide to SJR 8206, Budget Stabilization Account," by Jason Mercier, August 2007.

"Washington Votes for Fiscal Discipline, Against Tax Increases," by Jason Mercier, November 2007.

"State Lawmakers Should Return the Extra Money They are Taking from Taxpayers," by Paul Guppy, December 2006.

"New Audit Law to See Whether Government Agencies are Keeping Their Promises," by John Barnes, May 2006.

"The State Budget Tug-of-War," by Paul Guppy, January 2006.

"Guide to Initiative 900: Reviewing Government through Performance Audits," by John Barnes, October 2005.

"Overextended Government, Not Lack of Revenue, is the Reason for State's Structural Deficits," by Paul Guppy, March 2005.

"A Policy Guide for Budget Reform: Strategies for Improving State Government Services and Reducing the Deficit," by Eric Montague, January 2003.

"Ideas for Balancing the State Budget Without Raising Taxes," by Eric Montague, January 2002.

---

[1] "2007-09 Enacted Budgets," Office of Financial Management, at www.ofm.wa.gov/budget/legbudgets/0709biennial.asp. General fund figure includes Near General Fund accounts.

[2] "Gov. Gary Locke Announces 'Priorities of Government' Strategy for Lean, Results-Oriented State Budget," news release, Office of the Governor, Olympia, November 14, 2002, http://www.governor.wa.gov/press/press-view.asp?pressRelease=1222&newsType=1.

[3] Ibid.

[4] "Priorities of Government," Governor Gary Locke, news conference, November 14, 2002, at www.digitalarchives.wa.gov/governorlocke.

[5] "Biotech Cashes in on Real Estate: ZymoGenetics Sells, Leases Back HQ," by Luke Timmerman, *The Seattle Times*, October 8, 2002, p. C-1.

[6] "Washington State Government 2005-2006 Organizational Chart," Office of Financial Management, available at www.ofm.wa.gov/databook/pdf/orgchart.pdf.

[7] Under Initiative 601, state expenditures were limited to a growth rate at or below the average of the sum of inflation and population change during the previous three years.

[8] "The TABOR Legislative Handbook," The Independence Institute, Golden, Colorado, January 2000, http://i2i.org/articles/1-2000.PDF.

[9] "A Decade of TABOR, Ten Years After: Analysis of the Taxpayer's Bill of Rights," by Fred Holden, Independence Institute, Golden, Colorado, June 2003, p. 7, at www.i2i.org.

[10] Ibid., p. 7.

[11] "Overview of state tax and expenditure limits, 2007," National Conference of State Legislatures (NCSL), at www.ncsl.org/programs/fiscal/telsabout.htm, accessed May 14, 2008.

[12] Ibid.

[13] "Tax and Spending Limits: Theory, Analysis, and Policy," by Barry W. Poulson, Independence Institute, Golden, Colorado, February 2004, page 1, at www.i2i.org.

[14] Ibid.

[15] Senate Bill 6078, 2005 session, see www.WashingtonVotes.org for more information.

[16] This figure includes staff and faculty at state-funded universities and colleges. It does not include K-12 teachers and staff, who are considered employees of local school districts. See "FTE Staff for 1995-97 through 2007-09 Enacted Budget," Legislative Evaluation and Accountability Program (LEAP) Committee, at http://leap.leg.wa.gov/.

[17] "Salaries, Benefits and FTEs, FY 1998 to FY 2008, General Fund – State Only," e-mail communication from Pam Davidson, Washington State Office of Financial Management, available on request, May 21, 2008.

[18] "State Personal Income, 2007," Bureau of Economic Analysis, United States Department of Commerce, at www.bea.doc.gov. Per capita annual personal income for Washington residents was $40,414 in 2007.

[19] Office of Financial Management, Olympia, Washington, cited in "State government's hiring outpaces population growth," by Chris McGann, *Seattle Post-Intelligencer*, August 1, 2005, and Jason Mercier, "State government employment up 1,676: Ninth straight year employment has increased," Evergreen Freedom Foundation, available at www.effwa.org.

[20] "2008 Monthly Employee Premiums, PEBB Medical Plans," Public Employees Benefits Board, Washington State Health Care Authority, at www.pebb.hca.wa.gov/documents/rates/employee.pdf.

[21] "PEBB Enrollment Report, Report 1: Total Member Summary," Public Employees Health Benefits Board, Washington State Health Care Authority, March 2008, at www.pebb.hca.wa.gov/documents/mar2008.pdf.

[22] SHB 1417, HB 1644, SSB 5336, SB 5640 and E2SSB 5930, "Legislature expands access to PEEB coverage," PEBB Perspective, Public Employees Health Benefits

Board, Washington State Health Care Authority, July 2007, at
www.pebb.hca.wa.gov/documents/empjuly2007.pdf.

[23] Revised Code of Washington 41.80.100.

[24] "Collective Bargaining Agreement By and Between The State of Washington and
Washington Public Employees (WPEA)," July 1, 2005 through July 1, 2007, Article
36.3, at www.ofm.wa.gov/labor/agreements/05-07/wpea/wpea.pdf.

[25] "2007 Comprehensive Annual Financial Report," Message from the Director,
Funds of the State of Washington, Department of Retirement Systems, June 30,
2007, at www.drs.wa.gov/Administration/AnnualReport/CAFR/cafrIntro.pdf.

[26] Ibid., page 12.

[27] *Washington Federation of State Employees v. Spokane Community College*, 90 Wash. 2d
698, 585 P. 2d 474 (1978) and codified by the legislature in RCW 41.06.380.

[28] Substitute House Bill 1268, The "Personnel System Reform Act of 2002."

[29] For examples from other states of the effectiveness of contracting out, see
"Competing for Highway Maintenance: Lessons for Washington State," by Dennis
Lisk, Washington Policy Center Policy Brief, September 1998, and "Research Shows
Private Prisons Enable States to Improve Quality and Control Costs," Washington
Policy Center Legislative Memo, February 28, 2005, both at
www.washingtonpolicy.org.

CHAPTER 2

1. Guiding Principles of Taxation[1]

Recommendations

1. Adopt guiding principles based on equity and economic neutrality to shape changes in Washington's tax system, so the tax system is focused on raising needed revenue for core functions of government, not directing the choices and behavior of citizens.

2. Policymakers should seek to lower the overall tax burden to promote prosperity and opportunity for the benefit of all citizens.

Background

The people of Washington pay over 50 different kinds of taxes at the state and local level.[2] The largest single revenue source for state and local government is the general sales and use tax, representing about 55 percent of all taxes. The next largest revenue source is the Business and Occupation (B&0) tax. The chart shows the sources of state general fund revenue.

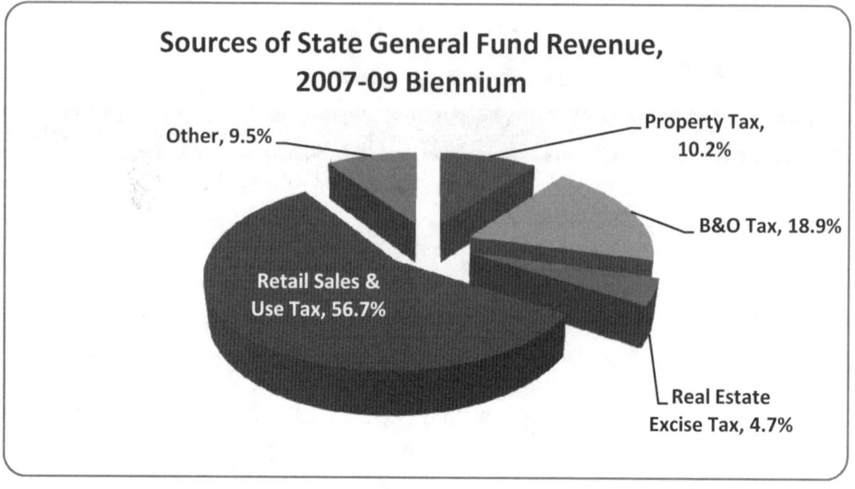

"Other" includes revenue from liquor sales, tobacco taxes, lottery proceeds, insurance premiums, etc. Source: Office of Financial Management.

The proper function of taxation is to raise money for core functions of government, not to direct the behavior of its citizens. This is true regardless of whether government is big or small, and this is true for lawmakers at all levels of government. Many lawmakers think of the tax code as a way to penalize "bad" behaviors and reward "good" ones. They have sought incessantly to guide, micromanage and steer the economy by manipulating the tax laws.

Taxation will always impose some damage on an economy's performance, but that harm can be minimized if policymakers resist the temptation to use the tax code for social engineering, class warfare and other extraneous purposes. A simple and fair tax system is an ideal way to advance Washington's economic interests and promote prosperity for its residents.

Policy Analysis

The fundamental principles presented here provide guidance for a fair and effective tax system; that is, one that raises needed revenue for core functions of government while minimizing the burden on citizens.

- **Simplicity** – The tax code should be easy for the average citizen to understand, and it should minimize the cost of complying with the tax laws. Tax complexity adds cost to the taxpayer, but does not increase public revenue. For governments, the tax system should be easy to administer, and should help promote efficient, low-cost administration.

- **Accountability** – Tax systems should be accountable to citizens. Taxes and tax policy should be visible and not hidden from taxpayers. Changes in tax policy should be highly publicized and open to public debate.

- **Economic Neutrality** – The purpose of the tax system is to raise needed revenue for core functions of government, not to control the lives of citizens. The tax system should exert minimal impact on the spending and business decisions of individuals and businesses.

- **Equity and Fairness** – Fairness means all taxpayers should be treated the same. The government should not use the tax system to pick winners and losers in society, or unfairly shift the tax burden onto one class of citizens. The tax system should not be used to punish success or to "soak the rich."

- **Complementary** – The tax code should help maintain a healthy relationship between the state and local governments. The state should always be mindful of how its tax decisions affect local governments so they are not working against each other – with the taxpayer caught in the middle.

- **Competitiveness** – A low tax burden can be a tool for Washington's economic development by retaining and attracting productive business activity. A high quality revenue system will be responsive to competition from other states.

- **Balance** – An effective tax system should be broad-based, without relying too heavily on a few sources of revenue. For the same reason, an ideal tax system should avoid special exemptions, preferring a low overall tax rate with few loopholes.

- **Reliability** – A high quality tax system should be stable, providing certainty in taxation and in revenue flows. It should provide certainty of financial planning for individuals and businesses.

While these guiding principles are important, there are inherent problems with any system of taxation. Basically, taxation reduces spending on private sector goods and services traded in the free market. The benefits of free exchange – to both the purchaser and seller – are reduced when trade is restrained by taxation. The way that taxes restrain private trade varies.

Income and property taxes reduce the incomes of taxpayers, lowering their demand for goods and services. Sales and excise taxes increase costs to suppliers, reducing their willingness to provide goods at any given prices. In any case, taxes reduce private trade and curtail job creation.

Since taxes lower the economic welfare of citizens, policymakers should try to minimize the economic and social problems that taxation imposes. Citizens then directly gain the benefits of a low tax burden. These benefits are summarized below:

<u>Benefits of a low tax burden</u>

- **Faster economic growth** – A tax system that allows citizens to keep more of what they earn spurs increased work, saving and investment. A low tax burden will mean a competitive advantage for Washington over states with high-rate, overly progressive tax systems.

- **Greater wealth creation** – Low taxes significantly boost the value of all income-producing assets and help citizens maximize their fullest economic potential, thereby broadening the tax base.

- **End micromanagement and political favoritism** – A complex, high-rate tax system favors interests that are able to exert influence in Olympia, and that can negotiate narrow exemptions and tax benefits. "A fair field and no favors" is a good motto for a strong tax system.

- **Increased civic involvement** – A complex, high-rate tax system makes it nearly impossible for the average citizen to understand how and why the state is collecting money. Citizens become cynical and alienated from their government. At some point, most citizens come to feel the state government no longer represents their interests. A simplified, broad-based, low-rate system encourages citizens to become re-engaged with government and to seek greater civic involvement.

The people of Washington work hard for what they earn. Money paid in taxes is, by definition, not available to meet other needs. As a matter of respect to citizens, policymakers should work to keep the overall level of taxation to the absolute minimum needed to pay for the core functions of government.

Recommendations

1) Adopt guiding principles based on equity and economic neutrality to shape changes in Washington's tax system, so the tax system is focused on raising needed revenue for core functions of government, not directing the choices and behavior of citizens. Basic to the concept of a fair tax system is that the state should take no more from citizens than it needs to pay for the core functions of government. This consideration goes beyond the need to balance the budget; it is a matter of fundamental respect and trust between citizens and their government.

2) Policymakers should seek to lower the overall tax burden to promote prosperity and opportunity for the benefit of all citizens. Washingtonians require and expect basic government services, and taxes must be collected to pay for these services. Government revenue should be limited to real public needs, so the tax system itself does not become one of the major problems of life. A fair and efficient tax system shows respect for the citizens of our state.

2. State Income Tax

<table>
<tr><td align="center">Recommendation</td></tr>
<tr><td>1. Avoid enacting a state income tax.</td></tr>
</table>

Background

Washington is one of only seven states that does not tax citizens' incomes. Doing so would fundamentally alter the state's tax structure, changing it from one that mainly taxes consumption to one that also taxes productivity.

Each state levies a different combination of taxes on the people who live, do business or travel within its borders. These different types and levels of taxation have a profound impact on the actions of residents and businesses and can significantly impede economic growth. More than any other type of tax, an income tax can stifle a state's economic growth, create instability in public revenues and limit people's take-home income.

Policy Analysis

Examination of long-term economic trends in states that have adopted income taxes indicate how a state tax on incomes may affect Washington. Since 1967, nine states have imposed an income tax.[3] In these states, government spending growth increased an average of 41.8 percent and personal income growth decreased an average of 64.2 percent after enacting the new tax.[4]

The following chart illustrates that the rate of government spending growth increases and personal income growth slows in states that impose an income tax, based on economic changes since adoption of an income tax through 1998.[5]

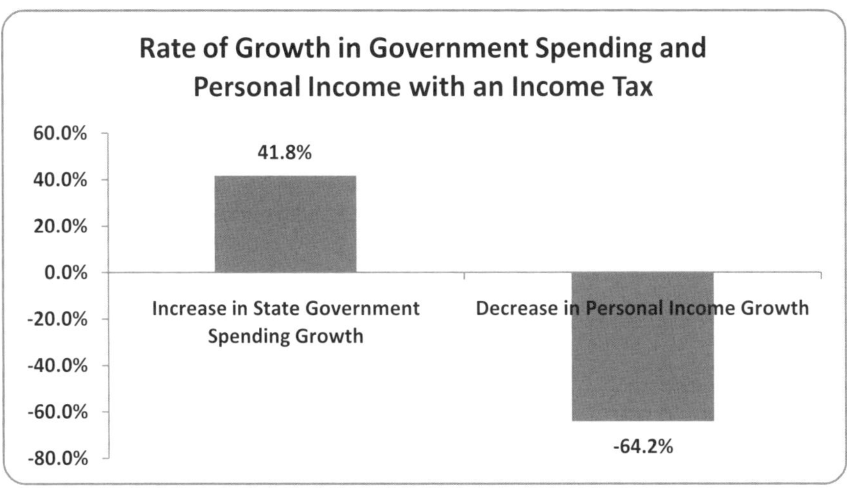

Government spending grows faster and personal incomes
rise more slowly in states with an income tax.

Why does personal income growth fall off faster in states that tax personal incomes? There are a number of reasons. Personal income growth is largely a function of market incentives. When government imposes a tax on earnings, individuals lose incentive to work harder and increase their wages. Similarly, when a share of interest earnings from savings is lost each year to taxation, individuals have less reason to save in the first place.

Why does government spending tend to increase faster in states that tax personal incomes? There are two primary reasons. First, an income tax adds one more way policymakers can incrementally increase tax revenues to fuel a faster rate of government growth. But over time, even small increases combine to stifle economic growth, transferring more money out of the productive economy and into the government sector.

Second, an income tax is not as transparent as other taxes. The tax is automatically deducted from workers' paychecks each month. The only time citizens may be aware of a how much they pay in income tax is when they complete a tax return once a year, and even then they may be more interested in any refund they might receive than in the amount of tax they paid in the first place. The obscure nature of an income tax increases the temptation for elected officials to increase the tax rate with less chance of provoking a negative public reaction.

Often lawmakers and special interest groups that rely on government spending say a state income tax is necessary because the growth of revenues from existing taxes are insufficient. But as the following charts show, money collected from Washington's major taxes – property, Business and Occupation and sales – are growing steadily and outpacing inflation. In addition to increases in tax rates, revenues have grown sharply due to the natural expansion of the economy.

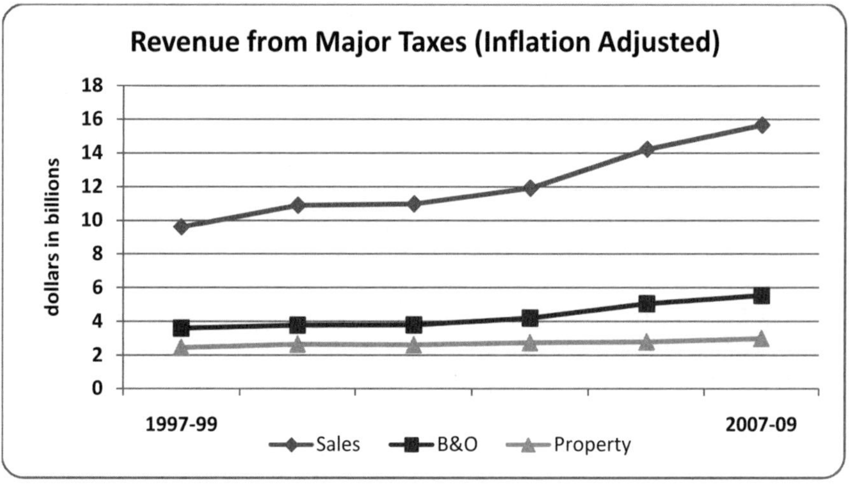

In most years, state revenue from major taxes grows faster than inflation.

The sales tax rate has grown since its inception in 1935 from two percent to 6.5 percent today. The following chart shows the growth of the sales tax rate. This upward trend contributed greatly to the growth in state revenues.

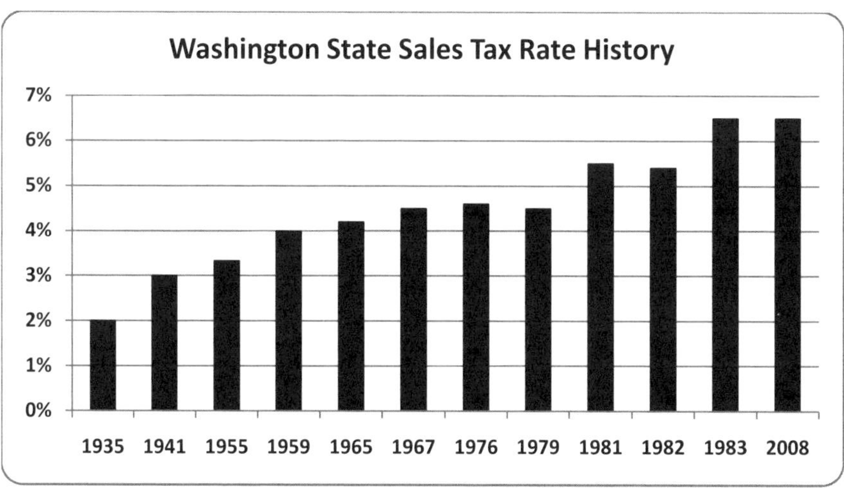

The state sales tax rate has more than tripled since 1935

State income taxes tend to reduce personal income growth, increase the rate of government spending and lower the competitiveness of the business climate. Avoiding an income tax allows people to spend more time working for themselves and their families, and less time working to pay for government.

Recommendation

1) Avoid enacting a state income tax. A state income tax would have a negative effect on the Washington economy. Comparisons among states show that income taxes reduce state competitiveness, add cost and complexity to the tax code, and reduce the incentive for people to work, save and invest. The absence of an income tax is one of the few clear advantages Washington's business climate has over those of other states.

3. Sales Tax Deductibility

Recommendation

1. Encourage Congress to promote equal tax treatment among states by making state sales tax deductibility permanent.

Background

In 1986, as part of a major overhaul of the tax code, Congress ended the deductibility of state sales taxes. For eighteen years, as residents of one of the seven states without a state income tax, Washington residents were unable to deduct what they pay in state sales taxes from their federal income tax. Since state income taxes are fully deductible, residents of other states received more favorable treatment under the code.

Policy Analysis

In 2004, Congress and the President resolved this inequity with passage of H.R. 4520, the American Jobs Creation Act.[6] A provision of the bill again made state sales tax deductible from the amount of personal income subject to the federal income tax. The deduction saves Washington residents an estimated $500 million per year.[7]

In practice, Washingtonians do not have to keep track of all their sales receipts through the year to calculate how much they pay in state taxes. The IRS issued a table that estimates, based on income, what dollar amount taxpayers can claim as sales tax costs on federal income tax forms. Additional deductions are allowed for sales tax paid on major purchases, such as automobiles.

The sales tax deductibility provision enacted in 2004 was only in place for tax years 2004 and 2005.[8] Congress has since temporarily extended the exemption for 2006 and 2007, but has not made the credit permanent.

Recommendation

1) Encourage Congress to promote equal tax treatment among states by making state sales tax deductibility permanent. The temporary sales tax deductibility provision is scheduled to expire once again. Unless Congress extends the provision or makes it permanent, residents in Washington and six other states will again be subject to unequal treatment under the federal tax code.

4. Property Tax Limitation

Recommendations

1. Enact property tax relief to reduce the financial burden government places on citizens to promote economic growth, homeownership, job creation and greater personal freedom.

2. Maintain Washington's uniformity principle when taxing property, so all classes of property owners are treated the same under the law.

Background

Many people believe their property value alone determines how much property tax they must pay, and when the county assessor updates home values to reflect market trends, their taxes automatically go up. This is not the case.

County assessors do not levy property taxes. Elected state legislators and the local board and council members of Washington's 39 counties and more than 1,720 cities and other taxing districts decide how much property tax citizens must pay.

Once elected officials in each taxing district decide the total dollar amount they feel they need to fund public operations for the following year, the assessor apportions that amount among the district's property owners, based on each land parcel's assessed value. It is a budget-based tax system, and that is the source of most of the confusion over who is responsible for rising property taxes.

Most people are familiar with rate-based tax systems, like the state sales tax or the federal income tax. Under a rate-based system elected officials first set a percentage rate which determines the fraction of each dollar of a given tax base that must be paid to the government. The revenue the government will receive from such a tax cannot be known in advance; it can only be estimated.

A budget-based system, like the property tax, begins at the other end. Elected officials *first* decide how much money they feel is needed for their government budget, then divide this among the tax base to determine what rate is needed to raise that amount of revenue.

The rate is expressed as so many dollars per $1,000 of assessed value. Under this system, the amount of revenue the government will collect is known from the beginning. It is the tax *rate* that is unknown until the assessor calculates it. The difference between the two systems can be expressed this way:

- **Rate-based system: rate x tax base = revenue**

- **Budget-based system: revenue ÷ tax base = rate**

Once the rate is determined, the county assessor applies it to the value of each owner's property. One piece of land may fall under the jurisdiction of as many as ten separate taxing districts.[9] The assessor adds the budget demands of the different districts together, calculates the tax rate, and then mails the final bill to each property owner. Property tax payments are due twice a year.

Voter-approved tax limitation

In recent years Washington voters have approved three popular measures to ease the growth of the property tax burden state and local governments place on their citizens.[10] Each measure set progressively more stringent limitations on how much state and local elected officials could increase the basic property tax each year. The relatively easy passage of these measures indicates public support for limiting property tax increases has remained stable over time.

The latest of these measures to become law was Initiative 747, passed by voters in 2001. It provides that a taxing district may not increase the total amount it collects in regular property taxes by more than one percent from one year to the next. Initiative 747's one percent limit replaces the earlier Referendum 47 limit, which held annual property tax increases to the lower of the rate of inflation or six percent.[11]

Judges overturn, and legislature re-enacts, Initiative 747

In June 2006, King County Superior Court Judge Mary E. Roberts struck down Initiative 747, saying the underlying law it was supposed to amend was ruled unconstitutional between the time Initiative 747 was filed in January 2001 and when it went to the voters that November. As a result, she said, voters were "incorrectly led" about what they were voting on.[12]

Judge Roberts' ruling was wrong on two counts. First, the voters were not misled. The ballot title clearly states what Initiative 747 would do: limit property taxes to 1 percent per year.[13] Second, Judge Roberts said the initiative didn't accurately reflect the law it sought to amend. But a separate court ruling changed the underlying law *after* Initiative 747 was filed, so initiative sponsors had no way of updating the text of the initiative before it appeared on the ballot.

Under Judge Roberts' hyper-technical legal reasoning, it is impossible to file a valid ballot initiative in Washington state, since initiative sponsors have no way of knowing how the legislature or a judge may change the law the initiative seeks to amend in the 10 months between the filing deadline and election day.

Judge Roberts' ruling, though flawed, was upheld by a sharply-divided state supreme court in 2007. The public reaction was so strong that lawmakers quickly convened a one-day special session for the purpose of re-enacting the Initiative 747 property tax limitation. Since Judge Roberts and the state supreme court justices had struck down Initiative 747 on a procedural technicality, the legislature's re-enactment of the measure makes it immune to further legal challenge.

Under the Initiative 747 law, local officials have three options when considering whether and how much to increase yearly property tax collections: 1) they can increase the amount collected by up to one percent; 2) they can increase the amount collected by more than one percent by drawing on unused taxing authority they banked in previous years; or 3) they can ask voters to approve a higher increase. There are no statutory limits on tax increase proposals sent to the voters. Such proposals need only a simple majority to pass.

Policy Analysis

Washington Policy Center research staff have tracked the results of voter-enacted property tax legislation for ten years. Our annual studies examine the extent to which elected leaders in Washington's 39 counties and 22 major cities restrict increases in regular property tax collections to voter-approved limits, or whether they choose to enact higher increases.

Our research finds that voter-passed initiatives have been successful in restricting how much the regular property tax burden grows each year. Well over 90 percent of Washington counties and major cities now limit their annual increase in regular property tax collections to one percent or less. This is a considerable change from 1998, when only six counties and two cities did so.

Yet while the annual rate of property tax increase has slowed, the amount of money collected by the state from this revenue source has sharply increased since 1980.

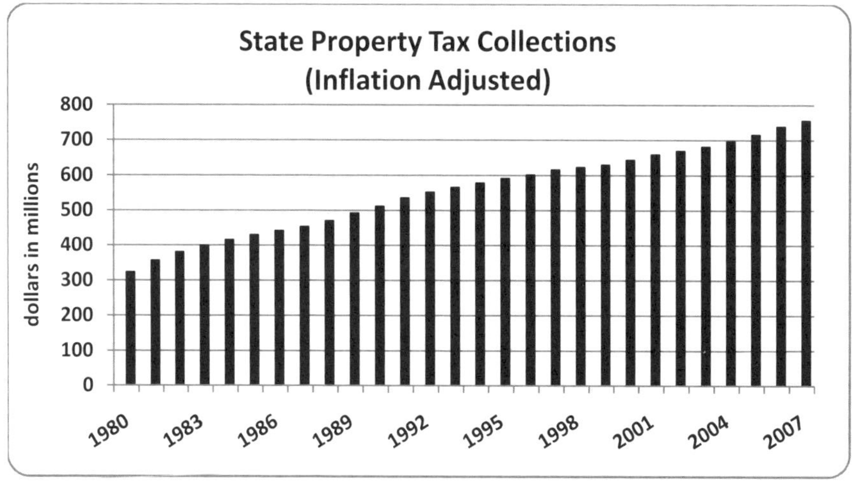

Property tax collection report from the Washington State Department of Revenue. 1980 base year using IPD inflation calculations from Washington's Legislative Evaluation & Accountability Program Committee (LEAP).

Because of tax limitation, property taxes are much lower today than they would have been under previous law. Limits on increases have brought well over $1.1 billion in tax savings for

Washington citizens, although the overall rate of property taxation remains high and taxpayers are demanding additional relief.

Maintaining property tax fairness

Some tax-relief bills introduced in the legislature seek to create a "split roll," in which, for the first time, different classes of property owners would be treated differently under the law. For example, some bills offer tax relief to homeowners, but not to business properties. If state tax collections remain the same, the result would not be broad-based tax relief at all, but merely an unfair shift of part of the existing tax burden from one group of property owners to another.

Efforts to provide property tax relief to Washingtonians should maintain the longstanding constitutional principle of treating the same class of taxpayers equally and uniformly. Lawmakers should avoid proposals that promise tax relief, but instead just shift the tax burden from one group of citizens to another, thus using tax policy to create winners and losers in society.

The simplest way lawmakers can ease the financial burden they place on citizens is to phase out the state property tax levy. Permanently phasing out the state property tax would not reduce local taxes collected by county and local governments. It would, however, induce state elected officials to set clear priorities in state spending.

Recommendations

1) Enact property tax relief to reduce the financial burden government places on citizens to promote economic growth, homeownership, job creation and greater personal freedom. Initiative 747 sought to limit but not reduce the overall property tax burden. Lowering the current level of property taxation would reduce the existing financial burden on citizens, free up money for investment in economic growth and job creation, and give Washingtonians greater personal freedom. One way to do this without impacting local government financing would be to reduce or phase out the state property tax levy.

2) Maintain Washington's uniformity principle when taxing property, so all classes of property owners are treated the same under the law. Washington tax law contains a fundamental principle of fairness: all property owners are treated equally when being taxed by state and local officials. Policymakers should defend this principle and resist proposals to create a so-called "split roll," in which separate classes of property owners are created and then taxed at different rates.

5. General Tax Limitations

> ## Recommendations
>
> 1. Adopt a constitutional amendment requiring a two-thirds legislative vote to raise state or local taxes.
>
> 2. Give tax increases an expiration date.
>
> 3. Like gas-tax revenue, toll revenue should be constitutionally protected.

Background

The voters have consistently voiced a desire to restrict the ability of government officials to unduly raise their tax burden. Initiative 601, passed by voters in 1993, required not only a two-thirds vote of the legislature to raise taxes, but also voter approval of any tax increase in excess of the state spending limit.

Despite this clear directive by the voters, lawmakers have suspended the two-thirds vote requirement twice (in 2002 and 2005) and the Democratic leader in the Senate, Senator Lisa Brown, has recently filed a lawsuit asking the State Supreme Court to declare the two-thirds vote requirement unconstitutional.

Instead of attacking and ignoring the will of the voters, government officials should enact meaningful restrictions on tax increases to help provide a restraint on excessive government spending and future tax increases.

Restrictions will help prioritize government spending and provide a legislative climate in which further increases in the government's financial burden are difficult to pass. Under such a restriction, if lawmakers felt they really needed to collect more money from people, tax increase proposals could be submitted directly to voters for approval.

Policy Analysis

Constitutional taxpayer protections

Since the legislature has repeatedly suspended the voter-approved requirement that tax increases require a two-thirds vote for approval, constitutional protections are needed. These protections, however, should not be limited to state taxpayers, but should extend to local taxpayers as well.

To encourage government officials to build a strong public consensus on the need for any proposed tax increase, a two tiered approach should be adopted. Government officials should utilize two different options to raise the tax burden:

1. with a two-thirds vote of the legislative body or;

2. with a simple majority vote pending ratification by the voters via a referendum.

Either option would help assure that a broad consensus is reached and the taxpayers are included on any policy decisions that would result in an increase in their tax burden.

Tax increase sunsets

Often, when Congress enacts a tax cut or a tax exemption, it includes a sunset clause, meaning the cut or exemption will expire on a certain date. Inevitably, a sharp political debate ensues when an expiration date nears, as lawmakers grapple with whether to vote to extend the tax reduction or to let it terminate. Often a tax break quietly expires without lawmakers having to vote it up or down.

Temporary tax cuts and exemptions create financial unpredictability for taxpayers from one year to the next. Ultimately, when tax cuts and exemptions are set to expire automatically, it is the same as building automatic future tax increases into the law.

In contrast, tax increases are rarely set to expire or "sunset" on a certain date. They tend to be permanent, thus allowing lawmakers to avoid addressing them or having to take an official position. Often taxes are created or increased for specific projects, but they do not expire automatically when the project is paid for or completed. Lawmakers then channel the revenue into the general fund or mark it for future spending. It becomes tax revenue in search of spending.

Citizens and businesses pay more than 50 different taxes in Washington.[14] Lawmakers routinely increase these taxes incrementally or create new ones, even during times when the natural expansion of the economy is pouring additional money into state coffers. For example, during the 2005 session, the legislature permanently raised taxes by $500 million, even though state revenues were growing by seven percent, due to normal economic growth.

By the time the legislature convened in 2006, the state economist was forecasting a $1.6 billion surplus. It turned out that the $500 million in new taxes was completely unnecessary. The new taxes became revenue in search of new spending, and lawmakers were more than happy to oblige.

If the 2005 tax increase had included a sunset provision, Washington citizens would be enjoying significant tax relief today, since the subsequent budget surplus showed that these additional taxes were not needed.

Instead of creating a permanent new expansion of the budget in order to spend away the surplus, lawmakers could simply have allowed the 2005 tax increase to expire. Washington citizens would have benefited by being allowed to keep more of their own money.

Protect toll revenue

State lawmakers are gradually adopting a system of funding transportation projects with toll revenue. Unlike gas-taxes, toll revenue is not constitutionally directed to be used only on public highways. The toll revenue can be redirected to any purpose, including non-transportation government spending, such as entitlement programs.

To ensure that vital transportation infrastructure needs are met, toll revenue should be protected from being tapped for general spending or other non-highway purposes. Toll revenue should receive the same protection that gas-tax revenue receives under the state constitution. If constitutionally protected, drivers would be more willing to accept a broad-based system of road tolls to help pay for and manage traffic congestion relief.

Recommendations

1) Adopt a constitutional amendment requiring a two-thirds legislative vote to raise state or local taxes. Since public officials often refuse to honor voter-approved taxpayer protections, the constitution should be amended to require a two-thirds vote of a state or local legislative body, or voter approval through a referendum, before any state or local tax increase takes effect.

2) Give tax increases an expiration date. When new taxes and tax increases are set to expire, lawmakers will have the opportunity to look at the facts and determine if the tax is serving its intended purpose. If collecting revenue from the tax is still justified, lawmakers can reauthorize it for a further period of time. If the project or goal for which the tax was imposed in the first place has been accomplished, citizens should be permitted to keep their money. If the legislature had followed this recommendation in 2005, the Washingtonians today would be benefiting from $500 million in tax relief.

3) Like gas-tax revenue, toll revenue should be constitutionally protected. To gain public support for funding transportation projects with road tolls and to ensure that road revenues are actually spent on reducing traffic congestion, toll revenue should receive the same constitutional protection afforded to gas-tax revenue.

6. Tax Advantages of Tribal Businesses

Recommendations

1. State leaders should negotiate an agreement with tribal casino owners so that a portion of Indian gambling profits are paid into the state general fund in lieu of taxes, as is common in most other states.

2. Policymakers should set up a review of the relationship between the state and tribal businesses, especially in new areas of commerce in which tribes compete with non-Indian citizens.

Background

For decades, tribal businesses (including casinos and hotels) have benefited from a system of rules and regulations that gives their owners significant competitive advantage over non-tribal citizens. Whether in the form of exemptions from unemployment insurance, business and occupation taxes, or workers' compensation taxes, many tribal businesses are able to take advantage of a reduced regulatory environment. Nowhere is this exemplified more than in the gaming industry.

In Washington there are 29 federally recognized Indian tribes. These tribes operate 27 casinos, with at least one additional major casino under construction, which together generated $1.33 billion in gross revenue in 2007.[15]

The total combined membership of the 29 tribes in the state is just under 55,000 people, or .009 percent of the people in the state. Some tribes have fewer than 200 members, while the largest have more than 9,000. Tribal membership is defined as the certified number of people who are officially recognized by tribal leaderships, based on their racial identity.

Who is an Indian?

There is no legal definition of who is an American Indian. Each tribe decides on and enforces its own membership rules. The National Indian Gaming Commission describes federal policy this way:

> "Indian tribes have the authority to determine membership requirements. Many tribes have a blood quantum requirement (i.e., one-fourth) and may have additional requirements relating to residency, place of birth, or enrollment deadlines. The Federal Government generally requires a person to be a member of a federally recognized tribe to be eligible for federal benefits."[16]

For example, leaders of the Snoqualmie Tribe, in a dispute over control of the tribe's anticipated casino profits, recently expelled 60 members because they "don't have the required one-eigth tribal blood to be members."[17] At the same meeting of designated "preferred voters," tribal leaders banished eight members, depriving them of all tribal benefits, including the right to be on tribal land, and the right to claim Indian identity.[18]

For purposes of the U.S. Census, the definition of who is an Indian is based on self-identification. In 2000, 2.4 million people identified themselves as American Indian or Alaska Native.[19] Only a small portion of people who self-identify, however, are registered members of a recognized Indian tribe.

Tribal businesses' tax status

In Washington, state and local governments are specifically prohibited by federal law from taxing any aspect of tribal gaming, whether it is a business and occupation tax on operations, or sales and use taxes for equipment. Also, no taxes are allowed on tribal gaming itself.

Some tribal businesses make limited impact mitigation payments to local governments to help cover the cost of community services. Unlike regular taxes paid by other citizens, however, these payments are voluntary, and the amount is negotiated between the tribal business owners and local governments.

Tribal business owners only make revenue-sharing and impact mitigation payments *after* their businesses have made a clear profit. In contrast, non-tribal business owners must pay the state Business and Occupation tax whether they make a profit or not.

Policy Analysis

Non-tribal card rooms and mini-casinos are subject to the full array of business taxes: sales tax on food and beverages, business and occupation tax, sales tax on construction and equipment purchases, etc. Additionally, local governments can levy a tax of up to 20 percent on gross receipts from gambling. More than half of local jurisdictions that tax non-tribal card rooms impose a tax rate of around 10 or 11 percent.

Some tribes are moving beyond their traditional core business of operating casinos and game rooms and branching out into other industries. Proposals for future tribal businesses include selling gasoline without collecting the 36 cents-per-gallon state gas tax, operating hotels and shopping malls without collecting state taxes, and opening a tax-exempt oil refinery to produce even cheaper gas for non-tribal consumers.

In 2006, the Squaxin and Swinomish tribes won a case in U.S. District Court (Judge Thomas Zilly) allowing them to keep revenue from gas taxes rather than forward them to the state.[20] Other Washington tribes could assert the same right and use their added profits to lower the price they charge drivers at the pump.

The Indian Gaming Regulatory Act

In 1988, Congress passed the Indian Gaming Regulatory Act prohibiting states from taxing tribal gaming revenues. However, tribes sometimes negotiate a voluntary profit-sharing agreement with states. This allows tribal leaders to mute public criticism about unequal tax treatment among businesses without giving up a valuable tax exemption.

In Washington, however, there is no profit-sharing agreement between the state and Indian tribes, as there is in most other states.

In 2005, the Washington State Gaming Commission reached a tentative agreement with the Spokane Tribe under which the Tribe would pay a percentage of its gaming profits, based on a sliding scale, to the state general fund.[21]

This agreement never took effect. On October 27, 2005, Governor Gregoire sent a letter to the Gaming Commission canceling the proposed agreement and instructing state negotiators to start over.[22]

In 2007, she signed a new agreement with financial terms far more generous to the Spokane Tribe.[23] Under the new compact, the tribal members will retain between $60 million and $90 million over ten years, which, under the canceled agreement, would have been paid to the general fund and used to fund state programs.

The canceled 2005 Spokane Tribe agreement could have served as a model for agreements with the state's other casino-owning tribes. If the state had such profit-sharing agreements with these tribes, the state general fund in 2006 alone would have received between $42 million and $490 million, depending on the net profits of individual casinos.

The following table summarizes the legal and regulatory advantages of tribal-owned businesses.

Comparison of Washington state regulations and taxes that apply to tribal businesses and non-tribal businesses

	Tribal Businesses	Non-Tribal Businesses
Must obey smoking ban	No	Yes
Must obey 1964 Civil Rights Act	No	Yes
Must obey voter-passed initiatives	No	Yes
Pay gaming taxes	No	Yes
Pay B&O tax	No	Yes
Pay sales tax	No	Yes
Pay tobacco tax	No	Yes
Pay workers' comp. taxes	No	Yes
Pay unemploy. tax	No	Yes
May offer slots	Yes	No
May offer keno	Yes	No
May offer craps	Yes	No
May offer roulette	Yes	No
May offer baccarat	Yes	No
Higher betting limit	Yes	No

Recommendations

1) State leaders should negotiate an agreement with tribal casino owners so that a portion of gambling profits are paid into the state general fund in lieu of taxes, as is common in most other states. By not following through with the model agreement negotiated with the Spokane Tribe in 2005, state leaders are depriving the state of important additional revenue that could supplement spending on essential public services, like public education and health care.

They are also missing an opportunity to serve the public interest, because there is no policy in place to redress some of the imbalance between the favorable tax treatment enjoyed by tribal businesses, and the high-tax environment in which all other business owners must operate.

2) Policymakers should set up a review of the relationship between the state and tribal businesses, especially in new areas of commerce in which tribes compete with non-Indian citizens. Policymakers should request a study to measure the economic and competitive impact of tax-free tribal businesses on non-tribal businesses in areas of commerce other than gambling. An objective assessment is needed to determine whether the special tax and regulatory treatment granted to tribal businesses is exceeding its intended purpose.

Additional Resources from Washington Policy Center

"Learning from the Past and Creating our Future" (keynote address at WPC's 2008 Government Reform Conference), by David Walker, April 2008.

"Assessing the Impact of the 1% Property Tax Limit," by Paul Guppy, February 2008.

"Review of Homestead Property Tax Proposals," by Jason Mercier, February 2008.

"Citizens Guide to Initiative 960, The Taxpayer Protection Act," by Jason Mercier, Policy Notes, 2007-16.

"New Tax Deferral Program Offers Little Hope to Hard-Pressed Homeowners," by Paul Guppy, December 2007.

"The Taxpayer Protection Act, Take 2," by Jason Mercier, September 2007.

"Failure to Enact Permanent 1% Limit Could Lead to $1.5 Billion Property Tax Increase," by Paul Guppy, March 2007.

"The Washington Policy Center Tax Cut Plan," by Paul Guppy, January 2007.

"Getting to the Bottom of Initiative 920 (Death Tax Repeal)," by Carl Gipson, October 2006.

"Relying on Sin Taxes Reveals the Contradictions in the State Budget," by John Barnes, June 2005.

"New Research Shows Voter-Passed Property Tax Limitation is Working," 2005.

"Property Tax Limitation in Washington State," by Paul Guppy, August 2003.

"The Economic Case against an Income Tax in Washington State," by David G. Tuerck, John S. Barrett, Sorin Codreanu, May 2003.

"A Policy Guide for Budget Reform: Strategies for Improving State Government Services and Reducing the Deficit," by Eric Montague, January 2003.

"Guiding Principles of a Fair and Effective Tax System," by Paul Guppy, January 2002.

"State Income Taxes Increase Government Spending and Reduce Personal Income Growth," by Eric Montague, June 2002.

---

[1] The text in this section is adapted from "Principles of Sound Tax Policy," by Dan Mitchell, Heritage Foundation, Washington, D.C., November 2001, "Guiding Principles of Taxation," Tax Policy and Research, Montana Department of Revenue, October 2001, and "Some Underlying Principles of Tax Policy" by Richard K. Vader and Lowell E. Galloway, Joint Economic Committee, United States Congress, Washington, D.C., September 1998.

[2] "Tax Reference Manual, Information on State and Local Taxes in Washington State," Revenue Research Report, Department of Revenue, Olympia, January 2007, p. 1, at www.dor.wa.gov/Content/AboutUs/StatisticsAndReports/2007/Tax_Reference_2007/default.aspx.

[3] These states are Connecticut, Illinois, Maine, Michigan, Nebraska, New Jersey, Ohio, Pennsylvania and Rhode Island.

[4] "Economic Impact of the Adoption of a State Income Tax in Washington," by Dr. Thomas R. Dye, Lincoln Center for Public Service, published by the National Taxpayers Union, Washington, D.C., June 2000.

[5] Ibid.

[6] H.R. 4520, "To amend the Internal Revenue Code of 1986 to remove impediments in such Code and make our manufacturing, service, and high-technology businesses and workers more competitive and productive both at home and abroad," passed by Congress and sent to the President, October 11, 2004, at www..thomas.loc.gov/cgi-bin/bdquery/z?d108:h.r.04520.

[7] Les Blumenthal, "State sales tax deduction cut from federal measure," *The News Tribune,* Tacoma, May 11, 2006. See also "Promoting State Sales Tax Deductibility," Office of Congressman Brian Baird, October 2003, at www.house.gov/baird/tax.htm.

[8] Conference Report on H.R. 4520, "The American Jobs Creation Act of 2004," Committee on Ways and Means, United States House of Representatives, October 7, 2004, at www.waysandmeans.house.gov/media/pdf/hr4520/hr4250confreptshortsummary.pdf.

[9] Examples of taxing districts include: the state, county, city, road, school, public utility, library, port, water, fire, sewer, parks, flood zone, hospital, airport, ferry, cemetery, mosquito control, park-recreation, emergency medical, irrigation, cultural-arts, agricultural pest and urban apportionment. In all there are 1,744 taxing districts in Washington.

[10] The three measures are: Referendum 47, passed November 1997 by 64 percent to 36 percent; Initiative 722, passed November 2000 by 56 percent to 44 percent (this

initiative was later invalidated by the courts); and Initiative 747, passed November 2001 by 58 percent to 42 percent.

[11] The measure of inflation required under Referendum 47 was the Implicit Price Deflator reported by the United States Treasury every October.

[12] *Washington Citizens Action of Washington et. al. v. State of Washington and William Rice, Director of the State Department of Revenue,* King County Superior Court, Judge Mary E. Roberts, No. 05-2-02052-1 SEA, June 13, 2006.

[13] "Proposed Initiatives to the People – 2001," text of Initiative 747, filed January 8, 2001, Index of Initiative and Referendum History and Statistics: 1914 – 2005, Office of the Washington Secretary of State, at www.secstate.wa.gov/elections/initiatives/statistics.aspx.

[14] "Tax Reference Manual: Information on State and Local Taxes in Washington State," Washington State Department of Revenue, January 2008, at www.dor.wa.gov.

[15] "Net Gambling Receipts for Gambling in Washington State in Fiscal Year 2007," Tribal Gaming (estimated), Washington State Gambling Commission, Agency Overview, December 2007, at www.wsgc.wa.gov/newsletters/brochure.pdf.

[16] "Who is considered a tribal member?" National Indian Gaming Commission, Frequently Asked Questions, Tribal Members, at www.nigc.gov/AboutUs/FrequentlyAskedQuestions/tabid/57/Default.aspx#q_01, accessed May 29, 2008.

[17] "Snoqualmies banish eight, disenroll 60," by Linda V. Mapes, *The Seattle Times,* April 28, 2008.

[18] Ibid.

[19] "Table 1: Total Population by Age, Race, Hispanic Origin or Latino Origin for the United States, 2000," Census 2000 Briefs and Special Reports, U.S. Census Bureau, at www.census.gov/population/www/cen2000/phc-t9.html.

[20] See also, "Tribes could escape gas tax," by Joseph Turner, *The News Tribune,* Tacoma, May 14, 2006, and "Tribes take over gas tax from state," *The Associated Press,* May 30, 2006.

[21] Spokane Tribe and the State of Washington Class III Gaming Compact 2005, Appendix.

[22] Letter from Governor Christine Gregoire to Mr. Curt Ludwig, Chairman, Washington State Gaming Commission, October 27, 2005.

[23] "Governor Signs Spokane Tribal Gaming Compact, Washington State Gambling Commission, February 16, 2007, at www.wsgc.wa.gov/docs/press_releases/spokane_compact_021607.pdf.

CHAPTER 3

1. Peer Review of Environmental Science

Recommendation

1. As the potential costs of policies regarding environmental issues increase, legislators should demand higher levels of scientific rigor.

Background

As the stakes increase, so does the need for peer review

In the coming years, Washington policymakers are preparing to spend billions of dollars on efforts to reduce carbon emissions. Billions more will be spent in time and money by residents who have to adjust to a myriad of regulations requiring them to change their driving habits, buy "green" building materials, pay more for energy and a range of other requirements.

Asking such commitments of Washington residents should mean that policymakers are demanding high levels of certainty about the potential costs of climate change. After all, it would make little sense to engage on an expensive crusade without some certainty about the harm the state is looking to avoid.

Unfortunately, proclamations about the risks from climate change have been revised again and again, always downward, and other information has been shown to be more about politics than science.

To make sure the policies being proposed are appropriate and effective, policymakers need to demand a more rigorous peer review of data they use to guide their decisions. Further, they should add an extra measure of caution when adopting policies that have high price tags for citizens. Policymakers should have accurate scientific information before they impose regulations that try to modify the lifestyles of the citizens they are supposed to represent.

A series of errors

During the past year, a number of scientific and financial errors have been found in climate change information being provided to the legislature. These errors are not trivial. They involve some of the most common claims being made about the supposed impacts of climate change.

The most often-repeated climate change threat in the Northwest is the predicted effect rising temperatures will have on snowpack. Electrical generation, recreation, drinking water and fish populations all rely on mountain snowpack. In 2007, Seattle Mayor Greg Nickels, using data from Oregon State University and the University of Washington Climate Impacts Group (CIG) claimed that, "The average snowpack in the Cascades has declined 50 percent since 1950 and will be cut in half again in 30 years." [1] This statement was incorrect, and it masked some statistical tricks.

The data Mayor Nickels used began in the high-snowpack years of the early 1950s and ended in the low-snowpack years of the mid-1990s, thus falsely exaggerating a downward trend. The statement also hid the fact that during the past two decades, when temperatures have been increasing, snowpack in the Cascades has shown a slight upward trend, with several years in a row of snowpack well above the average.

Ultimately, the chairman of the Atmospheric Sciences Department at the U.W. admitted that

> "reasonable statement about the part that we think is attributable to the warming associated with global warming is probably more like fifteen percent." [2]

The correction, however, was made only after an internal disagreement about the data became public and the mayor's staff was forced to revise their claim. This is not the only case of needed correction when it comes to public claims about climate change.

In its 2005 report, the Puget Sound Action Team and the Climate Impacts Group printed a graph indicating that the "mid-range" estimate of sea level rise in mid-Puget Sound was 39 inches over the next century. These groups even wrote that the projection was fairly certain, because sea level rise is one of the "best understood and predictable components of future climate."[3]

The graph using this data was used by staff at the Department of Ecology to back up their own estimate of the future effects of climate change. When the data were updated to reflect the science in 2008, however, suddenly the sea level numbers were dramatically lower.

In January 2008, the Climate Impacts Group and the Puget Sound Action Team estimated that the 90-year sea level rise in mid-Puget Sound would be just 13 inches, with only six inches attributed to climate change. This is one third of their 2005 projection. In fact, the previous certainty about the accuracy of the numbers was inappropriate, and the result was a significant error in the projections.

Officials in cities like Seattle and Olympia have used projections of severe sea level rise to push for more government spending on mitigation projects, like higher sea walls, as well as more regulations to try to reduce carbon emissions.

When a 500-year storm hit Lewis County in December 2007, the head of the Climate Impacts Group testified that the storm was not very significant, even telling a legislative committee that the rainfall was "not a top three event. I want to stress that."[4] His implication was that the storm was visible evidence of ongoing climate change, not a freak event.

He admitted, however, that he did not have all the data. When the data did come in, he was forced to change his position.

After examining the data from other sources, he wrote to the committee that he had changed his opinion, saying:

> "The damaging flood of December 3-4, 2007, on the Chehalis River resulted from exceptionally heavy rainfall that was confined to the vicinity of the Willapa Hills. Rainfall recorded by Weyerhaeuser and other gauges was about three

times that recorded outside of this small area. The exceptional nature of this event is confirmed by the USGS gauge at Doty, where flow exceeded twice the previous record."[5]

While ultimately this admission is appropriate, given the lack of data at the time of the hearing, the Climate Impact Group's statement that the rainstorm was not unusual was inappropriate.

Policy Analysis

This series of errors, all occurring within the past year, shows the real danger when data is not peer reviewed and public claims are made without subjecting them to critical examination by a third party. In each case, these inaccuracies could have been avoided through simple double checking by a trained eye.

None of these claims, however, received that review, and each found its way into the political decision-making process. A lack of peer review can lead to recklessness when drawing conclusions about environmental policy.

Preventing errors when the stakes are high

A number of elected officials have called climate change a "crisis." The seriousness of the problem, they argue, calls for serious and wide-ranging policies that change the way Washingtonians live and do business. One activist, praising Governor Gregoire's climate strategy, said that the goal was "remaking the economy of the nation, the whole globe."[6]

Politicians use the data they are given by scientists to gauge the level of response that is justified by the threat. If the data are exaggerated or skewed in one direction, it is likely that policies will be too expensive or inappropriate.

Often, politicians select the sources of their information because they simply want their beliefs reconfirmed, despite obvious conflicts of interest. In Washington, the legislature has selected the U.W. Climate Impacts Group, which openly calls for government intervention in climate change, as the group it funds to provide information on that issue.

The state's assessment of "green" building standards was written by Paladino and Company, which touts itself as one of the leading green building architectural firms in Washington. It is not surprising that when officials select biased groups, the data they provide are skewed, inaccurate and come without peer review. Policymakers need to demand better results, and ensure that the information they are receiving has been reviewed and critiqued.

Building in peer review can identify not only the accuracy or utility of information provided to the legislature, but also quantify the level of uncertainty involved. Even when data are accurate, important decisions may not be appropriate if the level of uncertainty is high.

Legislators should be skeptical about the quality of the data they receive from all sides of an issue, especially when scientists advocate for a specific policy direction. Expressing skepticism without alternative data can be difficult, but the more restrictive and costly an environmental policy will be on citizens, the greater the need to insure the science is accurate and has survived a rigorous review. Without independent peer review, legislators should not impose costly policy recommendations.

Recommendation

1) As the potential costs of policies regarding environmental issues increase, legislators should demand higher levels of scientific rigor. A critical peer review should be demanded of science being offered for use in policymaking, especially from groups who have already expressed policy preferences on their issue, and have an interest in the outcome.

2. Performance-Based Green Buildings

Recommendation

1. Eliminate the mandated "green" building standards for public buildings, which have failed to live up to their promise and cost more than initially projected.

Background

Promoting performance-based green buildings

As the push for policies that reduce greenhouse gas emissions grows, many policymakers are looking for reasons, other than environmental stewardship, to justify imposing more regulation. They argue that adopting "green" policies are not only good for environment, but they also create jobs and save money in the long term.

Too often, however, these claims are wrong. They are often based on faulty analysis and, as the data comes in, it becomes clear that there is a wide gap between green building claims and reality. Washington's push to mandate green schools is the latest example.

In 2005, the legislature required that all new Washington schools and state buildings receive "Silver" certification from the Leadership in Environmental an Energy Design (LEED) standard or the Washington sustainable school design protocol. The law said:

> "The legislature finds that public buildings can be built and renovated using high-performance methods that save money, improve school performance, and make workers more productive. High-performance public buildings are proven to increase student test scores, reduce worker absenteeism, and cut energy and utility costs."[7]

A wide range of studies were provided to back up these claims. In January 2005 the legislature received a study done by Paladino and Company and commissioned by the Washington State

Board of Education and the Office of the Superintendent of Public Instruction.[8]

The report claimed that the payoff from these "green" schools was significant. Their report claimed a "conservative" estimate of a 25 percent reduction in energy use, five percent increase in test scores and a 15 percent decrease in absenteeism. The small additional cost would be more than offset by the savings, leading to a predicted 150 percent return on investment.

Three years after those regulations were passed, however, the very schools used in the study are failing to meet the goals claimed. In many cases school districts have actually incurred higher costs for "green" design elements that added little benefit, but added greatly the cost of constructing that building.

Given that record, the legislature should move from a prescriptive, cookie-cutter approach to green buildings and provide incentives to build schools that meet some basic standards of efficiency. By focusing on outcomes rather than a district's ability to check off a certain number of "green" boxes during construction, the state is more likely to see actual improvements in energy efficiency, test scores and other academic measures. It also allows local school directors to use their expertise to customize buildings that fit local circumstances and local climate.

Rewarding performance, as opposed to requiring districts to meet an arbitrary set of standards regardless of outcome, will truly make Washington's schools "high performance."

Failing to make the grade

When developing a "green" standard for Washington's schools, the state hired Paladino and Company, which notes on its web page that "Our mission is simple: transform development into a sustainable process through collaboration on exemplary green building projects." The study focused on five school districts, examining the costs and benefits of various strategies at each school. Not surprisingly, they determined that requiring green building standards would yield large dividends to the state.

At the time of the study, however, the research was speculative, as many of the schools had not yet been opened or had been open less than a year. Using data through the 2006-07 school year, the actual results from the schools are significantly different from the projections promised in the report.

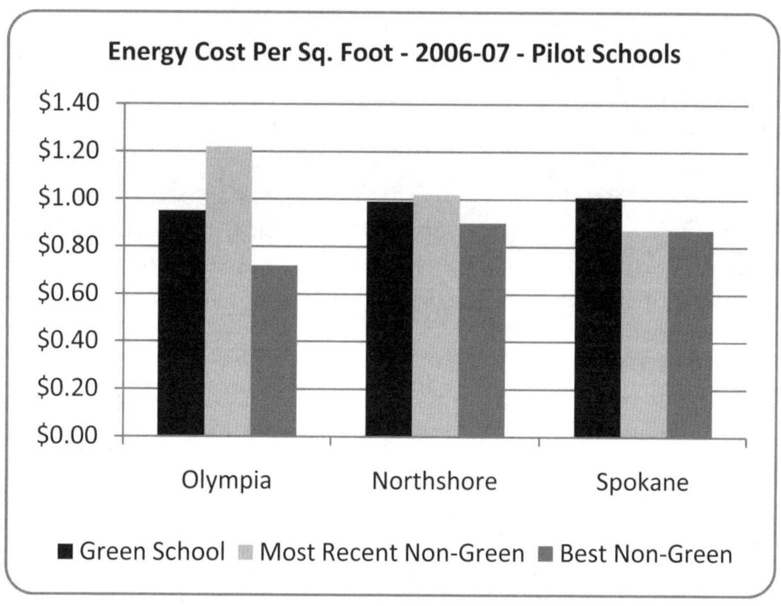

For instance, the study said "green" schools would reduce energy use by 30-50 percent. Recent energy data, however, shows that in Olympia, Northshore and Spokane the local "green" school, while more efficient than some buildings, was never the most efficient. Using energy costs per square foot, only in Olympia does the pilot school come close to being 30 percent more efficient than the most recent, non-green school. It, however, uses more energy per square foot than a school that was remodeled in 1991.

In the case of Spokane, the pilot school, which was one of three "green" schools recently built in the district, was actually 14 percent *less* efficient than the most recent, non-green school in the same area.

In Bethel, Thompson Elementary, a "green" school, did best at meeting the goals and was significantly better in energy costs per square foot than other buildings in the district, about 21 percent.

Ironically, the state complained that the building might not be up to the standards because its windows were too small.[9]

It should be noted that comparing schools effectively is difficult because the Bethel school district covers three different utility districts, each with different rates. Thus, there are only a few schools to compare to that pay the same rates. Only two of the fourteen other schools in the district are in the same utility district as Thompson.

This should not take away from Thompson's success. The numbers tell a clear story that a district willing to apply the rules with wide local discretion can see positive results. Given the difficulties found in other districts, however, we should be careful about drawing too many conclusions from this one school.

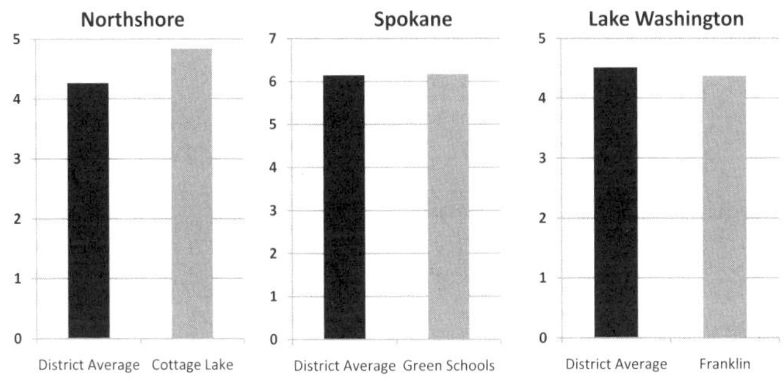

Similar results appear when examining the records related to student absences. Green schools are supposed to significantly reduce absenteeism, but the numbers show something else. In Spokane's three "green" schools, the average absentee rate per student is almost identical (slightly higher actually) to the district as a whole. In both the Northshore and Lake Washington school districts[10] the absentee rates are very similar, with the green school having slightly lower absentee rates in Lake Washington and slightly higher in the Northshore School District.

While the results have not been promising, the costs have been well above what was projected. Estimating the cost of the "green" elements of these schools is very difficult and no district we spoke with was able to measure these costs with confidence. Several districts, however, did offer an educated guess and everyone agreed that the best estimate was that "green" buildings cost about six percent more, not the two percent promised by Paladino and Company in its report.[11]

Policy Analysis

Why green standards fall short

There are a number of reasons green building standards do not live up to the promises made to the legislature in 2005. First, the initial cost projections were extremely rosy. It is likely that bill's supporters chose the most optimistic estimates in order to pass the legislation. Green building backers over-promised, so it is not surprising that school districts are now under-delivering.

Second, the standards rely on a cookie-cutter approach that requires spending that does little to achieve energy savings or other goals, but must be met to receive the required green certificate points. In Spokane, for instance, additional bike racks were installed to meet a requirement, but in reality the racks largely sit empty.

Third, the standards often try to impose contradictory goals. The rules call for larger windows in the belief that more daylight increases student test scores. The big windows, however, greatly increase energy costs by making a room colder in winter and hotter in spring and summer. Similarly, the schools recirculate air more frequently to improve the "health" of the buildings. That also means running the HVAC system more, increasing energy use.

Given these contradictory goals, it is not surprising that green buildings do not deliver the promised benefits. All of the goals may be desirable, but expecting that all can be met without tradeoffs is folly.

Rewarding success not effort

With energy costs rising, it is unlikely that school officials need much incentive to improve efficiency. In fact, average per square foot energy costs for Spokane schools has fallen in every decade, with schools dating from the 1930 being about 18 percent less efficient than schools built in the 1990s. Facility directors know their districts, and the data show that they successfully improve the energy efficiency of their buildings year after year.

Legislators should adopt a policy that rewards actual results after a school opens. This would not only engage the creativity and expertise of local officials, it would provide an incentive to improve if the school falls short. If a school building achieves 70 percent of the savings projected, state policy should act as an incentive for local officials to achieve the additional 30 percent. Currently, no such incentive exists. Schools that checked all the correct "green" boxes receive credit even when, as shown above, they do not actually save any energy.

Legislators should reexamine the standards they passed three years ago, providing districts with more flexibility and getting rid of the contradictory standards they put in place. Doing so is the surest way to achieve the promise of improving energy efficiency.

Recommendation

1) Eliminate the mandated "green" building standards for public buildings, which have failed to live up to their promise and cost more than initially projected. Provide performance-based incentives for school districts to meet energy efficiency targets, rewarding districts only after the data show they have achieved the promised energy savings.

3. Reducing Greenhouse Gas Emissions

Recommendation

1. Adopt a revenue-neutral carbon tax to encourage reduction of greenhouse gas emissions.

Background

A true market approach to reducing CO_2 emissions

If you hear the words "climate change" in Washington these days, the words "market-based" are sure to follow soon after. Lurking behind the proposed "market" approaches to climate change, however, lay a large number of solutions based on government subsidies, bureaucracies and sweeping political decisions about our lifestyles and economy.

The governor's Climate Advisory Team (CAT) recommends a "cap-and-trade" system that caps emissions and then allows companies that cannot reach the cap to purchase emissions allowances from those who are below the cap. While a cap-and-trade system appears "market-based," all the key decisions, setting the emissions cap and how to count carbon emissions, would actually be made by politicians.

The problem with such a mandatory approach is it depends on the supposed ability of government officials to make wise decisions about:

- A wide variety of diverse industries;

- The rapid pace of technical and economic development;

- The complex exchanges that occur daily in the economy;

- The unintended consequences of the decisions of millions of consumers.

There is a truly market-based system that can reduce greenhouse gases by harnessing the creativity of everyone in Washington, creating incentives for technological innovation and providing the flexibility needed to adapt to changing circumstances in the future. By increasing the price of carbon and cutting taxes to offset the price increase and encourage capital investment, Washington may take a significant step toward reducing CO_2 emissions in a way that is effective, efficient and truly creates jobs.

If, however, Washington follows the path it is on, relying primarily on a cap-and-trade system along with inflexible, top-down regulation and government officials picking winners and losers in areas not covered by a cap-and-trade system, we will find that we have spent a tremendous amount without meeting greenhouse gas reduction targets.

A patchwork of wishful thinking

The interim report released by the Washington Climate Advisory Team (CAT) in January 2008 is a patchwork of options covering a number of different areas. The CAT recommendations are limited by the expertise of a few dozen panel members and staff who identify potential improvements in areas with which they are partially familiar.

Worse, they actually hinder the creativity of those looking for technological solutions by narrowing the range of possibilities. For instance, the strategy calls for incentives with the goal of "maximizing in-state production of sustainable biofuels and biofuel feedstocks."[12] Recent studies, however, demonstrate that biofuels likely increase the amount of CO_2 emitted, because more energy must be used to grow and transport the fuel than is yielded.[13]

Government regulation and subsidies have skewed economic incentives to plant biofuel crops on marginal lands, increasing the need for energy inputs on the form of fertilizer, plowing, harvesting and transport.

Removing such incentives will be extremely difficult politically. Those who receive benefit from biofuel subsidies are likely to fight to keep them in place, meaning government officials are actually paying to increase CO_2 emissions as part of its climate strategy.

Put simply, subsidies and regulations, like those that form the foundation of the CAT's recommendations, fail to engage the public, are costly, stifle technological innovation and may actually be counterproductive.

Charting an unknown path

Additionally, the CAT often makes policy recommendations hoping that unintended consequences will not overwhelm the potential benefits. The most dramatic of these examples is transportation, which represents the single largest type of greenhouse gas emissions in Washington. The CAT report, however, leaves most of the transportation strategies undone.

There are two primary reasons.

First, the cap-and-trade system is less applicable to transportation-related emissions. The CAT report admits that "cap-and-trade market mechanisms being considered throughout the world at this time do not directly reduce transportation-related emissions."[14] As a result, policies that address transportation rely on central government planning and programs, not markets.

Second, developing such programs is extremely complex and historically they have failed to achieve their intended goals.

Ironically, despite the fact that CAT members do not know what strategy they will use, they did set targets for reducing vehicle miles traveled (VMT) and counted those in the final report as projected "reductions." In other words, they know where they want to go and believe they are likely to get there, but have no idea which path to take.

It is not surprising that CAT members would have difficulty developing an effective strategy. King County officials have for decades attempted to increase the percentage of commuters using transit and have continually failed. In fact, the percentage of daily commute trips in the Puget Sound region using transit is smaller today than in 1980.[15] Given the record of failure, it is difficult to see how any government-planned approach is likely to be effective in reducing VMT by 18 percent by 2020, the target set by CAT.

Policy Analysis

Cutting carbon emissions, risk and taxes

The problems outlined above can be overcome with an approach that is more flexible, creates strong incentives to innovate, and aggregates the dispersed information held by millions of Washington residents. This flexible approach is a revenue-neutral carbon tax that encourages reductions in emissions while reducing taxes on families and technical innovators.

A revenue-neutral carbon tax includes three elements:

1. Place a tax on carbon, including motor and heating fuels, while exempting biofuels;

2. Cut sales taxes to offset the increased cost to families of the carbon tax;

3. Cut taxes on capital investment to encourage new technologies, the replacement of inefficient equipment, and spur economic growth and job creation.

This approach would actually reduce taxes for consumers and technical innovators in Washington. Rather than relying on government regulations that try to alter our lifestyles, a revenue-neutral carbon tax recognizes that technological innovation must be central to our efforts to effectively reduce greenhouse gas emissions and grow Washington's economy.

The purpose of a carbon tax is to account for the costs associated with CO_2 emissions – costs that would otherwise not be felt by the carbon emitter. If one believes that CO_2 emissions are entirely benign, then the only reasons for such a tax would be other ancillary benefits, such as energy independence.

Many people, however, are skeptical of the claims of environmental activists, who have proven to be alarmist when it comes to climate change. Skeptics can still support a revenue-neutral carbon tax as a way to reduce environmental risk appropriately. The key is to approach the problem in a way that is efficient and creates appropriate, but not excessive, incentives to reduce the risks from greenhouse gases.

Getting the design and costs right

The goal of a carbon tax is to raise prices on consumption that creates risk of harm to the environment, instead of simply taxing to fund government programs. This approach encourages people to find alternatives to the use of carbon-emitting fuels and for innovators to create technologies that help reduce costs. Increasing the cost of using carbon adds extra incentive to be efficient by capturing the costs of the risk associated with carbon emissions.

The key is to design a carbon price so that it creates incentives without the negative impacts typical tax increases have on the economy and families. Policymakers should set the initial carbon tax low, in the range of $10-$15 per ton of carbon.[16] The tax would cover all forms of carbon emitting energy generation, both electricity and home heating oil and natural gas, as well as fuel consumption. This would amount to a three-to-four-cent increase in the price of a gallon of gas. Overall, a $10 per ton tax would generate about $250 million each year, which would be offset by reductions in other taxes. A $15 per ton tax would generate about $370 million.[17]

A low initial tax rate allows the flexibility to increase the tax if policymakers find that the incentives are too low. Of course, any increase in the carbon tax *must* be accompanied by offsetting cuts in other taxes.

Setting a carbon price is straightforward and it can be adjusted as new information emerges. Changing the rules for a myriad of government-imposed regulations as new evidence emerges would be virtually impossible.

A market approach to improve efficiency

A carbon tax has a wide range of advantages over the currently proposed system of cap-and-trade with government regulation and subsidies in areas not covered by caps. As a tax spreads throughout the economy wherever carbon-emitting energy is used, it creates incentives for every family and business in Washington. Instead of a few dozen politicians and planners deciding where Washington should cut CO_2 emissions, carbon tax incentives engage everyone in the effort to reduce costs and carbon emissions.

A cap-and-trade system would certainly create unintended consequences, and will create political constituencies that make it difficult to dislodge policies that are ineffective.

A carbon tax, with offsetting cuts in other taxes, avoids these problems. While providing broad incentives to reduce carbon emissions, it does not favor one business sector over another. Indeed, it rewards the constant drive of innovation, gradually making today's CO_2-emitting technology obsolete and driving carbon emissions ever lower.

Recommendation

1) Adopt a revenue-neutral carbon tax to encourage reduction of greenhouse gas emissions. A carbon tax, with offsetting cuts in other taxes, avoids economic shocks, while providing policymakers the flexibility to adjust the carbon tax rate up or down in response to better climate science. It promotes true economic growth, and avoids increasing the overall tax burden on families and business owners. It creates an incentive not only to innovate, but encourages every Washington resident to find inexpensive ways to conserve energy and reduce carbon emissions.

4. "Green-Collar" Jobs

Recommendation

1. Discard arbitrary jobs targets in favor of focusing on the real goals like reducing greenhouse gas emissions or increasing energy efficiency.

Background

As Washington develops its strategy to address climate change, some people have argued that not only will such an approach improve the environment, but it will actually generate new jobs.

They believe government spending on new projects and rules that steer investment into "green" technologies, will make Washington a leader in the area and bring jobs here. The governor's Executive Order 07-02 on the "Washington Climate Change Challenge" actually spells out the number of "green" jobs that will be created, calling for an increase by 2020 in "the number of clean energy sector jobs to 25,000 from the 8,400 jobs we had in 2004."[18]

There are some significant problems, however, in the way such jobs are calculated. First, the state does not look at the economy-wide impacts of the climate change rules, including job losses in non-energy sectors due to increased energy costs. It is likely that jobs will be "created" in the energy sector as investors move capital from other sectors to renewable energy, which has been granted protection and high returns due to favorable government rules. These jobs, however, would not be "new." They would simply be transferred away from other sectors of the economy.

Second, setting a jobs target for renewable energy without looking at whether those jobs are cost-effective virtually ensures that the state will see a net loss in jobs across all sectors and an increase in costs for Washington residents.

To create the necessary jobs, government officials will either spend taxpayer dollars to make job creation in that sector more attractive, or they will require energy companies to spend money on technologies that require more labor to produce the same amount of energy. In either scenario, taxpayers and ratepayers would pay more for the same product. The result would be an increase in jobs in one sector, but a reduction in the quality of those jobs and in the overall economic well-being of the people of Washington.

When it comes to reducing greenhouse gases, state officials should provide an honest economic assessment and discard arbitrary jobs targets that are likely to reduce Washington's overall prosperity.

Policy Analysis

Counting "new" jobs while ignoring lost jobs

Setting an arbitrary target for the number of jobs in the renewable energy sector is likely to harm the economy. If the people of Washington try to meet the governor's jobs goal, there are three potential outcomes, only one of which is economically benign.

If renewable "green" energy continues to be less efficient than hydro and other alternatives, government policies that seek to increase the number of jobs in this inefficient sector will increase energy costs for all Washington residents, because of the increased labor costs. Ratepayers and taxpayers will have to spend more of their money to get the same amount of energy, meaning they will have less to spend on other things.

Thus, creating "green-collar" jobs would reduce either the overall number of jobs in the economy or the quality of the jobs created. Government policies that direct money to renewable energy projects take capital away from other sectors.

Since renewable energy projects are not currently as efficient as the alternative, it will take more capital to do the same work. If the capital for these projects is simply shifted within the energy sector, the same amount of money would be distributed among a larger number of workers, putting downward pressure on salaries.

Such efforts also collect money from taxpayers and give it to favored businesses. When private investors decide where to put their capital, they look for the greatest return on their investment. In order to encourage investors to put their money into renewable energy, governments provide subsidies, in the form of cash or favorable regulations, to make the profit from "green" energy more attractive than competing investments. Such subsidies provide a favorable return to investors, but they increase costs to taxpayers. Taxpayers are paying more to receive the same level of energy.

If, on the other hand, renewable energy improves its efficiency, utilities may be able to meet electric demand or CO_2 reduction targets with fewer people, falling short of the 25,000 total job target. What then? Would the state require more jobs be created anyway? Would it provide subsidies to encourage utilities to hire more people to do busy work just to meet the 25,000 job target? Whatever strategy officials chose, it would involve inefficiently adding jobs to do the same amount of work. Again, the primary result would be to increase the cost of energy to consumers.

It could be that the target of 25,000 clean energy jobs by 2020 is extremely low and will be met with ease. If that is the case, then the target is meaningless, because meeting the target does not require government intervention. As such, the target's only value is political.

Setting the course of technological innovation

Proponents of government regulations attempt to address this concern by arguing that government incentives help investors look beyond short-term returns to longer-term investments that will create a higher rate of return over time. Further, they argue that government can capably guide investors to develop lucrative technologies.

Government officials, however, are very poor at determining the best direction of future technology. As with any political process, special interest lobbyists intervene in the decision making. Elected officials, who have the final say in determining the direction of technology subsidies, are typically not experts in these fields and often favor technologies that serve political goals, which may include those technologies most likely to benefit their local district or supportive special interest groups.

Even if these purely political considerations are not factored in, elected officials are rarely in the best position to judge the present and future direction of technological development. Choosing the right technology investments is difficult enough for individual investors and executives at private companies whose livelihood depends on it.

Asking elected officials, who are subject to a range of political pressures, to make similar judgments is unlikely to be effective, and is almost certain to be costly, thus reducing the prosperity of Washington residents.

The real economics of climate regulations

When making major decisions about the future of the state, elected officials and the public deserve to have a clear understanding of the economic impact of those policies. They should, however, be based on sound economic analysis.

Setting an artificial jobs goal serves primarily to distort policies designed to reduce carbon emissions and is likely to lead to increased subsidies and regulation and reduce prosperity. The policies currently being offered to create "green-collar" jobs are likely to be costly to taxpayers and ratepayers, reduce the overall economic well-being of Washington residents, and will simply create jobs in one sector at the cost of jobs in other sectors.

This does not necessarily mean that policies that reduce greenhouse gases are unnecessary or not worth the cost. It simply means that policymakers should make decisions based on an honest assessment of the costs and benefits of these policies rather than using analysis that only looks at one side of the ledger. True economic effects can then be weighed against the environmental and political benefits of any climate change policies.

The only way to make that comparison honestly is to engage in a complete examination of the economic impacts or avoid the process altogether. Doing otherwise is simply misleading.

Recommendation

1) Discard arbitrary jobs targets in favor of focusing on the real goals like reducing greenhouse gas emissions or increasing energy efficiency. Any economic analysis of climate policy should include all economic impacts, not just increasing jobs in favored "green" sectors while ignoring economic sectors that are likely to lose jobs.

5. The Role of Science in Environmental Policy

Recommendation

1. Policymakers should recognize the limits of science and use it appropriately to guide the public decision making process, not to dictate policy outcomes or to silence their political critics.

Background

One of the most common claims made by advocates of particular environmental policies is that "the science says" policymakers should follow a particular course of action, so there is no need for any further public debate.

This is especially true in the debate over climate change, where the phrase "scientific consensus" has become a shield used by advocates of all manner of policies to fend off objections. Geneticist David Suzuki of Canada even went so far as to argue that those concerned about climate change should

> "put a lot of effort into trying to see whether there's a legal way of throwing our so-called leaders into jail because what they're doing is a criminal act."[19]

Science is, of course, extremely important when judging the seriousness of environmental challenges. However, science is only one part of the discussion and is often one of the least important elements in determining the final policy undertaken by government. Finding the correct policy also involves judging the values and priorities of the public and understanding the most effective way of translating those values into appropriate policy solutions.

Policy Analysis

Given those balances, policymakers should follow some guidelines in understanding the reliability of scientific information provided to them and how that information can be weighed. By understanding the strengths and limitations of scientific information, policymakers are more likely to find solutions that not only offer effective solutions but solutions that preserve other values and ensure that resources are available to tackle other challenges as well.

Myopia and margins of error

As scientific knowledge improves, scientists consistently refine their expertise; they become more and more specialized in particular fields. That specialization allows scientists to become experts and push the bounds of scientific knowledge, but it also comes with a cost. Specialization can breed a myopic focus and that narrowness can lead to view society's priorities in a way that naturally puts their own specialty at or near the top.

It is not surprising, for instance, that a fish biologist would oppose economic development that effected salmon habitat, or that a climatologist would be especially concerned about possible human influence on the atmosphere.

What is problematic is when scientists express value preferences, not science. A fish biologist is free to oppose economic development, but he cannot claim that such opposition is based on "science," when it is really based on his value preferences and is borne of a career focusing on a particular animal species.

Negative impact of value preferences on science

Individual value preferences can have a negative impact on the quality of science in three important ways.

First, it can lead them to overestimate a scientific specialty's role in describing the world. During the 1990s, salmon biologists frequently referred to salmon as the "canary in the coal mine," indicating that as salmon go, so goes human society and nature.

With regard to climate change, experts tend to emphasize their own field as most important. Climatologists generally regard atmospheric changes as central to the debate. Astrophysicists tend to emphasize solar activity. One expert on polar issues indicated that he felt recent temperature increases were due in large part to patterns of ice flows at the North Pole. This is expected, but it makes it difficult to sort out what is science and what is the by-product of a scientist's narrow, specialized view.

Second, scientists may offer policy solutions because they are certain they understand the nature of a particular problem. Indeed, scientists who are unsure about causes are also less likely to offer solutions. The problem arises when scientists overestimate their level of certainty. For instance, in 2005 the University of Washington's Climate Impacts Group released a study with a graph estimating that, due to climate change, Puget Sound's sea level would rise 39 inches over a hundred years.

At the time they called this projection "one of the best understood and predictable components of future climate."[20] Just over two years later, the estimates had been cut by one-third, to a predicted 14-inch sea-level rise over one hundred years. In 2005, members of the Climate Impacts Group felt very comfortable demanding far-reaching and costly public policies because they overestimated the certainty of their own projections.

Third, the corollary to underestimating uncertainty is to overestimate the risk from a particular environmental threat. Scientists, for whom a particular subject is the focus of their career, are likely to have a very low tolerance for threats to the particular animal they study or the topic area of interest to them.

For example, when University of Washington geologist David Montgomery testified in 2008 on severe floods in Centralia, he particularly lamented what he considered the human causes of some of the landslides.

In his testimony before the Washington state Senate he argued for changes in a number of activities, but said that such events did not occur frequently enough for people to change rules relating to development and forestry. In other words, he was admitting that his level of risk tolerance was far lower than the tolerance of the community at large, even those living in the flood zone. The issue at hand, therefore, was not the science but the level of risk tolerance based on what Dr. Montgomery feels is important (geology) compared to what other people feel is important (forestry and economic development).

Uncertainty about the accuracy, relevance and timeliness of scientific information makes it difficult for policymakers to know when and how they should use science in making policy decisions.

Indeed, policymakers often find it easier to simply take the scientists at their word, especially when it is used to justify a policy outcome policymakers already favor. When policymakers take scientists' statements on blind faith, however, they are avoiding responsibility for the policy decisions they impose on society.

Policymakers are also likely to misfire, because policy decisions based on poor information are likely to result in mandatory programs and regulations that are less effective and more costly than is appropriate, leaving the underlying problem unsolved, while needlessly absorbing economic resources that could be used to address legitimate issues.

The costs of this approach are not hard to imagine. When developing strategies to address environmental problems, policymakers need to have a good understanding of the causes and risks associated with those challenges. If the science being provided is distorted by the personal values and perspective of the scientists, policymakers end up spending public money on efforts that provide little benefit and drain resources from other important issues. Imagine the difference in costs of a public policy designed to address a 39-inch sea level rise, compared to one directed at a 14-inch rise.

Science should not set policy priorities

Even when the science is accurate, it does not indicate that the problem ought to be addressed or that particular policies should be followed.

Consider the case of pesticides. Scientists may be certain that particular pesticides will lead to a certain number of incidents of cancer. Even this knowledge, however, may not make it an important issue or even a call for immediate action. If the rate of cancer is much smaller than the potential damage done from starvation due to destroyed crops, the pesticide risk, although known, is not the most important risk to society. Indeed adopting the use of pesticides in such a circumstance is an instance of trading a high risk (i.e. crop failure) for a low risk (incidents of cancer). Any rational person would make such a tradeoff.

This is not only a case of judging one threat versus others, but of the unintended consequences of a policy. Removing the risk associated with the pesticide might also lead to increased crop failure, or might encourage farmers to turn to other, more toxic pesticides that are actually more harmful to humans.

Finally, economists and others are more likely than scientists to understand how the incentives created by the range of potential policies will actually play out in the real world. The policy approach recommended by scientists might not be the best way to achieve particular environmental goals. Scientists, rightly, speak with authority only when it comes to their areas of expertise. When it comes to implementing policy, however, they are no more knowledgeable than the general public.

A scientist who argues for a cap-and-trade system to reduce CO_2 emissions is no more qualified to argue than a baseball player, and both are less qualified than an economist to address the pluses and minuses.

Policymakers can also judge the policies in context of the values held by the public. In the United States, policies that provide more individual freedom and choice are likely to be more popular with the public than those that severely restrict personal freedom. Those are not scientific choices, but economic and value choices. Public policy that ignores these considerations, even when based on sound science, is likely to fail.

As the fields of environmental science improve, policymakers will receive data that is more reliable and complete. Policymakers, however, should continue to follow some simple principles when using science to formulate policy:

- Scientists, reflecting their specialty, can overestimate their level of scientific certainty and the risk associated with problems in their particularly field;

- The existence of scientific evidence about an environmental problem does not indicate the relative importance of that problem compared to other challenges society faces;

- Science does not automatically lead to a particular policy solution for solving environmental problems. Policies perceived as the most "direct" response to a problem might also have large unintended consequences, or might meet strong resistance from competing social values.

Recommendation

1) Policymakers should recognize the limits of science and use it appropriately to guide the public decision making process, not to dictate policy outcomes or to silence their political critics. By recognizing the limits of scientific information, policymakers are more likely to develop policies that are effective and efficient. Following a few simple guidelines makes it clear why arguments about what "the science says" are not the sum total of discussion about any environmental issue.

6. Restoring Salmon Habitat

Recommendation

1. Policymakers should adopt and fund a plan to require state Department of Transportation officials to enlarge culverts on state roads, to open at least 500 miles of wild salmon habitat a year for the next five years.

Background

Each year, Washington legislators spend millions of public dollars in the name of protecting salmon, but for more than 15 years, they have made only minimal progress on one simple method that would immediately open thousands of miles of critical river and steam habitat to spawning salmon.

Across the state, nearly 2,500 miles of high-quality salmon habitat are blocked by state highways, roads and other Department of Transportation (WSDOT) construction. The obstructions are in the form of 1,676 culverts which are too narrow to allow migrating salmon to swim farther upstream. Despite the potentially dramatic gains from removing these barriers, the pace of repair has been slow.

The problem is that the mundane work of enlarging road culverts does not garner the same media and political attention as grander schemes like the Puget Sound Partnership. Further, the pace of culvert rebuilding depends on the willingness of legislators to devote funding to it. With predicted budget deficits in the years ahead, it is more likely lawmakers will assign this routine, but important, road work to a low funding priority.

Inadequate funding and slow progress

Over the decades, WSDOT has built hundreds of fish blockages that need to be removed in order to open salmon habitat. The pace of culvert rebuilding, however, has been extremely slow. A little over 10 percent of the barriers created by WSDOT engineers have been removed, and the department's current plan calls for opening only 200 miles of habitat a year for the next 12 years. The legislature is devoting only about eight to twelve million dollars a year to culvert widening.

The problem is that these repairs compete with other transportation projects and fixing culverts simply is not very attractive politically. Other agencies, in contrast, have had much more success. Department of Natural Resources officials, who manage money earned from state timber harvests, have already fixed more than half of the 1,840 stream blockages they identified in 2001, more than ten times the number repaired by WSDOT.

The pace of culvert work is so slow that earlier this year state leaders lost a lawsuit brought by Washington's Indian tribes.[21] As a result, state leaders are negotiating a court settlement to speed up the pace of culvert repair.

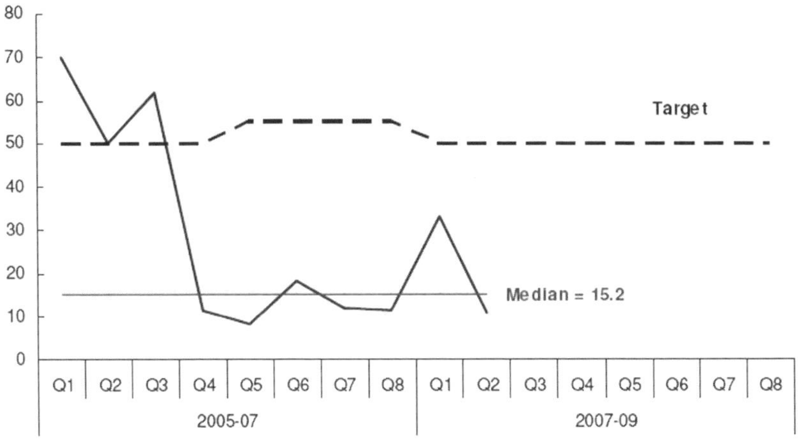

The court's ruling should not have been a surprise to state officials. On Earth Day 2005, Washington Policy Center reported that fixing culverts would, "open up hundreds, and perhaps thousands, of miles of needed habitat for the recovery of wild salmon. The problem is that legislative funding for such projects has been squeezed out in favor of other priorities."[22]

Policy Analysis

Even at the present low level of funding, WSDOT is not meeting its own targets for the amount of salmon habitat it is supposed to be opened each year. The target set by Governor Gregoire is 50 miles of habitat opened each quarter. Even at the planned rate, it would take about 12 years to complete the work.

WSDOT's actual rate for the last year and a half, however, has been only about 15 miles of salmon habitat opened per quarter. At this even slower pace, it will take 41 years to complete the work, sometime around 2050.

Instead, the legislature should increase culvert funding to $30 million a year for five years, sufficient money for WSDOT officials to rebuild enough culverts to open 2,500 miles of wild salmon habitat.

Speeding the pace of WSDOT's culvert rebuilding projects would set the stage for even greater expansion of salmon habitat. Private landowners whose roads block salmon streams are not required to make any improvements as long as there is a downstream impediment. Rapidly making repairs on WSDOT roads would immediately force the removal of barriers on private land farther upstream.

Taking the common sense route

As long as wild salmon populations continue to recover slowly, environmental advocates will push for dramatic and costly policy proposals to open more habitat. For example, the more radical groups within the environmental movement have long called for tearing down the hydroelectric and flood-control dams on rivers in Eastern Washington. This extreme step would have a large and negative effect not only on the state economy, but on people's supply of clean water and carbon-free energy.

If the state continues its inadequate funding and lackluster performance in opening thousands of miles of immediately-available habitat, there will continue to be calls for grand but destructive gestures, like dam removal. These gestures may seem politically attractive, but they carry heavy costs and may be much less effective in helping wild salmon than simply enlarging state-owned road culverts.

Recommendation

1) Policymakers should adopt and fund a plan to require state Department of Transportation officials to enlarge culverts on state roads, to open at least 500 miles of wild salmon habitat a year for the next five years. Lawmakers should require WSDOT to increase the pace of its culvert rebuilding program by devoting $30 million a year to it for the next five years. This level would be enough to open 2,500 miles of wild salmon habitat. Removing WSDOT's barriers to spawning salmon is the most immediate and cost effective way to increase the water habitat salmon need to continue their recent population recovery.

Additional Resources from Washington Policy Center

"The Hidden Costs of the Push for 'Green Collar' Jobs," by Todd Myers, April 2008.

"Promoting Personal Choice, Incentives and Investment to Cut Greenhouse Gases," by Todd Myers, April 2008.

"Celebrate Earth Day by Giving Up Eco-Fads," by Todd Myers, April 2008.

"Comments on State's Climate Advisory Team Draft Recommendations," by Todd Myers, January 2008.

"Climate Advisory Team Misses Opportunities for Real CO_2 Reductions," by Todd Myers, January 2008.

"Analysis of SHB 1032: Adding Subsidies for Renewable Energy Production," by Todd Myers, February 2008.

"A Sea Change in Sea Level Projections: 2005 Puget Sound Estimates Cut by Two-thirds," by Todd Myers, January 2008.

"Role of Economic Growth in Reducing CO_2 Greenhouse Emissions," by Todd Myers, Policy Note 2007-07.

"Why Don't Greens Care About Global Warming?" by Todd Myers, March 2007.

"Reducing Carbon Emissions through Consumer Choice," by Todd Myers, January 2007.

"April Was a Bad Month for Environmental Accuracy," by Todd Myers, April 2007.

"Oregon State University – Mixing Science and Politics in Forestry and Climate Change," by Todd Myers, February 2007.

"Seattle Peak Oilers: 'World to End Soon – And This Time We Mean It,'" by Todd Myers, January 2007.

"A Citizens Guide to Initiative 933: Washington Green Energy Quotas," by Todd Myers, October 2006.

"Using Precaution to Highlight the Problem Can Prevent a Solution," by Todd Myers, December 2006.

"Environmental Interest Group Writes Story about Itself – *New York Times* Publishes It as News," by Todd Myers, November 2006.

"A Cure Worse Than the Disease," by Todd Myers, August 2006.

"Northwest Global Warming Data Isn't Clear as Some Claim," by Todd Myers, February 2006.

"A Long-Running War Appears at an End," by Todd Myers, June 14, 2006.

"Oregon State University Salvage Logging Critique Suppresses Own Date and Mixes Politics with Science," by Todd Myers, March 2006.

"Politics Kills Science on Forest Fire," by Todd Myers, March 22, 2006.

"Northwest Global Warming Data Isn't As Clear As Some Claim," by Todd Myers, February 2006.

"Analysis of News Reporting on Habitat Conservation Plans by the *Seattle Post-Intelligencer*," by Todd Myers, July 2005.

"Bringing Coal to Newcastle; Emission Standards Fight Comes with an Environmental Cost," by Todd Myers, April 2005.

"Washington State Earth Day 2005: Abundant Red Herring Threaten Salmon," by Todd Myers, April 2005.

"Oregon's Measure 37 Property Rights Law: Lessons from the First Eleven Months," by Todd Myers, December 2005.

"Should the State Follow LEED or Get Out of the Way?," by Todd Myers, February 8, 2005.

"A Responsible Approach to Climate Change," by Peter Geddes, September 2004.

"Clearing the Air on New Source Review," by Eric Montague, 2004.

"Private Land Trusts: A Free-Market Forest Conservation Tool," by Eric Montague, October 2002.

---

[1] "State should find ways to protect City Light's climate-protection efforts," by Seattle Mayor Greg Nickels, guest op-ed, *The Seattle Times*, February 7, 2007, at www.archives.seattletimes.nwsource.com/cgi-bin/texis.cgi/web/vortex/display?slug=nickels07&date=20070207.

[2] "Scientists Say Cascade Snowpack Has Not Declined 50% Afterall," news report by Austin Jenkins, National Public Radio, KUOW, aired March 15, 2007, at www.kuow.org/DefaultProgram.asp?ID=12439.

[3] "Uncertain Future: Climate Change and its Effect on Puget Sound," by A.K. Snover, P. W. Mote, L. Whitely Binder, A.F. Hamlet, and N. J. Mantua, 2005, page 21, at www.cses.washington.edu/db/pdf/snoveretalpsat461.pdf .

[4] Testimony before the Washington State Senate Natural Resources, Ocean and Recreation Committee by Phil Mote, Washington State Legislature, January 10, 2007.

[5] Letter to the Washington State Senate Natural Resources, Ocean and Recreation Committee, by Phil Mote, February 13, 2008.

[6] Becky Kelly, spokesperson for the Washington Conservation Voters quoted in "Bill orders firm steps to make state 'greener,'" by Lisa Stiffler, *Seattle Post-Intelligencer,* February 20, 2008.

[7] Revised Code of Washington 39.35D.010, "High Performance Buildings: Findings – Intent."

[8] "Washington High Performance School Buildings," Report to the Legislature, Office of the Superintendent of Public Instruction, January 31, 2005, at www.k12.wa.us/SchFacilities/pubdocs/OSPIFinalReport.pdf.

[9] Author interview with Bethel school district officials, January 8, 2008.

[10] Lake Washington was not one of the pilot schools, but has been favorably cited as an example by supporters of green building standards in Washington.

[11] Author interviews with district officials in Bethel, Lake Washington and Spokane school districts, November 2007 – January 2008.

[12] Washington State Department of Ecology, "Leading the Way: A Comprehensive Approach to Reducing Greenhouse Gases in Washington State," February 2008, http://www.ecy.wa.gov/pubs/0801008a.pdf, page 27 (Accessed June 20, 2008).

[13] See for example, "Sustainable Biofuels: Prospects and Challenges," January 2008, The Royal Society, www.royalsociety.org/displaypagedoc.asp?id=28632, and "Use of U.S. Croplands for Biofuels Increases Greenhouse Gases Through Emissions for Land Use Change," by Timothy Searchinger, Ralph Heimlich, R.A. Houghton, Fengxia Dong, Amani Elobeid, Jacinto Fabioisa, Simla Tokgoz, Dermot Hayes and Tun-Hsiang Yu, *Science Magazine*, February 7, 2008, at www.sciencemag.org/cgi/content/abstract/1151861.

[14] Washington State Department of Ecology, page 50.

[15] U.S. Department of Transportation, "Chapter 4. Means of Travel to Work," http://www.fhwa.dot.gov/ctpp/jtw/jtw4.htm (Accessed June 20, 2008)

[16] It should be made clear that this is not the CO_2 price, but the carbon price. This range would equate to about \$2.73 to \$4.00 per ton of CO_2.

[17] These numbers are generated using the projected 2010 carbon emissions from energy emissions, which account for 87 percent of total CO_2 equivalent (CO_2e), and includes non CO_2 greenhouse gases, emissions in Washington. Costs per ton were multiplied by CO_2 emissions, then divided by 3.67, to yield a cost per ton of carbon. Emissions data taken from Washington State Department of Ecology, "Leading the Way: A Comprehensive Approach to Reducing Greenhouse Gases in Washington State," February 2008, http://www.ecy.wa.gov/pubs/0801008a.pdf (Accessed June 20, 2008).

[18] "Washington Climate Change Challenge," Executive Order 07-02, Office of Governor Christine Gregoire, February 7, 2007, at www.governor.wa.gov/execorders/eo_07-02.pdf.

[19] "Jail politicians who ignore climate science: Suzuki," by Craig Offman, *National Post*, February 7, 2008, at www.nationalpost.com/news/story.html?id=290513.

[20] "Uncertain Future: Climate Change and its Effects on Puget Sound," by A.K. Snover, P. W. Mote, L. Whitely Binder, A.F. Hamlet, and N. J. Mantua, a report for the Puget Sound Action Team by the Climate Impacts Group (Center for Science in the Earth System, Joint Institute for the Study of the Atmosphere and Oceans, University of Washington, Seattle), 2005, page 20.

[21] "Tribes win ruling on salmon, State ordered to fix culverts for fish passage," by Robert McClure, *Seattle Post-Intelligencer*, August 23, 2007, and *United States et al v. State of Washington et al.*, United States District Court, Western District of Washington, Case No. CV 9213RSM, Subproceeding No. 01-01.

[22] "Washington State Earth Day 2005: Abundant Red Herring Threaten Salmon," by Todd Myers, Washington Policy Center, April 22, 2005, at www.washingtonpolicy.org/Centers/environment/opinioneditorial/05_myers_earth day.html.

CHAPTER 4

1. Health Care Mandates

<table>
<tr><td>

Recommendations

1. Authorize low cost, mandate free health insurance.

2. Require an independent cost-benefit analysis of existing health care mandates.

3. Adopt a moratorium on new health care mandates.

4. Urge Congress to allow the interstate purchase of health insurance, so Washington residents can shop for health coverage in any state.

</td></tr>
</table>

Background

Paying for health care coverage is one of the fastest-rising costs facing businesses and citizens in Washington. At the same time health insurance is one of the most heavily regulated sectors of our state's economy. These two trends are linked, with increasing state regulation playing a major role in driving up the cost and reducing the accessibility of health care coverage.

In 2007, national health care spending grew 6.9 percent, twice the rate of inflation, to an estimated $2.3 trillion.[1] Health care spending now makes up about 16 percent of the national economy, and is projected to increase to $4.2 trillion, or 20 percent of GDP, by 2016.[2] In 2007, employers saw their cost of providing health insurance increase by 6.1 percent, the latest in a series of yearly increases at well above the annual rate of inflation.[3]

Although some of the cost drivers of health care are beyond the control of policymakers, there is one key factor which state policymakers directly control: the cost and impact of state-imposed mandates. Mandates are state laws listing benefits for specific conditions or services that every health insurance policy sold in the state must cover, whether insurance purchasers have requested the coverage or not. Independent research shows that mandates can increase the cost of basic health coverage by about 20 to 50 percent overall, depending on the state, or by about 0.5-1.0 percent per mandate.[4]

State-imposed mandates interfere with the normal voluntary relationship between buyers and sellers. Mandates mean insurance purchasers are forced to pay for medical coverage they may not otherwise choose, and patients are made to bear the cost of services they do not want and may never use. This creates a "crowding out" effect, by which some health care services are not available because insurers must offer the benefits mandated by the state.

Moreover, mandates may encourage health providers to follow fixed clinical procedures and services, depriving doctors of the discretion they need to practice medicine. By doing so, they increase the likelihood that medical resources are misallocated, and that care provided through existing health care insurance plans is not flexible, innovative or efficient.

Beginning with a single access-to-provider mandate in 1963 (for chiropody), the number of new mandates and enacted changes to existing mandates in Washington has grown to 53 in 2008. During two distinct periods the number of new mandates surged. Between 1982 and 1990 the number of mandates tripled from 10 to 30, and from 1993 to 2001 their number increased a further 50 percent.[5]

From 2004 through 2008, an additional mandate has been added each year: a ban on denying insurance coverage for injuries caused by narcotic and alcohol abuse, a requirement for mental health parity, and a requirement for prostate cancer screening. The yearly increase in the number of health care mandates is shown in the following chart.

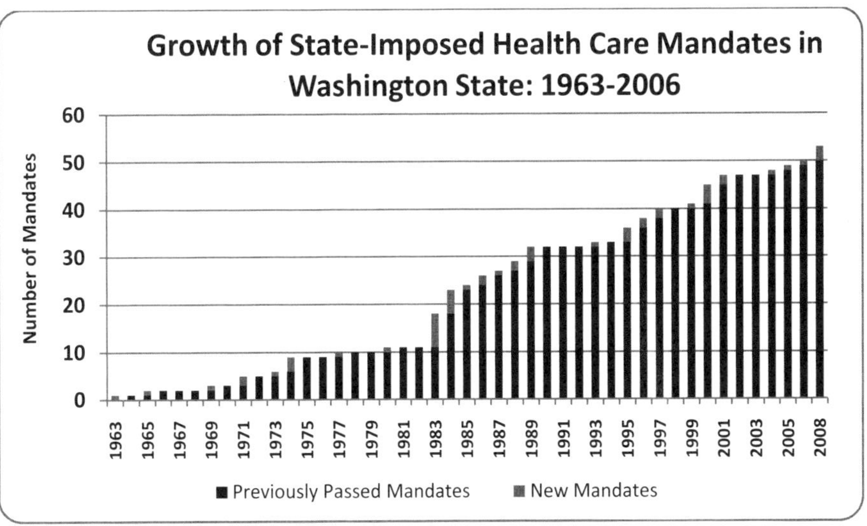

The cumulative effect of state-imposed mandates contributes significantly to the cost of health insurance in Washington.
Source: Washington State Office of the Insurance Commissioner.

An extensive set of state-imposed restrictions on what consumers can buy would have a substantial impact on any industry. It is not surprising, then, that these mandates have considerable impact on health insurance prices and availability in Washington.

Research by the Congressional Budget Office (CBO) found that "government regulation at both the state and federal levels can also increase the costs of health insurance and lead to higher premiums." CBO cites "mandates to cover specific benefits such as chiropractic services or minimum hospital stays for births" as examples of such high-cost insurance regulations.[6]

Mandates and their associated costs contribute to the number of uninsured people in Washington. Since 1992, the number of new mandates and changes to existing mandates rose, as noted, by more than 50 percent, increasing from 30 to 53. Over the same period the number of uninsured people in Washington has increased to approximately 593,000 people in 2007, including 73,000 children, or nearly 10 percent of the population.[7]

The authors of one national study found that state-imposed mandates may account for as many as one in four Americans who are uninsured. "Mandates are not free," they report, "they are paid for by workers and their dependents, who receive lower wages or lose coverage altogether."[8]

Another study found a strong correlation between higher health coverage costs and increases in the uninsured population. Professors Frank A. Sloan and Christopher J. Conover of Duke University found that, "the higher the number of coverage requirements placed on plans, the higher the probability that an individual was uninsured, and the lower the probability of people having any private coverage, including group coverage. The probability that an adult was uninsured rose significantly with each mandate present."[9]

Policy Analysis

Because of mandates and other state-imposed regulations basic health insurance is not available in Washington. State law contains a "value" or "bare-bones" insurance provision dating from 1990, but it includes many detailed regulatory requirements and is not free of all mandates.[10]

A policy allowing true basic health insurance free of state-imposed mandates has the following advantages:

- **It promotes the public interest** – the public benefits when government policies allow greater, rather than fewer, choices in the health care market;

- **It encourages personal freedom** – citizens would have greater say in one of the most personal and sensitive areas of life;

- **It enhances market efficiency** – health care consumers would be able to seek the coverage they need at a price they are willing to pay;

- **It reduces the number of uninsured** – individuals, families and small business owners who are currently priced out of the market would have new opportunities to gain access to health insurance.

Letting Washingtonians buy health coverage in any state

State law makes it illegal for people in Washington to buy health insurance in another state, no matter how good a deal that policy might be for them. This prohibition generally does not apply to other types of insurance, like auto, homeowners and life insurance.

Today the internet makes access to choice, price competition and product information easier than ever. Dozens of easy to use websites provide health coverage information. Examples of consumer-based health insurance websites are:

- eHealthInsurance.com.
- HealthQuoteUSA (at nwinc.com)
- HealthInsuranceSort.com. (BlueCross)
- HealthInsuranceInfo.net
- HealthInsuranceFinders.org

These websites allow consumers to shop among a wide range of health coverage options, all with varying prices and benefit levels. One site alone (eHealthInsurance) lists at least 215 plans.

Other insurance models work this way. Multi-state companies selling auto, homeowners and life insurance offer choice, good prices and quality service for one reason only. The consumer is in charge, and insurers know they have to please the customer, not government regulators or company benefits managers, in order to get business.

Greater market choice and better prices in health care are available across the country and easily available through the internet. Washington lawmakers should remove the legal barriers and let their citizens tap into a nationwide market in affordable health care.

Recommendations

1) Authorize low cost, mandate free health insurance. Insurance should be available to individuals and businesses without state-imposed mandates, with pricing that reflects its actual value to consumers. Allow insurance companies to tailor their policies to include mandates or not.

2) Require an independent cost-benefit analysis of existing health care mandates. As has been done in other states, an independent cost-benefit analysis would more accurately determine the role of mandates in increasing the cost of health coverage.

3) Adopt a moratorium on new health care mandates. A moratorium on new mandates would create a much-needed "time-out" in the growth and complexity of health insurance regulations. This, in turn, would give policymakers and the public the opportunity to learn more about the long-term impact of mandates on the price and availability of health care coverage.

4) Urge Congress to allow the interstate purchase of health insurance, so Washington residents can shop for health coverage in any state. The number of mandates varies widely from state to state. By gaining access to a national market in health coverage, Washington residents could select policies from states with fewer mandates, thereby decreasing costs and increasing choice in the marketplace.

2. Health Savings Accounts and High Deductible Plans

Recommendations

1. Encourage insurance companies to enter Washington's HSA/HDHP market to promote choice and price competition benefiting consumers.

2. Exempt high deductible health plans from state community rating requirements.

3. Urge Congress to make premiums for individually purchased health insurance plans, such as those accompanying HSAs, tax deductible.

4. Cut the state tax on individual insurance policies.

Background

The current system of employer-based health care coverage dates from when the federal government imposed wage controls during World War II. Since employers were barred from offering higher wages to attract workers, they began offering non-monetary benefits such as free health care. In 1943, the IRS ruled that the cost of these benefits was a legitimate business expense, making health coverage fully tax deductible for businesses, but not for individuals.

That ruling, later confirmed in law by Congress, created three interconnected economic distortions in the health care market:

• It prevented patients from knowing the actual cost of the care they received;

• It created the third-party payer problem, encouraging patients to demand care, regardless of whether it is necessary or cost effective. Most weekend warriors do not need a $1,000 MRI for their aches come Monday morning;

• It undermined the true understanding of health insurance. People tend to see their health benefits as a pre-paid service, not as a way of mitigating risk. People reason, "It's a free benefit. I'll use as much as I want;"

• It caused health insurance to actually become health "maintenance" whereby it covers all health related activities, not just unexpected or catastrophic problems.

An effective tool to dismantle these distortions did not exist until Health Saving Accounts (HSAs) were established on December 8, 2003, when President Bush signed the Medicare Prescription Drug, Improvement and Modernization Act. The law became effective January 1, 2004, when the first HSA was sold, allowing consumers to purchase health coverage with the same tax advantage as businesses for the first time in 61 years.

Citizens in Washington and throughout the country can now make pre-tax deposits into an HSA that can be used to pay for routine health care expenses. HSAs must be accompanied by a high deductible health plan (HDHP). In 2008, this means a plan with an annual coverage deductible of at least $1,100 for an individual or $2,200 for families. In Washington, the legislature enacted a bill creating an HSA benefit option for the state's 106,000 employees and their families.

In 2008, annual HSA deposits cannot exceed the amount of the insurance deductible or $2,900 for individuals and $5,800 for families, whichever is less. These latter limits are indexed to inflation and will increase in future years. Also, individuals 55 years old and older can make an additional "catch-up" contribution of $900 in 2008, and a "catch-up" contribution of $1,000 in 2009 and in every year thereafter.[11]

Savings in an HSA can earn interest or be invested in stocks or mutual funds just like savings in Individual Retirement Accounts. Interest and investment earnings are tax-free.

HSA balances belong to individual account holders and remain theirs if they change jobs, become unemployed or retire. The funds can be used to pay qualified medical expenses and unspent funds carry over to the next year. Below is a summary of how HSAs work.

An Overview of Health Savings Accounts

• Each HSA must be accompanied by a high-deductible health plan (HDHP).

• Annual tax free contributions can be made up to the lesser of:
- the amount of the HDHP deductible, <u>or</u>
- $2,900 for individuals and $5,800 for families (indexed to inflation).

• HSAs are portable. HSA funds belong to the account holder and travel with the person from job to job.

• Contributions to an HSA may come from any source, including: self, parent, spouse, grandparent, or employer.

• Funds may be spent tax free on qualified medical expenses.

• Investment earnings in the account accumulate tax free.

• Unspent funds in an HSA carry over to the next year; there is no "use it or lose it" limitation.

The idea behind HSAs is simple. Individuals should be able to manage some of their own health care dollars through accounts they own and control. They should be able to use these funds to pay for health care expenses such as prescriptions, x-rays and other diagnostic tests, and office visits to their health care provider. Consumers who have more direct control over their health care dollars are more likely to take responsibility for their health care decisions.

Health Savings Accounts have several additional advantages for consumers. Besides making health coverage more affordable, HSAs build financial assets. The money in an HSA belongs to the account holder, not to an employer, insurance company, or government agency. Because unlimited annual rollover is allowed, unspent funds in an HSA can accumulate tax free for years and be available at retirement.

HSAs are popular, and, in recent years, the number of people purchasing them has increased rapidly. In the last nine months of 2005, the number of Americans with HSAs tripled to 3.2 million.[12] In 2008, 6.1 million Americans are covered by HSAs and similar high-deductible plans, a 35 percent increase over the previous year.[13]

In Washington state in 2008, 101,254 people, or 2.5 percent of those covered by private plans, are enrolled in HSA plans.[14]

Recent data shows that people covered by HSAs effectively accumulate money to pay for their routine medical expenses. In 2007, on a twelve-month average basis, 87 percent of HSA holders had more than $1,000 in available cash in their accounts.[15]

After retirement, HSA money may be spent on any non-medical purpose subject only to income tax. There are never taxes for medical costs, including long-term care expenses or Medicare premiums. Unspent money in an HSA can be inherited by heirs or a surviving spouse.

HSAs also carry advantages for employees and employers. The accounts provide flexible service to employees, giving them more choice and control over their health care spending. Through HSAs, employers can encourage a more health conscious and productive workforce. Moreover, any employer contributions to an HSA are not taxable to the employee.

Employers benefit by having lower administrative costs and less paperwork. HSAs are managed by employees or their financial advisors, not by the employer. Employers also see HSAs as a method of controlling their growing health care costs. Whole Foods, the grocery chain, covers all of its employees through personal, high-deductible plans while providing cash to employees for the deductible, and spends only half of the national corporate average for health care costs.[16]

Policy Analysis

Consumer directed Health Savings Accounts bring price and service competition to the health care market. Doctors, clinics, and hospitals have an incentive to provide high quality, price transparent care to patients. As consumers begin shopping more for their basic health care, providers will get questions they usually do not hear from patients such as, "How much does that cost?"

As the number of patients with HSAs rises, so will the amount of transparent information that is available to these patients. Already, websites exist which compare hospital prices and prescription drugs for a given disease or condition. The emergence of in-store mini-clinics provides consumers with straight forward pricing for a limited number of health care services.

Examples of mini-clinics in Washington are SmartCare Centers in Fred Meyer stores and MinuteClinic, located in select Bartell Drug Stores. Examples across the country include Express Clinic, Quick Clinics and Checkups.[17] For an advertised fee, mini-clinics provide vaccines, diagnoses, and the treatment of relatively minor ailments such as pink eye, strep throat and athlete's foot. Such consumer friendly sources of health care are an example for the entire health care system.

In addition to making coverage more accessible, Health Savings Accounts have civic and social advantages. HSAs make people more independent and self-reliant, rather than dependent on government or employers for a vital life necessity. HSAs encourage people to be more accountable and responsible in their own lives.

Recommendations

1) Encourage insurance companies to enter Washington's HSA market to promote choice and price competition that benefit consumers. Over the years insurance companies have steadily left the state, leaving consumers with fewer choices. The advent of HSAs offers a way to reverse that trend. The legislature should encourage more insurers to enter the state's emerging HSA market.

2) Exempt high deductible health plans from state community rating requirements. This would allow fair and accurate pricing of

HSA health coverage because the cost of insurance policies are based on the actual health risk people bring to the insurance pool.

As a good first step toward helping the uninsured, the exemption could be limited to people who had no health coverage in the previous six months. Extending the exemption to small businesses buying first-time HSAs for their employees would further reduce the uninsured population.

3) Urge Congress to make premiums for individually purchased health insurance plans, such as those accompanying HSAs, tax deductible. Under current federal law, money paid for the high deductible health plan that must accompany each Health Savings Account carries no tax advantage, yet all other financial aspects of HSAs – contributions, interest earnings and payouts – are tax free. State policymakers should encourage Washington's congressional delegation to make premiums for all individually-purchased health insurance plans tax deductible.

4) Cut the state tax on individual insurance policies. State lawmakers charge a 2 percent insurance premiums tax on all health insurance policies sold in Washington, thus artificially adding to the already rising cost of health coverage. The legislature should eliminate this tax on individual policies. This would immediately make individual health care more affordable and would help reduce the number of uninsured people.

3. Certificate of Need Law

Recommendations

1. Repeal Washington's Certificate of Need law.

2. Short of repeal, scale back Certificate of Need restrictions to allow doctors, clinics and hospitals to respond to patients' needs more quickly and efficiently.

Background

Imagine your community is home to a nursing care facility that has operated for years with optimal customer satisfaction. It provides quality care and assistance, its facilities are modern and clean, and the staff is excellent. The nursing home is exceeding capacity and its operators look at the growing demand and decide to expand the facility by adding five beds. The administrators consult experts, study options and cost projections and, after careful consideration, secure a building permit and begin construction. It sounds reasonable, except they just broke the law.

Currently it is illegal to open or expand most kinds of medical facilities in Washington, unless the state grants a special Certificate of Need (CON). Washington is one of thirty-seven states (including the District of Columbia) that require specific government permission to open, expand or modify most kinds of health care facilities.

Dating back to New York in 1964, CON laws grew out of the belief that surplus supply of medical facilities and services meant providers would pass the excess cost on to patients. Limiting supply, some believed, would cap rising health care costs.

Eventually, every state adopted CON laws. Washington adopted its law in 1972. It is administered by the state Department of Health. The National Health Planning and Resources Development Act of 1974 directed each state to examine proposed health care facilities and determine the need for such services.

Typical Steps in the CON Need-Determination Process for Building or Expanding a Hospital in Washington

- Compile historical hospital use data for area during previous ten years;

- Compute average use rates for each year and for each age group: 0-64 & 65+, at a minimum;

- Forecast each area's hospital use rates for a target year (in some cases as far out as 10+ years);

- Adjust use rates for population trends from the Office of Financial Management;

- Adjust projections and use rates based on presence of a Health Maintenance Organization;

- Adjust use rates for residents who use out-of-state hospitals;

- Distribute forecasted patient days to hospital planning areas based on market share;

- Use average occupancy standards to determine each planning area's bed need;

- Add psychiatric bed need forecast (determined in a separate process) to non-psychiatric need forecast;

- Make necessary final adjustments for population, use rates, market shares, out-of-area use rates, and shifts in occupancy rates.

By 1982, however, the federal government recognized the failure of CON laws to reduce health care costs and repealed the national health planning requirements. Since then, 14 states have followed suit and eliminated their CON requirements.

Washington retains its original 1972 statute, even though the law has demonstrably failed in its stated goal of reducing costs and increasing access to health care. The state, not doctors or hospital administrators, decide whether anyone may build, expand, sell, purchase, or significantly modify 15 different kinds of medical facilities and services, including hospitals, nursing homes, outpatient surgery centers, retirement communities, and organ transplant services.

The CON application process lasts up to two years or more and costs hundreds of thousands of dollars, which is added to the price of health care. The process itself is extremely arcane.

The CON process is just one phase of a much larger set of regulatory requirements. The following table shows the many additional permitting, licensing, building code, environmental and zoning requirements that must be completed before a clinic or hospital is built in Washington.

Non-CON requirements for clinic and hospital construction in Washington[18]

<u>Licensure and Physical Plant Requirements</u>
- Finishes (carpet, tile, wall covering)
- Heating and ventilation system
- Hot water system
- Medication handling
- Nurse call system
- Room size, furniture and equipment
- Shower and toilet fixtures

<u>Fire / Life Safety Requirements</u>
- Automated sprinkler system
- Electrical generator system
- Fire alarm system
- Fire / life safety structural design
- Life support system
- Medical gas system
- Smoke control system

<u>Standards Adopted by State Building Code Council</u>
- 2003 International Building Code
- 2003 International Fire Code
- 2003 International Mechanical Code
- 2003 International Plumbing Code
- Barrier-free requirements
- National electrical code
- Washington state energy code
- Washington state ventilation code

These regulations are important to protecting public health and safety, and there is no suggestion that this list should be shortened or eliminated. The purpose here is to show that the lengthy and complicated Certificate of Need process is imposed *in addition* to a long list of existing requirements.

Policy Analysis

Three decades of experience shows that Washington's CON laws have not worked as intended. A 1999 study by the Washington State Joint Legislative Audit and Review Committee (JLARC) and a 2005 study by Seattle's Mercer Human Resource Consulting Group both concluded that Washington's CON laws have neither reduced the cost of nor increased access to health care.

A 2004 report by the Federal Trade Commission and the Department of Justice came to the same conclusion. It suggested that in some states CON laws have contributed to higher health care costs by reducing supply and stifling competition. [19]

The program's record indicates CON no longer serves the public interest, if it ever did. The stated purpose of the program is to control costs and meet changing conditions. Yet to succeed, our health system requires the very flexibility CON is designed to prevent.

In a state experiencing rapid growth and demographic change, CON prevents providers from adapting to the changing health needs of the community.

For example, in 2006, Cancer Treatment Centers of America wanted to build a $76 million, 24-bed state-of-the-art medical facility on a 10-acre site in Kent. City leaders strongly supported the proposal, which would have created 250 new jobs. State regulators, however, concluded that the hospital was not needed, twice rejecting it through the CON process. [20]

CON laws create the opposite of their intended purpose, actively blocking citizens' access to health care choices and modern health care facilities. The laws also bog down health care providers in stacks of regulation and paperwork.

A special Task Force created in 2005 by the legislature (SB 1688) failed to improve the restrictive nature of state law. Far from streamlining health care regulation in Washington, the Task Force recommended the opposite, calling for a "state health planning process supported by an adequate data reporting system." [21]

The failure of the Task Force to reduce CON barriers to health care, and instead to add to them, shows how the CON process has become arcane and politicized. Influential medical organizations holding a Certificate of Need frequently use the CON process to keep competitors out of their area.

In contrast, when health care organizations are allowed to compete in a system that functions more like a normal market, consumers of health care win because there are incentives for providers to innovate and grow more efficient.

Competition builds a nimble, community-responsive system that readily adapts to changing needs. Bureaucratic red tape and inflexible planning and regulatory structures that keep competitors out cannot achieve these ends.

In practice, Washington's CON laws do not improve health outcomes for citizens. Instead, they are used to control access to health care. State regulators – not communities and health care professionals – pick winners and losers in health care by deciding when and where medical facilities can be built.

Recommendations

1) Repeal Washington's Certificate of Need Law. Washington should join the 13 states like Pennsylvania, California and Texas that have repealed their Certificate of Need regulations. Citizens in those states benefit from a faster and less-bureaucratic process for opening new hospitals and clinics. Washington citizens would similarly benefit if our state's failed CON law were repealed.

2) Scale back Certificate of Need regulations to allow doctors, clinics and hospitals to respond to patients' needs more quickly and efficiently. If retained, the CON law should be limited to only a few types of medical facilities or only apply at a higher expenditure threshold. This could be done as a precursor to full repeal or with the intention of streamlining the CON process to make it more workable.

4. Medical Liability Reform

Recommendations

1. Cap the amount of noneconomic damages that can be awarded by a jury to $350,000 or less.

2. Eliminate joint and several liability.

3. Encourage far-reaching medical liability reforms such as schedules of damages, "early offer" programs and specialized medical courts.

4. Strengthen the effectiveness of the Medical Quality Assurance Commission.

Background

Currently, individuals may file civil lawsuits against doctors, clinics and hospitals for unlimited amounts of money for breaches of duty that cause injury. This legal system has two primary purposes – deter doctors and other health care providers from acting negligently, and compensate injured people for the losses they have suffered.

Although not required by state law, most doctors in Washington buy malpractice insurance to protect themselves and their practices against expensive jury verdicts. The high cost of malpractice insurance contributes to the rising cost of health care, and is having a harmful effect on doctors, patients and payers.

The American Medical Association includes Washington on the list of states facing a medical liability crisis, threatening the viability of the medical community and the health of patients. This is the third malpractice crisis in 30 years, following the ones in the mid-1980s and the mid-1970s. It is a recurring problem in desperate need of a long-term solution.

Although fewer medical malpractice claims have been filed in recent years, the monetary value of each claim is rising. Over the past ten years, the average jury verdict in Washington has increased by almost 70 percent and the average settlement cost has increased by over 50 percent. Likewise, the number of verdicts and settlements over $1 million increased by tenfold in roughly this same time period. High jury awards are not isolated events; they influence future court cases as well as out-of-court settlements.

Higher claim costs are the primary reason for increased malpractice insurance premiums. Moreover, in Washington, because of joint and several liability rules, each defendant in a medical malpractice lawsuit is potentially responsible for paying the total jury award to a patient, regardless of how small that defendant's role was in causing the patient's injury.

This rule encourages injured patients and their lawyers to seek full payment from the defendant with the "deepest pockets," not necessarily the one most responsible for causing harm.

Malpractice lawsuits affect physician behavior, contributing to the practice of defensive medicine and driving up health care costs. Defensive medicine refers to a doctor ordering diagnostic tests, procedures, specialist referrals or prescription drugs mainly to reduce malpractice liability, not to serve their patients better.

A recent study found that medical liability costs and defensive medicine account for at least 10 percent of medical care costs.[22] Additionally, physicians in a state with a malpractice crisis, like Washington, are more likely to retire early, leave the state, or reduce their scope of practice. Patient access to health care is then restricted by fewer physicians in the community.

In 2005, two contentious medical malpractice initiatives, Initiatives 330 and Initiative 336, appeared on the November ballot. Each took a radically different approach to changing Washington's medical liability laws. Both initiatives failed, prompting the governor to negotiate and the legislature to pass a health care liability bill in 2006.

The new law makes modest changes to patient safety, liability insurance and the legal process. Most of these changes, however, are minimal and will not truly resolve the medical malpractice crisis in Washington.

Policy Analysis

Twenty-nine states have adopted some limitation on jury awards, primarily on noneconomic damages. Many states model their tort reform on California's Medical Injury Compensation Reform Act (MICRA), enacted in 1975. MICRA caps noneconomic damages at $250,000 and limits attorneys' fees based on a sliding scale.

Because of MICRA, malpractice claims in California are settled in one-third less time than the national average of more than five years, and malpractice insurance rates have dropped by 40 percent since its inception. The result is a system that better serves the needs of patients by reducing the cost of litigation and speeding compensation payments.

Noneconomic damage caps reduce the average size of an award and limit malpractice insurance premium growth. Caps have been demonstrated to result in a 23 percent to 31 percent reduction in the amount of an average jury award. Moreover, states with caps of $350,000 or less on non-economic damages saw increases in malpractice insurance premiums of 13 percent in 2000-01, while states without caps experienced a 44 percent increase in premiums.

In 2003, Texas capped malpractice jury awards for noneconomic damages at $250,000. As a result of this and other reforms, the state's largest malpractice insurance company cut its premiums by 35 percent, resulting in $217 million in savings to doctors, and their patients, over a four year period.[23]

Officials at one nonprofit hospital, Christus Health, report malpractice reform has saved them some $100 million, which they can now devote to charity care, instead of fighting lawsuits. Limiting jury awards has made Texas a much more attractive place to practice medicine. In the last three years, about 7,000 doctors have entered the state, many to serve in rural areas.[24]

Joint and several liability

Over the last 20 years, the majority of states have reformed their joint and several liability laws. In states that abolished joint and several liability, physicians are not held liable for the negligent acts of other doctors. This approach is fair because it allocates financial damages in proportion to each defendant's actual level of fault. It also reduces costs because malpractice insurers, when issuing policies, know how much risk each doctor is assuming.

Washington needs reforms similar to those in other states that are successfully reducing costs while protecting patients. Practical reforms include reasonable limits on non-economic damages and eliminating joint and several liability. These recommended reforms represent an important start.

More comprehensive medical liability reform

The medical liability system is complicated, and it currently does not meet its two objectives of deterring medical negligence and compensating injured patients.

Policymakers should consider broader, long-term reforms that address the fundamental problems with the medical liability system. Effective long-term reforms include:

- A regular schedule for determining noneconomic damages, with financial awards increasing with the seriousness of the patient's injury;

- "Early offer" programs that allow fast payment of compensation with an injured patient's agreement not to seek further payments; and,

- Specialized medical courts where independent medical experts can make faster, more consistent decisions about awarding just compensation to injured patients.

Improving the Medical Quality Assurance Commission

The purpose of the medical liability system is to secure fair compensation for injured patients, punish negligent or incompetent doctors, and deter future acts of negligence. The court system by itself, however, is ill equipped to police the medical profession and ensure the good conduct of doctors. The enforcement powers of the executive branch are best suited for that purpose.

Washington regulates physicians through the Medical Quality Assurance Commission (MQAC). The Commission is responsible for establishing, monitoring and enforcing qualifications for licensure, consistent standards of practice and continuing competency.

While patient complaints and out-of-court malpractice settlements may not be widely known to the public, they are no secret to the members of MQAC. Acting on this information, the state should investigate, impose limits on practice and, if need be, revoke the licenses of negligent doctors *before* they do serious and lasting harm to patients.

There must be a system in place to protect those physicians testifying against incompetent doctors from legal retribution. Competency should be decided by the MQAC, not the courts.

Recommendations

1) Cap the amount of noneconomic damages that can be awarded by a jury to $350,000 or less. As in other states, the goal is to make future awards more predictable, which in turn will make insurance premiums more predictable.

2) Eliminate joint and several liability. Defendants should be liable only for their own decisions and actions, not the decisions and actions of others. This will decrease the need for patients to bring a marginal suit against a "deep pocket."

3) Encourage far-reaching medical liability reforms such as schedules of damages, "early offer" programs and specialized medical courts. Longer term solutions need to be developed if the goals of the medical liability system are to be achieved.

4) Strengthen the effectiveness of the Medical Quality Assurance Commission. Physician competency and quality are regulated by state law. Regulators need to make greater efforts to assure the public that the few substandard physicians in the medical profession are identified and removed from the health care system.

5. Medicaid Reform

Recommendations

1. Adopt a state voucher program to give Medicaid recipients control over their health care dollars.

2. Encourage Congress to allow block grants of federal funds instead of matching funds to the states.

Background

The Medicaid program, which was created by the Medicare Act of 1965, provides federal and state funding on a matching basis for health care for the poor and disabled. Today, over 55 million people receive services through the Medicaid program.[25]

Four groups of people receive assistance through the Medicaid program. These groups are: the poor, the disabled, mothers and children, and individuals needing long-term care. Although mothers and children make up most of the beneficiaries, long-term care accounts for 70 percent of yearly Medicaid dollars.[26]

Physician participation in Medicaid is voluntary. Medicaid payments to doctors have always been lower than those of any other insurance carrier, including Medicare. Consequently more and more physicians are withdrawing from the program, thus decreasing access to health care and freedom of choice for low income and disabled people.

The cost of Medicaid is not sustainable. In 1966, its first year, the cost was $1 billion. The cost of the program exploded to $330 billion by 2007.[27] In many years, the financial burden of Medicaid grows at twice or three times the rate of inflation. It is estimated that at its present rate of growth, Medicaid-funded nursing home expenditures in 2030 will equal the size of the entire Social Security program today.

Policy Analysis

Medicaid has a number of harmful effects on the very people it is intended to help. First of all, it discourages work and job improvement for low paid employees, since with increasing income, workers lose their Medicaid benefits.

It also encourages employers of low-income workers not to offer health benefits. They assume, or hope, that taxpayers will provide these benefits instead.

Medicaid also discourages private insurance companies from offering nursing home policies. As the government program crowds out private carriers, this insurance market gets smaller every year, resulting in less choice for consumers.

Lastly, Medicaid discourages charity care and philanthropic giving in the health care sector. If the government is assumed to be already giving health care to low-income people, private donors tend to shift their money to other causes.

State lawmakers unfortunately are caught in a vicious cycle. The more of state tax money they devote to Medicaid, the more money they receive from the federal government. If Washington state spends one of its own dollars on Medicaid benefits, it gets another dollar in matching funds from federal taxpayers, seemingly doubling the state's spending on health care.

The federal matching fund mechanism makes state lawmakers feel like they are receiving "free" money, so it is no surprise that Medicaid is the largest budget item for virtually every state in the country. In reality, of course, the "free" matching money is provided by federal taxpayers, who are the same people as state taxpayers.

In 1996, the federal government reformed welfare and repealed the Aid to Families with Dependent Children (AFDC) program. The AFDC was a means-tested entitlement with state and federal matching funds, very similar to Medicaid. Opponents of AFDC repeal predicted tragedy for low-income families. That didn't happen. In fact welfare caseloads decreased dramatically and poverty across all demographic groups declined as well. More families became economically independent and entered the workforce.

Much can be learned from the welfare reform of 1996. Federal funding for Medicaid should be given as block grants, not as matching funds. This would induce states to budget for the truly needy and not rely on a blank check from federal taxpayers.

To introduce responsible use of Medicaid funds, recipients should be given individual vouchers so they can control their own health care spending. These vouchers could be used to purchase private insurance policies and to fund personal Health Savings Accounts. Dollars not spent could be rolled over from year to year and could be taken from one job to another.

Like welfare reform, this change in the Medicaid program would help lift poor families out of poverty, by making them independent and giving them ownership of their own health care coverage.

Recommendations

1) Adopt a state voucher program to give Medicaid recipients control over their health care dollars. Vouchers would allow Medicaid recipients to choose the health insurance policies that work best for them, and to participate in consumer driven health care. It would also increase access by giving Medicaid recipients a broader choice of doctors.

2) Encourage Congress to allow block grants of federal funds instead of matching funds to the states. Medicaid costs will continue to spiral out of control unless a meaningful ceiling is placed on spending. A simple method to accomplish this is to use federal block grants instead of unlimited matching funds. This change would cause states to be better stewards of their own health care budgets, since state lawmakers would no longer feel they are getting "free" money from federal taxpayers.

6. Innovations in Health Care Services

Recommendation

1. Avoid heavy-handed state regulations that block innovation in the delivery of health care services.

Background

Although 86 percent of health care in the United States is paid for by a third party, usually an insurance company or a government agency, a growing number of free market health care models are becoming common in Washington and across the country. These alternative ways of delivering health care services allow the patient to make all the key decisions in how to access care: where to go, when to go, who to see, how to pay, and how much to pay.

It is interesting to note that these alternatives are thriving outside the financing and regulatory structure of government, and largely beyond the notice of state legislators. In fact, public officials, even those working in health care regulation, are often among the last to comprehend how the health care marketplace is changing.

At the same time, patients seeking alternative forms of health care delivery have the full protection of all the consumer laws, professional licensing requirements, quality of service standards and truth-in-advertising rules that apply to any legitimate business activity.

Following is a short description of the innovations and patient-centered conveniences emerging in the private health services market.

Policy Analysis

Medical tourism

Patients have traveled to the United States to receive health care for many years. Over the last decade, though, a growing number of Americans have sought medical care in foreign countries. The driver obviously is reduced cost in other countries compared to the United States.

In one example, a knee replacement that costs an average of $30,000 in the U.S. can be obtained for 40 to 60 percent less in another country, such as India, including costs for all medical procedures, doctor fees and the hospital stay.[28]

Today, the most common medical reasons for traveling are joint replacement, cosmetic procedures, cardiac surgery, dental services and organ transplants.

International medical travel began with under-insured or non-insured Americans. As health coverage costs have risen, a few employer-based insurance programs have recently encouraged their employees to travel overseas for major surgical procedures, saving both the plan, and its members, money.

Medical travel agencies are increasing in number and international hospital certification is adding credibility to international health care. However, foreign physician training and the experience of hospital personnel remain significant variables in the quality of care internationally.

Concierge medicine

Under concierge medicine, consumers pay a fixed amount of money per month to have 24-hour access to a dedicated primary care physician. Same-day appointments, e-mail access and more time with the doctor are standard services. The vast majority of concierge patients also have affordable, high-deductible insurance to cover hospitalizations and major medical expenses.

This model is now being applied across a wide range of socioeconomic levels. The movement started with the wealthy, but today many concierge practices are affordable. A clinic in Seattle charges adults in their 40s only $768 a year, or just $64 a month.[29] Some charge as little as $35 per month.

Doctors are able to build successful practices because of the volume of patients. The low cost and 24-hour access make it much easier for doctors to practice preventive medicine. Patients with long-term health conditions are more likely to keep their illness from getting worse, thus saving the system money in the long run.

Convenient care clinics

A convenient care clinic is a small health care facility located in a common shopping area, like a mall or large retail store. They are often open seven days a week, take walk-in visits and offer affordable services. They are generally staffed by qualified nurse practitioners under the supervision of a doctor. They provide simple medical procedures, testing, immunizations, physicals and preventive health screenings.[30]

Unlike traditional doctors' offices, convenient care clinics openly post their prices, and accept payment by cash, credit card or insurance. Convenient care members report a 98 percent patient satisfaction rate.[31]

Large retailers such as Wal-Mart are opening in-store clinics to treat customers with routine medical problems. From a patient standpoint, the convenient location and the reduced cost are major attractions.

Although a relatively new concept, last year there were about 800 convenient care clinics in the U.S. Those in the profession expect this number to grow to 1,500 in 2008, as the idea of going to a retail storefront for health care gains consumer acceptance.[32]

Use of the internet

Transparency in health care is becoming a major issue with payers as well as patients. There are growing concerns with quality issues and high costs and people are demanding more information.

Multiple sites are appearing on the internet to meet the growing demand for a huge volume of reliable, high-quality health care data. Within a few years, anyone who has access to the internet will be able to research their own medical condition, compare results and outcomes for various procedures and providers, and perform cost comparisons before making important care decisions.

The internet is one of the most promising tools for informing people about their own health and options for treatment. For this reason it is important for policymakers not to place regulatory roadblocks or new taxes on this growing and cost-effective source of consumer information.

Value-based medicine

There is much data to show a definite decrease in health care costs for payers that use a value-based model for their employees. By financially rewarding healthy behavior, like an improved diet, getting more exercise, or giving up smoking, employers have seen a significant drop in their rate of increase in medical related expenses.

Pitney Bowes began a value-based benefits program in 2001 centered on employees with diabetes and asthma. The company saw its annual costs decrease for treating both conditions within the first year, and it experienced $4 million in health care savings by the fourth year of the program.[33]

Executives at Quad Graphics identified obesity as a major driver of employee health care expenses. In the late 1990s, they began a program of waiving insurance co-payments for workers who joined a weight and diabetic management program or a smoking cessation program. Total cost for participants has ranged from 17 to 21 percent below previous estimates for each year of the program. The company plans to add asthma, hypertension and hyperlipidemia to the list of conditions requiring no co-payment from employees.[34]

Although it is too early to know the overall impact of value-based health care, the trend is encouraging and warrants further utilization.

Conclusion

Allowed to function on its own, the free market has the ability to develop solutions to the ongoing problems of funding and access to health care. Policymakers should encourage more free market activities, letting private innovators in the market explore what works and what doesn't, and then pass the benefits on to health care consumers.

In particular, state lawmakers and the insurance commissioner should not place a stifling regulatory burden on these innovative and practical ideas, as they have done to hospitals and clinics with the time-consuming Certificate of Need process.

Recommendation

1) Avoid heavy-handed regulations that block innovation in the delivery of health care services. Over-regulation by the state prevents doctors and clinics from developing new ways to build relationships with patients. It also prevents medical professionals from using new technology, such as electronic medical records, or talking to patients through e-mail, to improve the way they practice medicine.

Additional Resources from Washington Policy Center

"Healthcare in the United States Today: Problems and Solutions," by Roger Stark, MD, November 2007.

"Testimony on Establishing the Washington Health Partnership," by Paul Guppy, February 2008.

"Moore's *Sicko* Offers No Cure for U.S. Health Care," by Paul Guppy, October 2007.

"A Capitalism Prescription," by Dr. David Gratzer, M.D., June 2007.

"Washington State Barriers to Health Savings Accounts: Key Changes that Would Make Health Care More Affordable for All Washington Residents," by David Hogberg, PhD, June 2007.

"Price Controls Threaten Popular Drug Discount Program," by Paul Guppy, February 2007.

"Analysis of the Health Care Connector Bill," by Paul Guppy, February 2007.

"Bulletproof? Health Savings Accounts in 2007 and 2008," by John R. Graham, February 2007.

"A Snapshot of Health Insurance Costs in Washington State," by Tanya Karwaki, JD, August 2006.

"A Pocket Guide to Health Savings Accounts (Revised Edition)," by Liv S. Finne, JD, June 2006.

"The Doctor is Out," by Tanya Karwaki, JD, May 2006.

"The Failure of Government Central Planning: Washington's Medical Certificate of Need Program," by John Barnes, January 2006.

"'Fair Share' Bill is Unfair and Impractical," by Paul Guppy, January 2006.

"Overview of Initiatives 330 and 336: Proposals to Reform Washington's Medical Liability Law," by Paul Guppy, September 2005.

"SB 6130 – To Allow State Employees to Choose Tax-Free Health Savings Accounts," by Paul Guppy, February 2006

"Drug Formulary Law is Blocking Patients' Easy Access to Prescription Drug Treatment," January 2006.

"Health Savings Accounts Will Revolutionize American Health Care," by John C. Goodman, 2004.

"Ten Tools for Achieving Consumer-Driven Health Care," by Greg Scandlen, June 2003.

"Treatment Denied: State Formularies and Cost Controls Restrict Access to Prescription Drugs," by Linda Gorman, February 2003.

"An Analysis of the Impacts of the Medical Malpractice System," by Eric Montague, 2003.

"How Mandates Increase Costs and Reduce Access to Health Care Coverage," by Paul Guppy, June 2002.

"The Ten Billion Dollar Entitlement: Assessing the Cost of Single-Payer Health Care," by Paul Guppy, November 2000.

---

[1] "Health Spending Projections Through 2016: Modest Changes Obscure Part D's Impact," by John A. Poisal, et al., the National Health Expenditure Accounts Projections Team, *Health Affairs*, 26, No. 2 (2007): w242-w253, February 21, 2007, at www.content.healthaffairs.org/cgi/content/abstract/hlthaff.26.2.w242.

[2] Ibid.

[3] "Employer Health Benefits, 2007 Annual Survey," by Gary Claxton et. al., The Henry J. Kaiser Family Foundation and the Health Research and Educational Trust, 2007, www.kff.org/insurance/7672/upload/76723.pdf.

[4] "Health Insurance Mandates in the States," by Victoria Craig Bunce, Director or Research and Policy, and J.P. Wieske, Director of State Affairs, Council for Affordable Health Insurance, March 2008, at www.cahi.org/cahi_contents/resources/pdf/HealthInsuranceMandates2008.pdf.

[5] "How State Imposed Mandates Increase Costs and Reduce Access to Health Care," by Paul Guppy, Washington Policy Center Policy Brief, June 2002, at www.washingtonpolicy.org/HealthCare/PBGuppyHealthCareMandates.html.

[6] "Health Care Costs and Insurance Coverage," testimony by Dan L. Crippen, Director, Congressional Budget Office, before the Committee on Education and Workforce, United States House of Representatives, June 11, 1999.

[7] "Our Charge," Washington Blue Ribbon Commission on Health Care Costs and Access, Final Report, January 2007, at www.leg.wa.gov/documents/joint/HCCA/Final%20Report.pdf.

[8] "Mandated Benefit Laws and Employer-Sponsored Health Insurance," by Gail A. Jensen, Ph.D., Wayne State University and Michael A. Morrisey, Ph.D., University of Alabama-Birmingham, Health Insurance Association of America, January 1999.

[9] "Effects of State Reforms on Health Insurance Coverage of Adults," by Frank A. Sloan and Christopher J. Conover, *Inquiry 35*, No. 3, Fall 1998, pages 280 to 293.

[10] Revised Code of Washington, 48.44.023(b), "Mandatory offering providing basic health plan for employers with fewer than twenty-five employees – Exemption from statutory requirements – Premium rates – Requirements for providing coverage for small employers."

[11] "Health Savings Accounts," HSA Contributions, U.S. Department of the Treasury, January 2008, at www.ustreas.gov/offices/public-affairs/hsa/pdf/HSA-Tri-fold-english-07.pdf.

[12] "January 2006 Census Shows 3.2 Million People Covered by HSA Plans," survey of 96 AHIP companies, Center for Policy and Research, America's Health Insurance Plans, March 2006, at www.ahip.org/content/default.aspx?docid=15302.

[13] "January 2008 Census Shows More than Six Million People Covered by HSA/High-Deductible Health Plans," Center for Policy and Research, America's Health Insurance Plans, April, 2008, at www.ahipresearch.org/pdfs/2008_HSA_Census.pdf.

[14] Ibid., page 9.

[15] Ibid., page 12.

[16] "A Lesson for Government: How Consumer-Based Health Care is Benefiting Workers in the Private Sector," by Sally Pipes, Washington Policy Center Policy Note, 05-01, at www.washingtonpolicy.org/Centers/healthcare/policynote/05_pipes_consumerhc.html.

[17] "Locating a Mini-Clinic Near You," AARP Bulletin, AARP, April 12, 2007, www.bulletin.aarp.org/yourhealth/articles/express_lane_sb.html.

[18] "Facilities and Services Licensing," Washington State Department of Health, Construction Review Services, at www.doh.wa.gov.

[19] "Improving Health Care: A Dose of Competition," A Report by the Federal Trade Commission and the Department of Justice, July 2004, at http://www.justice.gov/atr/public/health_care/204694.pdf.

[20] "Patients see hope, but the state says there's no need," by Peter Neurath, *Puget Sound Business Journal*, May 12, 2006.

[21] "Washington State Certificate of Need Program Task Force Report," November 1, 2006, under "Recommendations, Purpose and Goals," page 8, at www.hca.wa.gov/doc/CONfinalreporta.pdf.

[22] "The Factors Fueling Rising Healthcare Costs, 2006," prepared for American's Health Insurance Plans, January 2006, PriceWaterHouseCoopers, at www.pwcglobal.com/extweb/pwcpublications.nsf/docid/e4cofoo4429297A852571090065A70B.

[23] "Why Doctors are Heading for Texas," by Joseph Nixon, *The Wall Street Journal*, May 17, 2008.

[24] Ibid.

[25] "The Medicaid Program at a Glance," Medicaid Facts, Kaiser Commission on Medicaid and the Uninsured, March 2007, www.kff.org/medicaid/upload/7235-02.pdf.

[26] Ibid.

[27] "Medicaid spending jumps sharply," by Dennis Cauchon, *USA Today*, October 8, 2007.

[28] "What are the cost savings for medical tourists?" Global Surgical Solutions, LLC, http://www.globalsurgicalsolutions.com, accessed May 23, 2008.

[29] "Small practice evolution: Making the switch to concierge medicine," by Robert Lewis, *Medical Economics*, May 2, 2008, at www.medicaleconomics.modernmedicine.com/memag/Small+practice+evolution/Small-practice-evolution-Making-the-switch-to-conc/ArticleStandard/Article/detail/512299?contextCategoryId=8485.

[30] "About CCCs," Convenient Care Association, at www.convenientcareassociation.org/index.htm, accessed May 23, 2008.

[31] "CCC's Benefit Patients," Fact Sheet, Convenient Care Association, at http://www.convenientcareassociation.org/CCA%20General%20FACTSHEET.pdf accessed May 23, 2008.

[32] Ibid.

[33] Presentation by David Hom, Center for Health Value Innovation on Value Based Health Benefit Design, at "Health Care 08," 6th Annual Health Care Conference, panel on "New Trends in Health Care," Washington Policy Center, Sea-Tac, Washington, May 13, 2008.

[34] Ibid.

CHAPTER 5

1. K-12 Education Spending

Recommendations

1. Return the education system to its core function by focusing resources on classroom instruction.

2. Reform basic education funding to allow money to follow the child to the public school of the family's choice. Allow principals to control their budgets, and to assemble their own teaching teams.

3. End rigid separation of programs to eliminate costly and wasteful administrative oversight. Allow more flexibility in spending education dollars, especially by local principals.

4. Remove restrictive class size requirements and other legal restrictions to allow more flexibility and innovation in spending education dollars.

5. Create a transparent accounting system to inform policymakers and the public about how education dollars are spent.

Background

Public schools were established in Washington in 1854 by the first territorial legislature. The system started with 53 schools and about 2,000 students.[1] A century and a half later, there are just over a million (1,026,000) K-12 public school students attending 2,275 schools in 296 districts across the state.[2]

The state's total population has grown at a much faster pace than the number of students, creating a larger tax base to pay for educating a proportionately smaller number of students. Between 1971 and 2006, the state population increased by almost three million people (82 percent),[3] while K-12 public school enrollment increased by only little over 200,000 students (25 percent).[4] These trends are shown in the chart below.[5]

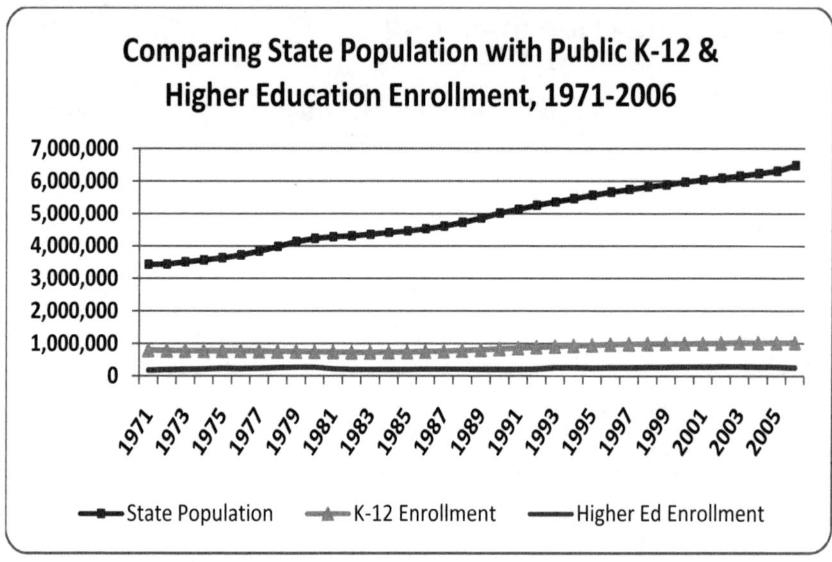

State population has grown much faster than public school enrollment, creating a larger tax base to pay for educating a proportionately smaller number of students.

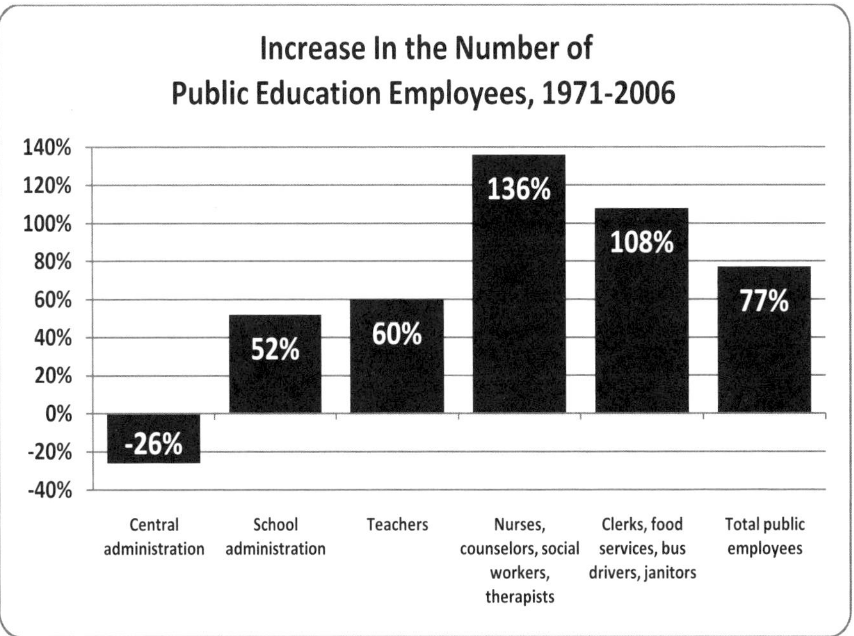

Source: "Preliminary School District Summary Reports 2007-08 School Year, Historical Comparison of Statewide School District Personnel," OSPI.[6]

While the number of students enrolled in public schools since 1971 increased 27 percent, the number of public school employees increased by 77 percent, more than twice as fast.

The rise in K-12 spending

K-12 education is the largest single expenditure in the state budget. For 2007-09, the total budget for public schools is $17.9 billion, including state, local and federal grant funding. The bulk of K-12 education spending, over $13.52 billion, comes from the state general fund budget.[7] About $1.6 billion comes from federal grants, and about $2.8 billion is provided by local funding, raised primarily from property taxes.[8]

Details on how the state portion of education funding is spent are shown in the following table.

2007-09 State Basic Education Programs (in millions)		
General Apportionment	$ 8968.6	66.3%
Special Education	1112.9	8.2%
Transportation	550.7	4.1%
Learning Assist. Program	189.9	1.4%
Bilingual Education	134.5	1.0%
Institutions	36.8	0.3%
Subtotal: Basic Education Programs	$10,993.5	81.3%
2007-09 Non-basic Education Programs (in millions)		
Student Achievement Fund (I-728)	$869.8	6.4%
Initiative 732 COLA (3.2%, 2.9%) and Other Compensation	380.0	2.8%
Levy Equalization	414.7	3.1%
Education Reform	265.2	2.0%
K-4 Enhanced Staffing Ratio	233.3	1.7%
Health Care Benefit Increases	66.4	0.5%
Two Learning Improvement Days	66.0	0.5%
Salary Equity Increases (2007-09)	64.2	0.2%
Promoting Academic Success	49.0	0.4%
Statewide Programs/Allocations	41.7	0.3%
State Office and Ed Agencies	33.5	0.2%
Highly Capable	17.2	0.1%
Educational Service Districts	16.0	0.1%
Food Services	6.3	0.0%
Summer & Other Skills Centers	5.7	0.0%
Pupil Transportation Coordinators	1.7	0.0%
Subtotal: Non-Basic Education Programs	$2530.6	18.7%
TOTAL – STATE FUNDS	**$13,524.1**	**100.0%**

Altogether, average spending per student in Washington public schools is about $9,500 a year, not including capital spending.

Of the money for public schools, about 59 percent is spent on classroom instruction. The rest of the public school budget is spent on administrators, maintenance personnel, special education, counseling, transportation, food services and interest on debt. An additional $1.33 billion is spent on school construction. The state spends a further $9.6 billion on Higher Education and "Other Education" programs.[9]

Yet, even with higher levels of funding, and fewer students in school in proportion to the number of taxpayers paying for public education, high school drop-out rates are very high. The state reports that 67 percent of our students graduate from high school,[10] and an independent estimate shows that only 66 percent are graduating from Washington's high schools.[11] Washington is ranked 37th in the nation in graduation rates.[12]

Thirty-seven percent of freshmen attending a four year university or two year community college must take high school level remedial math or reading courses. Many students are unable to overcome this handicap and do not complete their college degree.[13]

Policy Analysis

Advocacy groups argue that K-12 public education in Washington is underfunded. Yet by most measures, K-12 public education in Washington is very well-funded.

The problems that continue to plague the public education system require fundamental changes to the way public money is spent. Directing more dollars into the current entrenched system, no matter how carefully targeted or lavishly spent, will not improve student achievement.

Rising trend in spending

K-12 education funding in Washington has increased significantly in recent decades, even after accounting for inflation. Between 1980 and 2000, state and local spending on K-12 schools increased by 94 percent in inflation-adjusted dollars, from $3.96 billion in 1980 to $7.67 billion in 2000.[14] The rising trend continues. As mentioned, general fund K-12 spending in the current biennium exceeds $13.52 billion.[15]

Yet, while spending has almost tripled since 1980, the number of K-12 public students over the same period increased only 36 percent, increasing from 756,500 K-12 students in 1980 to 1,026,000 in 2007.

Washington public schools are well-funded

Advocates for increased spending argue that education is underfunded because it makes up a smaller share of the state budget than in the past. Their choice of statistics is selective, however, and it is only by looking at broad measures that an accurate picture emerges.

As the state expands spending on non-education programs, the *proportion* of the budget going to pubic education falls, even as the *amount* spent on education is increasing. Public schools in Washington are receiving more public money than in the past, even as total state spending on other programs expands.

Despite claims that schools have been "cut," state education funding has steadily increased over time, and in no year has the legislature reduced the amount of money devoted to public schools.

In fact, per-pupil spending is higher than ever, and therefore school district administrators have more resources than in the past to educate a given number of students. In addition, there are more taxpayers paying into the system than ever before. By almost every reasonable measure, public schools in Washington receive more than adequate funding.

More spending does not lead to better learning

While education spending in Washington has increased sharply in recent decades, there has been little or no increase in student performance. Nationally, the money spent on K-12 schools has also been dramatically increasing, even after figures are adjusted for inflation.

Between 1960 and 2000, real expenditures per student in the United States more than tripled from $2,235 in 1960 in inflation-adjusted dollars to $7,591 in 2000.[16] Per-student spending continues to rise. As noted, Washington is spending about $9,500 per student in 2007. Yet state and national test scores show no significant improvement in student performance.[17]

In 2007 only 36 percent and 34 percent of Washington's 8th grade students achieved proficiency or better on the reading and math portions, respectively, on the National Assessment of Educational Progress test (NAEP). This assessment is the recognized gold standard for assessing the achievement of U.S. students.[18]

Despite increased spending and costly class size reductions, the "achievement gap" between white and minority students on the 4th and 8th grade NAEP reading and math tests from 2002, 2003, 2005, and 2007 has not decreased, but has actually increased.[19]

Placing an effective teacher in every classroom

Policymakers have focused money on reducing class sizes, particularly in grades K-3, but independent research shows that placing an effective teacher in every classroom is more important than any other factor in improving student learning, including smaller class sizes.[20]

Shifting from funding staff ratios to funding children

Currently, Washington allocates money to the schools by funding a certain number of certified instructional staff (teachers) and classified staff (bus drivers, janitors, cafeteria workers and other support personnel) for every 1,000 students. This funding is adjusted for inflation and staff pay is based on a pre-set statewide salary grid, which blindly pays teachers based on seniority and number of degrees and credits, not ability to convey knowledge to students.

For example, the current (general apportionment) ratio of teachers to students is 49 teachers for every 1,000 students. Other funds add 15 teachers, for a current total of 63 teachers per 1,000 students.[21]

In this system no account is taken of actual student needs at the local level, or in recognizing and rewarding particularly talented teachers. It also does not account for ineffective teachers. If parents complain, bad teachers are simply transferred to another classroom.

Staffing schools by allocating ratios allows central school district bureaucracies to control the assignment of personnel to individual schools. Schools have little flexibility to alter the mix of resources in a way that would most benefit students. As a result, principals in Washington are hamstrung by lack of control over their budgets, and over their personnel choices. Principals control less than five percent of the money allocated to their schools.[22]

Washington's Joint Legislative Audit and Review Committee (JLARC) reports that:

> "In most cases, central administrators determine the number of certificated and classified staff assigned to individual schools. Almost 96 percent of districts responding to JLARC's survey said that central administrators determine whether to hire additional teachers and 89 percent said central administrators determine the number and type of classified staff employed at each school."[23]

The JLARC study reveals that in almost all cases central administrators decide which teachers will work in a particular school. Local principals have almost no control over which teachers are assigned to their schools, or whether a particular teacher's skills and experience match with the needs of students.

A better way is to "fund the child"

A better, innovative method of school finance, called "fund the child," or "weighted-student formula," has revitalized schools across the country. This approach has proved successful in Cincinnati, San Francisco, Houston, St. Paul, Seattle (in the past) and Oakland, and there are pilot programs in Boston, Chicago and New York City.

Under this system, education funding follows the child to the public school of his family's choice. Schools which are successful attract students and dollars. Schools which do not teach students and do not satisfy students see declining enrollment. This signals to the district superintendent that the leadership of that school needs to be replaced.

Funding for each child can include a dollar multiplier to account for children who are more difficult to teach, such as disabled children and children with limited English proficiency. Devoting these dollars to the local school level allows principals to decide how to best educate these children.

Funding the schools in this way allows principals to control their budgets, and to hire teachers who best meet the needs of their students. The results in San Francisco and other cities are promising. Student achievement and parent satisfaction and involvement rates are soaring.[24] Accountability is built in. Schools which do not to educate children are reorganized and their failed leadership is replaced.

End separation of categorical spending programs and eliminate waste.

In addition to six Basic Education programs, the Washington legislature currently funds sixteen non-basic education programs, as listed in the table. One of these categories, "Education Reform," funds twenty-five programs. The Office of Superintendent of Public Instruction and Statewide Programs includes 25 programs controlled by that office, including funding to the Professional Educator Standards Board to "strengthen teacher preparation requirements in cultural understanding" and a program to create a program to recognize "outstanding classified staff across the state."[25]

Numerous categorical spending programs are a bureaucrat's dream come true, as explained by UCLA Professor of Management Bill Ouchi:

"When a state legislator or governor runs for office and talks about education, he or she will usually promise voters to allocate more money for whatever is the concern of the day…After the legislature allocates the new money, that cash doesn't go directly to individual schools – it goes to the district central office. There, the bureaucrats don't send dollars to the schools. Instead, they hire people to perform new tasks in the schools. The problem with doing it this way is that the decisions on exactly what kind of staff each school needs aren't made at the local school, they're made far away in the central office.

"One school might need only 0.6 of a specialist, while another school might need 1.3 – but each school will get one whole person. Not only that, but the schools might have a better, more creative way of using that money to meet the goal – but they don't have the freedom to do so. And here is the topper: before the central office bureaucrats assign the new personnel out to the schools, they'll create several new positions in headquarters – with several new executive positions to oversee the new offices – and to make matters worse, those newly created central office bureaucrats will proceed to tell the new teachers in the schools how to do their jobs!"[26]

Combining categorical programs into fewer revenue streams would allow school superintendents to remove central staff now employed to track and oversee spending for over 50 different sources of revenue. It would also relieve local principals from having to apply and account for all the supplemental funding for their schools. Instead, categorical funding should be provided to principals without strings attached, so they can enhance the quality of their teaching staff.

Create a transparent accounting system

It is impossible for policymakers or the public to make informed decisions about K-12 spending, because the Office of Superintendent of Public Instruction does not show how spending relates to student learning. A recent Joint Legislative Audit and Review Committee (JLARC) study identifies the kinds of data needed to inform the public and policymakers:[27]

- School expenditure data;
- Staff/teacher descriptive data;
- Student descriptive and outcome;
- School/community descriptive data.

For example, school-level spending is not reported to the state, so important information, such as actual spending per teacher is not available. Better information about teacher and staff costs is needed, including their academic degrees and majors, and routes to certification. Also, the state superintendent does not keep track of whether high school students are ready for college, even though most people assume possessing a Washington public high school diploma should mean a young person is prepared for college-level work.

Recommendations

1) Return the education system to its core function by focusing resources on classroom instruction. Independent research shows that placing a good teacher in the classroom is the single most effective way to educate children, especially if that teacher has mastery of the subject matter. Over the years, the school system has been given more and more social tasks to make up for failures in other policy areas. Education leaders should be allowed to focus their money on academics, and not be asked to solve other problems facing society.

2) Reform basic education funding to allow money to follow the child to the public school of the family's choice. Allow principals to control their budgets, and to assemble their own teaching teams. Policymakers should allow parent choice among public schools, not staffing ratios, to guide funding of schools. They should also give local principals control over their own budgets, and over the hiring and firing of teachers and staff in their own school.

3) End rigid separation of programs to eliminate costly and wasteful administrative oversight. Allow more flexibility in spending education dollars, especially by local principals. This policy change would allow more flexibility and innovation in spending education dollars at all levels of decision-making.

4) Remove restrictive class size requirements and other legal restrictions to allow more flexibility and innovation in spending education dollars. Reducing class sizes has not resulted in improvements in student learning, as education advocates promised. Instead, policymakers should remove legal restrictions which micro-manage schools, and let local principals implement the kind of learning program that works best for their students.

5) Create a transparent accounting system to inform policymakers and the public about how education dollars are spent. The Office of Superintendent of Instruction should do a better job of collecting relevant information about the funding and performance of local schools, especially how spending on teachers relates to student learning, and make this information easily available to policymakers, parents and the general public.

2. Teacher Quality

Recommendations

1. Raise teacher quality by reforming teacher pay.

2. Hire teachers based on their proven experience and mastery of academic subject matter, particularly in math and science, rather than on the number of teaching certificates earned or school of education requirements met.

3. Put local principals in charge of hiring the teaching staff for their own schools, so they can select teachers based on the learning needs of their students.

4. Allow local principals to fire or suspend bad teachers, and hold principals accountable for teacher performance and yearly progress in student learning.

Background

Research consistently shows that placing an effective teacher in the classroom is more important than any other factor, including class size, in raising student academic achievement.[28] A good teacher can make as much as a full year's difference in students' learning growth.[29] Students taught by a high-quality teacher three years in a row score 50 percentile points higher than students of ineffective teachers.[30] Students taught by a bad teacher two years in a row may never catch up.

Two decades of research show that the qualities of an effective teacher are:

- mastery of the subject matter being taught;
- five years or more of teaching experience;
- teacher training that emphasizes content knowledge and high standards of classroom competency;
- strong academic skills, intellectual curiosity and an excitement about learning for its own sake.[31]

Policy Analysis

In Washington, only half of the class scheduled to graduate in 2009 was able to pass the 10th grade WASL.[32] This is in part because public school teachers often do not have mastery of the subjects they teach. Only 40 percent of math teachers hold math degrees from college, and only 77 percent of science teachers hold college science degrees.[33] School officials regularly report they are unable to find people who hold a teaching certificate and who are qualified to teach math and science in high schools.

Many Washington professionals are highly qualified to teach these subjects but, because they do not have a formal certificate, it is illegal for public school officials to offer them teaching positions. Getting a teaching credential requires months of additional classroom work, something many qualified professionals have neither the time, money nor inclination to do.

Another major factor causing qualified teacher shortages is the single-salary "time and credits" pay grid the legislature requires school districts to use. The limitations of teacher pay policy are discussed further in the next section.

Meanwhile, schools of education require students training to be teachers to spend most of their time learning pedagogical techniques, not on gaining mastery of the subject they will teach when they graduate and enter a classroom.

School of education administrators defend the current system by saying someone who knows a subject may not be able to teach the subject. The research shows, however, that experienced professionals, like an engineer who wants to teach high school math, can quickly be taught classroom procedures, and that his mastery of mathematics is the most important factor in whether his students will learn.

Putting the local principal in charge of the teaching staff would allow the principals easily to remove any teacher who was not working out. Principals should then be held accountable for teacher performance and student learning.

If a district superintendent finds that a local school is consistently failing to teach students, he should dismiss the principal and hire a new one. The lines of responsibility should be clear to public school employees and to the public. Teachers and principals who are unable to educate children to the standard required by the state should be removed from the system, and their places taken by people who can be effective educators.

Recommendations

1) Raise teacher quality by reforming teacher pay. See Section 3 on Teacher Pay for details.

2) Hire teachers based on their proven experience and mastery of academic subject matter, particularly in math and science, rather than on the number of teaching certificates earned or school of education requirements met. Current state credential requirements make it illegal to hire many highly-qualified people to teach in a public school. Mid-career professionals, former military service members, retired business owners and others are all potential teachers, if they show mastery of their subject and acquire the necessary classroom skills. Professionals bring life experiences into the classroom and help students understand the complex grown-up world they will enter upon graduation.

3) Put local principals in charge of hiring the teaching staff for their own schools, so they can select teachers based on the learning needs of their students. Local principals should be encouraged to be education leaders, rather than routine government employees skilled at navigating the education bureaucracy. Principals should be able to hire the best person to teach in the classroom, and be able to hold all faculty members accountable for whether students are learning.

4) Allow local principals to fire or suspend bad teachers, and hold principals accountable for teacher performance and yearly progress in student learning. In order to assemble and maintain a high-quality, highly-motivated educational team, principals must be allowed to weed out teachers who are unwilling or unfit to do the hard work of educating children. Also, it is unfair and demoralizing to effective, hard-working teachers when poor-performing teachers are kept on staff, often with the same or higher level of pay.

3. Teacher Pay

Recommendations

1. Change the automatic single-salary pay grid so that teacher pay is based on ability to educate children, not on arbitrary degree requirements or years of employment.

2. Give local principals management control over their own school's budget and teaching staff.

3. Establish school oversight at the district level and an appeals process to ensure fair treatment of teachers. Allow superintendents to fire ineffective or abusive principals.

Background

More than half of the people employed by public school districts in Washington are not classroom teachers. In 2005-06, there were approximately 48,558 teachers working in elementary and high school classrooms, or only 47 percent of the 103,000 workers employed in public school education.[34] The average salary of public K-12 teachers for a nine-month work year (2006-07) is just over $48,000.[35]

School districts supplement teacher pay for additional time, responsibilities and incentives (known as "TRI"), most of which is paid from local levy revenue. The average additional salary paid to teachers under this arrangement is $7,476, bringing the total average salary for a nine-month work year to $55,487.[36]

Policy Analysis

The current pay structure for Washington public school teachers was established in the 1920s to "ensure fair and equal treatment for all." The system stresses equality over excellence.

This salary structure has changed little over the last 85 years. During that time, the world has changed, becoming more innovative and competitive, yet teacher pay today is based on seniority and training level, not actual effectiveness in educating children.

The quality of the teacher is the most important factor in whether children learn, but the method of paying teachers actually deters people with technical knowledge from entering teaching, and it encourages those with such skills to leave teaching for work in the private sector.

Teachers with strong backgrounds in math and science sacrifice far more financially under the single-salary schedule than their college peers who did not go into teaching.[37] For example, four years after college, graduates with technical training who are not teachers earn almost $13,500 more than their peers who entered the teaching profession. After ten years the pay gap grows to almost $28,000.[38]

University of Washington researcher Dan Goldhaber notes how non-teacher professionals are rewarded based on ability:

> "Not surprisingly, the non-teacher labor market rewards ability at a much higher rate than the teacher labor market, with the teacher labor market actually giving a slight premium to those with the lowest SAT scores in 2003."[39]

He also notes that better-qualified teachers use their clout to avoid having to work in high-poverty schools:

> "Teachers with more labor-market bargaining power – those who are highly experienced, credentialed, or judged to be better – will therefore tend to be teaching in nicer settings with lighter work-loads. As a consequence, the most-needy students tend to be paired with the least-qualified teachers."[40]

A teacher-pay system designed to ensure "fair and equal treatment for all" has resulted in placing the least effective teachers in the classrooms of the neediest students.

Performance pay

Leaders of Washington's teachers' unions strongly oppose paying teachers based on ability, but this approach is now common in many parts of the country. Douglas County, Colorado has had such a system since 1994. There, the system is designed to "reward teachers for outstanding student performance, enhance collegiality, and encourage positive school and community relations."[41]

In Douglas County, unions do not oppose merit pay. The president of the area's teachers federation says that under performance pay, "Teachers must demonstrate how their work is being used to drive instruction, and they are rewarded for employing new skills."[42]

Several states, including Tennessee, Arizona, Colorado, Iowa, Ohio, Florida, and North Carolina, have adopted similar performance-based pay systems for teachers.

The advantage of performance pay is that it encourages teachers to develop their talents and acquire new skills. Performance pay also allows school administrators and parents to recognize quality educators and encourage them to excel in the classroom. At the same time, performance pay improves the quality of the teaching profession by encouraging underperforming teachers to seek a different line of work.

There are four different approaches to creating an effective performance pay system:[43]

- **Merit pay**. Individual teachers are evaluated and given bonuses based on improvements in their effectiveness in the classroom;

- **Knowledge- and skills-based pay**. Teachers receive a salary increase when they acquire new levels of education and training. In Washington, teacher contracts often include automatic knowledge-based pay increases;

- **Performance pay**. Teachers are rewarded when their students show measurable improvement on standardized academic tests;

- **School-based performance pay**. All the administrators, teachers, and staff at a particular school receive a bonus if their students meet certain academic standards.

To determine performance fairly, teachers should be assessed frequently on student achievement, teaching skills, subject knowledge, classroom management and lesson planning. An appeals process should be put in place so teachers receive an independent review if they feel they have been unfairly treated. Principals who abuse the performance pay system to benefit themselves or to unfairly enrich their friends should be disciplined or dismissed.

Policymakers who support equitable performance pay systems show respect for students, parents and taxpayers who have a right to expect that public schools will consistently and effectively educate children.

Recommendations

1) Change the automatic single-salary pay grid so that teacher pay is based on ability to educate children, not on arbitrary degree requirements or years of employment. The pay schedule should be changed to reward and retain top-performing teachers and attract talented teachers to high-need schools.

2) Give local principals management control over their own school's budget and teaching staff. It is almost impossible for principals to dismiss low-performing teachers. Using fair and objective measures of job performance, principals should be given the authority to hire, fire and promote teachers, and be held accountable for the quality of their teaching staff.

3) Establish school oversight at the district level and an appeals process to ensure fair treatment of teachers. Allow superintendents to fire ineffective or abusive principals. Teachers and other school employees should have the right to contest unfair treatment. Independent oversight by superintendents and school boards is needed to avoid favoritism, unmerited raises and management harassment of individual teachers. Principals who abuse the merit pay system should be disciplined or dismissed.

4. Student Testing and Achievement

Recommendations

1. Improve or replace the WASL with an objective test based on the highest-quality academic standards available, so that students are fairly judged based on an objective test which does not change from year to year.

2. Offer more practical career and technical education classes for graduating high school students who choose to enter the workforce instead of going on college.

3. Make a Washington state diploma a recognized sign of a good education, by raising the academic standard of the WASL or by choosing a better test, so it more closely matches respected, national tests, like the NAEP.

Background

Student testing and the WASL

The WASL was developed in the mid-1990s to assess whether Washington's children are adequately being taught reading, writing, math and science. While some educational activist groups oppose standardized tests, the WASL has been beneficial by placing student achievement front and center in the policy debate over Washington's schools, and by providing a clear basis for assessing whether education officials are fulfilling the paramount duty of the state.

The WASL shows that in general public schools are failing to educate children to the standard set by the legislature:[44]

- In 2007, only 76.6 percent of fourth grade students met the reading standard, 60 percent met the writing standard and 58 percent met the math standard;

- In eighth grade, 65 percent met the WASL reading standard and 50 percent met the math standard in 2007;

- In tenth grade, 81 percent met the reading standard, 84 percent met the writing standard, and 50 percent met the math standard in 2007.

In all three grades, less than 45 percent of students met the WASL standard in science.[45]

Research by the Thomas B. Fordham Foundation reveals wide gaps in state standards as states have succumbed to the temptation to water down the rigor of their tests in order to meet the high expectations of federal law.[46] Washington lawmakers did exactly that in 2007, when they canceled the math portion of the WASL.

The wide disparities between achievement on the National Assessment of Educational Progress (NAEP) test and on the WASL shows that Washington's statewide test inflates student achievement and makes it appear Washington children are learning more than they really are.

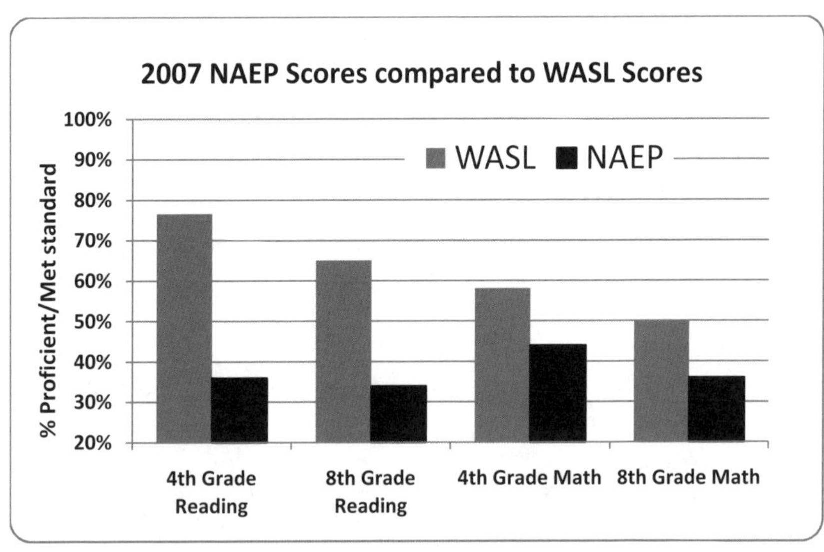

*WASL scores shown are those which are deemed to have "met the standard."

The WASL is subjectively graded, and thus cannot be considered scientifically valid and reliable. The Superintendent of Public Instruction admits the lack of objectivity in the test:

> "The WASL uses far more open-ended questions than other states' tests to measure the higher-level thinking, reasoning and communications skills intrinsic to Washington's academic standards."[47]

In addition, in 2004, The Office of Superintendent of Public Instruction lowered the bar for passing the WASL test, by reducing the score needed to "meet the standard."[48]

In 2007, the governor and the legislature, seeing that nearly half of students in the class of 2008 would probably fail the 10th grade WASL in math, and realizing this would be unacceptable to the public, cancelled the math requirement for that year.

The math standard is under review, and the governor has announced that no new standard need be in place until 2013. In the meantime, at least 340,000 Washington students will be issued high school diplomas without meeting the WASL standard in math.

State leaders have not maintained the quality of the WASL and they are not providing the level of education they have promised to Washington's children. The WASL should be improved or replaced by an objective test based on the highest-quality academic standards, such as those developed by the states of Massachusetts, Indiana, and California.

Dropout rates are very high

The world that our children face today is far different than the world their parents faced. In 1950, 60 percent of jobs were "unskilled" and required a high school diploma or less. Today, less than 15 percent of all jobs are considered "unskilled" and roughly two-thirds of jobs require some amount of college education.[49]

Yet, today, more than one-third of Washington public school students fail to graduate, and another third graduate without the knowledge and skills necessary for college or the workplace.[50]

- About 33 percent of public high school student drop out.[51] In 2007, about 29,800 students did not graduate.[52]

- Over half (52 percent) of students entering community or technical colleges have to take remedial math, English or reading courses to catch up.[53]

- 37 percent of students entering our two-year and four-year colleges must take remedial math or English courses.[54]

The National Association of Manufacturers' Skills Gap Report finds that 84 percent of employers say that public schools are not doing a good job of preparing students to succeed in the workplace.[55]

Public education leaders have failed to teach math effectively because of poor curriculum choices and by placing artificial limits on who is allowed to teach math in the classroom.

Policymakers should set a goal that 90 percent of high school students pass the math portion of the WASL. Today, less than half are able to pass this portion of the test, even though it measures only middle school math skills. A better standard is needed, so that children receive the education they have been promised.

In Washington, a government-issued diploma should, at a minimum, certify that a young adult entering college or the workforce has received an adequate education.

Not all graduating students are college-bound; many must earn a living after leaving high school. Career and vocational education opportunities should be expanded, and these programs should be rigorous enough to provide students with the math and writing skills they need for success.

Finally, instead of watering down the WASL test, state education leaders should pick a high academic standard and stick to it because that is what's best for students. As education researcher Chester Finn put it:

"It's really squalid to see states set 'tough' requirements and then back off, defer, or punch holes in them. Our kids deserve to grow up in a country where policy makers do what they say."[56]

Recommendations

1) Improve or replace the WASL with a test based on the highest-quality academic standards, such as those developed by other states. Students should be fairly judged by an objective test which does not change from year to year. The legislature and state education leaders should pick a high academic standard for graduation and stick to it. Lawmakers should refrain from repealing sections of the standard chosen, as they did by canceling the math section of the WASL, and instead apply and maintain a consistent standard of learning. This approach would give students a valuable educational asset, a Washington state diploma, as they go on to college or enter the workforce.

2) Offer more practical career and technical education classes for graduating high school students who choose to enter the workforce instead of going to college. Public education leaders should encourage all students to graduate, but not all graduates need or want to go on to college. A basic Washington high school education should open career opportunities and prepare graduating students for success in the workplace, if that is the path they choose.

3) Make a Washington state diploma a recognized sign of a good education by improving the WASL or choosing a better test, so it more closely matches respected, national tests, like the NAEP. Over the years, lawmakers and the Superintendent of Public Instruction have gradually weakened the WASL academic standard, putting Washington students at risk of falling bchind their peers across the country and around the world. A better test more closely aligned to a respected standard like the NAEP would ensure that Washington's children are receiving the level of education they need and deserve.

5. Universal Preschool and All-Day Kindergarten

Recommendations

1. Public policy should support stable, long-term relationships between parents and young children.

2. Encourage voluntary participation and avoid programs based on universal or mandatory participation.

3. Respect parental choice by making early learning public assistance portable and child-centered, not fixed and provider-centered.

4. Build on innovation in the private market, as providers compete to offer flexible, high-quality services that serve the needs of families.

5. Allow voluntary professional memberships, so child care providers are not required to join a union against their will.

Background

In 2007, the legislature created a new Department of Early Learning, with initial two-year funding of $329 million. The Department's program includes an expanded, by 2,250 places, Early Childhood Education and Assistance Program (ECEAP), at a subsidy rate of $6,500 per child. It also increases payments to providers, creates a Quality Rating and Improvement System, and devotes $51 million to an all-day kindergarten program.[57]

Advocates of early learning programs argue that some young children are entering school at a disadvantage, and that this contributes to the state's low academic achievement and high drop-out rate. Advocates plan to spend $100 million to develop public opinion to support broad, permanent state programs. Their stated purpose is:

"to create the public and political will to develop a
sustainable system of affordable, high-quality early learning
across the state."[58]

Policy Analysis

Research indicates, however, that any benefits to children of
institutional-based early learning programs are short-lived. Early
academic gains fade quickly, and by the fifth grade, children who
attended early learning programs show no measurable improvement
over children who did not attend these programs.[59]

Oklahoma, New Jersey and Georgia have all recently tried
highly-regulated universal preschool programs, some providing
taxpayer subsidies of as much as $11,000 per child per year. The
results are not encouraging. Any short-term gains for disadvantaged
children fade out over time, especially if children were slated to
attend low-performing public schools.

Early learning advocates point to three studies, High/Scope
Perry Preschool, Abecedarian, and Chicago Child-Parent, to claim
that these programs can achieve long-term success. However, they
overlook three key aspects of these programs that make them
impractical for application in Washington state.

First, each program delivered an intensive level of center-
based care to severely disadvantaged children, with low student-to-
teacher ratios and intensive parent involvement and education over
several years. These programs stayed involved with particular
families for six years in the case of the Chicago study, and for five to
eight years in the case of the Abecedarian program. This level of
involvement is not practical for the much larger child populations
that would be covered by a universal early learning program.

Second, the main benefit to children of these programs was a
stronger relationship with parents, not being part of a universal
institutional program. As psychologist Dr. Matthew Thompson
points out:

"It is possible that parental involvement explains more of the
variance in outcome among inner-city children than do
structured programs...

"If policy makers mistakenly accept the conclusion that preschool intervention results in less criminal activity later, they may mistakenly invest in these programs when the money might be better invested in parenting skill programs and other interventions to increase parental involvement."[60]

Third, these specialized early learning programs involved very high costs; $11,000 per child in the Abecedarian program, and $12,300 per child in the High/Scope Perry program. The Chicago program had a student/teacher ratio of 8.5 to one, and the High-Scope Perry program included 90-miniute weekly home visits.

These are key features that would be impractical in a statewide, universal program. The positive results of these three studies could not be duplicated on a larger scale.

Fostering strong bonds to parents

Policymakers should avoid public programs that separate parents from their very young children for long periods of time. Social science and brain research shows that the healthy development of very young minds depends on the quality and reliability of a young child's relationships with the important people in his or her life, especially with parents.

A strong parent-child relationship is associated with better cognitive skills and enhanced social competence and work skills later in school. The science shows a direct connection between the social and emotional development of young children and their intellectual growth.

Conversely, too much time away from parents and in institutional care can inhibit a small child's social and emotional development. Social scientists at U.C. Berkeley and Stanford found that more hours in center-based care, 15 to 30 hours a week or more, resulted in, "no cognitive gains and substantially greater behavioral problems associated with additional hours of attendance."[61]

Elementary school teachers depend on the eagerness and natural curiosity of young children in order to impart important skills and knowledge. It is important to protect these social attributes of very young children. Natural excitement can be stifled by exposure to an over-structured environment, such as center-based care. Child development researcher Bruce Fuller notes that:

> "Institutions, no matter how small and warm and fuzzy, start to regulate kids' behaviors. Once you rigidify and routinize that, then kids start to shut down, and their cognitive growth starts to slow down."[62]

The vast majority, 77 percent, of Washington's 442,000 children under age five are cared for in family-based, non-institutional settings.[63] Most parents in Washington choose individual home-based care, usually from a parent or relative, or less than four hours a day of an institutional preschool setting, for their very young children. These children tend to learn self-control and socializing behaviors from their families, which prepare them for the classroom, without dampening their natural curiosity.

The downside of all-day kindergarten

A recent study by the RAND Corporation shows that developing nonacademic readiness skills, as opposed to spending time in all-day kindergarten, is important to raising overall achievement and narrowing the learning gap between minority and white children.[64]

Nonacademic readiness skills are significantly related to reading and mathematics achievement in the fifth grade. Nonacademic readiness skills include a child's motivation, his ability to exercise self-control, to interact positively with others, and the avoidance of negative behaviors.

The RAND researchers found that in some cases a child attending all-day kindergarten later experienced *reduced* mathematics achievement when nonacademic skills are considered.[65]

Attending an all-day kindergarten program hindered the development of these important nonacademic school readiness skills. Children who participated in all-day kindergarten demonstrated poorer dispositions toward learning, lower self-control and poorer interpersonal skills than children in part-day programs.

Children in all-day programs also showed a greater tendency to engage in externalizing and internalizing negative behaviors (acting-out, defiance, arguing, fighting) than children in part-day programs.

Thus researchers found that all-day kindergarten is not a solution to the widely-touted lack of learning readiness of many kindergarteners.

Recommendations

1) Public policy should support stable, long-term relationships between parents and young children. Research shows that one-on-one relationships with parents and close family members contribute to the social and educational development of very young children. Policymakers should build on this research and encourage, or at least not create programs that disrupt, these important early relationships.

2) Encourage voluntary participation and avoid programs based on universal or mandatory participation. Public assistance to low-income families seeking early learning programs should be individual, portable and voluntary. Decisions about whether a child should participate should be made by parents, not program managers. Programs based on universal or mandatory participation should be avoided.

3) Respect parental choice by making early learning public assistance portable and child-centered, not fixed and provider-centered. Early learning public assistance should be child-based, not provider-based. Parents should be able to select the program or learning institution that best serves their child. If parents become dissatisfied, they should be able to transfer their child to another program, with public aid following the child.

4) Build on innovation in the private market, as providers compete to offer flexible, high-quality services that serve the needs of families. Private, for profit entities tend to be much more creative and nimble than government agencies. Early education programs should build on choice, innovation and constructive competition among private providers, as they seek to develop flexible solutions that serve the needs of families. Similarly, policymakers should avoid imposing top-down restrictions that tend to stifle innovation and drive providers out of the market.

5) Allow voluntary professional memberships, so child care providers are not required to join a union against their will. In order to draw high-performing and talented people to the early learning field, policymakers should insure that membership in any private outside professional organization, such as a union, is voluntary. The state should not force early learning teachers and care providers to join such a private organization as a condition of employment.

6. Online Public Education

Recommendation

1. Encourage public school officials to expand online public education opportunities, so this learning option is available to any willing student.

Background

In May 2005, the legislature unanimously passed, and Governor Gregoire signed, SB 5828, to allow public school districts to offer online learning programs. Students in an online program study from home and receive lessons, submit homework and communicate with teachers by computer. Currently, about 6,600 students in Washington are enrolled in online public education.

Online public education programs must comply with all the academic rules and standards that apply to traditional public schools, including civil rights protections, oversight by certified teachers and state-mandated testing.[66]

Lawmakers passed the bill to allow students to take advantage of emerging internet technologies, particularly for students who have dropped out, or who otherwise were not being served by traditional schools. Online programs are effective in reaching:

- Students who have dropped out or are at risk of doing so;

- Students who do not perform well in large, traditional school settings, or do not connect socially in such settings;

- Homeschooling families who want to re-connect with public education (there are more than 17,000 homeschooled children in Washington);

- Gifted students who need more challenging coursework, or slower students who need more time to master a subject;

- High school students who have jobs or family responsibilities;

- Students who have long-term health conditions or physical handicaps;

- Students pursuing high-level training in sports or the arts and who cannot attend regular school hours (for example, Olympic gold medallist Apolo Ohno is an online graduate).

Online education in Washington

The three largest online programs are operated by the Federal Way School District, the Steilacoom School District and the Quillayute School District.

A large percentage of students in the Steilacoom and Quillayute programs, 45 percent and 38 percent respectively, had previously left the public education system.[67]

In addition to full-time online learning programs, 12,097 other students in the 2006-07 school year were enrolled in one or more online classes through their local public school district.[68]

Online public education is popular

Nationally, online public education is popular, as the number of families enrolling their children in online programs has rapidly increased in just a few years. In 2001, an estimated 50,000 K-12 students were engaged in distance learning. By 2003, that number had grown to 327,670 students.[69]

In 2006, the number of K-12 students taking online courses ballooned to 700,000.[70] The number of families choosing online public education courses increased more than tenfold in only six years.

In addition, officials in 72 percent of public school districts offering distance learning programs report they plan to expand their online courses in the future, in response to growing demand from parents in their area.[71]

Policy Analysis

While the explosive growth of online enrollment shows this public education choice is popular, online education still represents a small percentage of the 48.6 million students attending public schools across the country.[72]

Online public education programs are providing a high-quality, rigorous educational program for students who do not fit well in a traditional public school. These programs have proved successful in persuading families that had previously rejected public education to enroll their children in a public school program.

Online programs are academically successful for students, financially sustainable for taxpayers, and popular with parents. As such, they play an important part in fulfilling the state's paramount duty to make ample educational provision for all children within its borders.

Recommendation

1) Encourage public school officials to expand online public education opportunities, so this learning option is available to any willing student. Washington policymakers have a paramount duty to make ample provision for the education of all children. Online education is effective at reaching hard-to-serve student populations. In addition, the choice of online education is popular with parents.

Policymakers should encourage school districts to offer the option of online courses to any willing student. Lawmakers should not place limits on how many students can enroll, as some have proposed, or impose restrictions on the ability of school districts to create or expand these programs. Online education has proven successful in drawing families back to the public system, and in providing rigorous, high-quality learning for children.

Additional Resources from Washington Policy Center

"Learning Online: An Assessment of Online Public Education Programs," by Liv Finne, March 2008.

"Second-Rate Math Curricula and Standards Have Failed to Educate Our Students," by Liv Finne, January 2008.

"Proposed Bill Would Unionize Foster Parents," by Paul Guppy, February 2008.

"Bill to Unionize Daycare Workers Violates the National Labor Relations Act," by Liv Finne, February 2008.

"Unionizing Daycare, Requiring Union Membership and Collective Bargaining in the Provision of State Subsidized Daycare Services," by Liv Finne, February 2008.

"Early Learning Proposals in Washington State," by Liv Finne, December 2007.

"Reviewing the Research on Universal Preschool and All-Day Kindergarten," by Liv Finne, Policy Note 2007-24.

"Reducing education Standards Denies Learning Opportunities to Students," by Liv Finne, Policy Note 2007-07.

"The Coming Crisis in Citizenship," by Professor Mathew Manweller, July 2007.

"How to Fix the Coming Crisis in Citizenship," by Professor Mathew Manweller, August 2007.

"Better Use of Education Money, Not More of It, Will Improve Student Learning," by Paul Guppy, September 2006.

"Overview of Public Education Spending in Washington State," by Liv Finne, August 2006.

"Referendum 55 and Initiative 884 Failed, So What Can We Do about Education?" by John Barnes, December 2004.

"Creating New Opportunities to Learn: Charter Schools and Education Reform in Washington," by Melissa Lambert Milewski, September 2004.

"A Citizen's Guide to the $1 Billion Education Initiative: An Analysis of Initiative 884 and public education funding in Washington," by Melissa Lambert Milewski, July 2004.

"K-12 Public Education Spending in Washington," by Melissa Lambert Milewski, 2004.

"K-12 Public Education: Ignoring Good Management Practices and Risking America's Future," by Julia Rindlaub, Policy Note 04-15, 2004.

"Innovative School Facility Partnerships: Downtown, Airport, and Retail Space," by Matthew D. Taylor and Lisa Snell, Introduction by Eddie Reed, M.S., December 2001.

---

[1] "Organization and Financing of Schools," Office of the Superintendent of Public Instruction, 2004, pages 127-9.

[2] "Student Demographics, Enrollment, October 2006," Washington State Report Card, Office of the Superintendent of Public Instruction, at www.reportcard.ospi.k12.wa.us/summary.aspx?year=2006-07.

[3] In 1971, the total population in Washington was 3,436,300. By 2006, the population had increased to 6,395,798, "Fact Sheet, Washington," American Community Survey, United States Census Bureau, 2006.

[4] "K-12 Enrollment," Office of Financial Management, www.ofm.wa.gov/trends/tables/fig402.asp and, "2007 Washington State Higher Education Trends and Highlights, Office of Financial Management, February 2007, at ofm.wa.gov/hied/highlights/section1.pdf.

[5] "State Population By Age and Sex: 1970-2030, From November 2003 Forecast," "K-12 Enrollment," and "Public Higher Education Enrollment," Office of Financial Management, November 2007.

[6] "Preliminary School District Summary Reports 2007-8 School Year, Historical Comparison of Statewide School District Personnel," Table 2, OSPI, January 17, 2008, accessed at http://www.k12.wa.us/safs/PUB/PER/0708/ps.asp.

[7] "Omnibus Operating Budget Comparisons, 2007 – 2009, Total Budgeted Funds," 2007 Washington State Legislative Budget Notes, Legislative Evaluation and Accountability Program Committee, at www.leap.leg.wa.gov/leap/budget/lbns/2007toc.asp, page 284.

[8] "A Citizen's Guide to Washington State K-12 Finance 2008," Senate Ways and Means Committee, January 2008, page 15, at www.leg.wa.gov/documents/Senate/SCS/wml/swmwebsite/publications/budget guides/2008/K12Guide2008FINAL.pdf.

[9] "Omnibus Operating Budget Comparisons, 2007 – 2009, Total Budgeted Funds," 2007 Washington State Legislative Budget Notes, Legislative Evaluation and

Accountability Program Committee, at
www.leap.leg.wa.gov/leap/budget/lbns/2007toc.asp, page 284.
[10] "On-Time Graduation Rate 2005-6," Washington State Report Card, Office of the
Superintendent of Public Instruction, 2006-07, at
www.reportcard.ospi.k12.wa.us/summary.aspx?year=2006-07.
[11] "Ready for What? Preparing Students for College, Careers, and Life After High
School," Diplomas Count, The Graduation Project 2007, *Education Week*, page 4,
athttp://www.edweek.org/media/ew/dc/2007/wa_SGB07.pdf.
[12] "Washington High Schools," Alliance for Excellent Education, February 2008, at
www.all4ed.org/files/washington.pdf.
[13] "Key facts about higher education in Washington, 2007," Washington Higher
Education Coordinating Board, page 38, at
www.hecb.wa.gov/news/newsfacts/KeyFacts2007.asp.
[14] "A Citizens' Guide to the $1 Billion Education Initiative," by Melissa Lambert
Milewski, Washington Policy Center, July 2004, at
www.washingtonpolicy.org/Centers/education/policybrief/04_milewski_i884.html.
[15] "Omnibus Operating Budget Comparisons, 2007 – 2009, Total Budgeted Funds,"
2007 Washington State Legislative Budget Notes, Legislative Evaluation and
Accountability Program Committee, at
www.leap.leg.wa.gov/leap/budget/lbns/2007toc.asp.
[16] "The Failure of Input-based Schooling Policies," by Eric A. Hanushek, Stanford
University and National Bureau of Economic Research, July 2002, pages 5 and 6.
[17] Ibid., pages 6 and 7.
[18] "State Profiles," 2007 National Assessment of Educational Progress, National
Center for Education Statistics, at
www.nces.ed.gov/nationsreportcard/states/profile.asp.
[19] "Washington State Reports on the National Assessment of Educational Progress,
2002, 2003, 2005, and 2007," Office of the Superintendent of Public Instruction, at
www.K12.wa.us/assessment/NAEP/Reports.aspx.
[20] "Teacher Pay Reforms, The Political Implications of Recent Research," by Dan
Goldhaber, University of Washington and the Urban Institute, The Center for
American Progress, December 2006.
[21] "Overview of K-12 Finance," Legislative Fiscal Staff, October 22, 2007, page 7.
[22] "K-12 School Spending and Performance Review, A Preliminary Report," State
of Washington Joint Legislative Audit and Review Committee (JLARC), September
14, 2005.
[23] Ibid., page 17.
[24] "The Agony of American Education, How per-student funding can revolutionize
public schools," by Lisa Snell, *Reason Magazine*, April 2006.
[25] "Omnibus Operating Budget Comparisons, 2007 – 2009, Total Budgeted Funds,"
2007 Washington State Legislative Budget Notes, Legislative Evaluation and
Accountability Program Committee, at
www.leap.leg.wa.gov/leap/budget/lbns/2007toc.asp, p. 287.
[26] "Making Schools Work: A Revolutionary Plan to Get Your Children the
Education They Need," by William G. Ouchi, Simon & Schuster, 2003, page 91.
[27] "K-12 Data Study, Report 07-6," Report Digest, Joint Legislative Audit and
Review Committee (JLARC), February 21, 2007.
[28] "Teacher Pay Reforms, The Political Implications of Recent Research," Dan
Goldhaber, University of Washington and Urban Institute, The Center for American
Progress, December 2006.

[29] Ibid.

[30] "Cumulative and Residual Effects of Teachers on Future Student Academic Achievement," by William L. Sanders and June C. Rivers, November 1996.

[31] "Teacher quality and student achievement research review," by Policy Studies Associates for the Center for Public Education, November 2005.

[32] "Washington State Report Card 2006-7," Office of the Superintendent of Public Instruction, at www.reportcard.ospi.k12.wa.us/summary.aspx?year=2006-07, accessed May 22, 2008.

[33] "Learning to Teach with Technology," by Vaishali Honawar, *Education Week*, March 27, 2008, page 30.

[34] "Personnel by Major Position and Racial/Ethnic For School Year 2005-2006," Office of the Superintendent of Public Instruction, at www.k12.wa.us/DataAdmin/pubdocs/personnel/stateFTEreport2005-2006.pdf. Accesses May 20, 2008

[35] "A Citizen's Guide to Washington State K-12 Finance 2008," Senate Ways and Means Committee, January 2008, page 19, at www.leg.wa.gov/documents/Senate/SCS/wml/swmwebsite/publications/budget guides/2008/K12Guide2008FINAL.pdf.

[36] Ibid, page 18-19.

[37] "Teacher Pay, The Political Implications of Recent Research," Dan Goldhaber, University of Washington and Urban Institute, The Center for American Progress, December 2006, pages 7 and 8.

[38] Ibid., page 8. The pay gap after four years is $13,469; after ten years it is $27,890.

[39] Ibid.

[40] Ibid., page 11.

[41] "Pay for Performance: It Can Work – Here's How," by Ellen R. Delisio, *Education World*, January 29, 2003, at www.educationworld.com/a_issues/issues/issues374c.shtml.

[42] Ibid.

[43] "Pay for Performance: What Are the Issues?" by Ellen R. Delisio, *Education World*, January 30, 2006, at www.education-world.com/a_issues/issues/issues374a.shtml.

[44] "2004-2005 WASL Results (administration info)," Washington State Report Card, Office of the Superintendent of Public Instruction, at www.reportcard.ospi.k12.wa.us/, accessed July 3, 2006.

[45] Ibid.

[46] The Proficiency Illusion," by John Cronin, Michael Dahlin, Deborah Adkins, G. Gage Kingsbury, Thomas B. Fordham Institute, October 4, 2007.

[47] "What Works? Creating Successful Public Schools," by Marsha Richards, Evergreen Freedom Foundation, August 2005, page 3.

[48] Ibid.

[49] "Math Education in Washington State: Where We Are and Where We Need to Be," College and Work Ready Agenda, at www.collegeworkready.org/downloads/cwra_mathfact_v03.pdf, page 1, accessed April 18, 2008.

[50] "Washington State Card," Alliance for Excellent Education, February 2008, at www.all4ed.org/files/Washington.pdf.

[51] "State Information," Alliance for Excellent Education, citing Editorial Projects in Education Research Center 2007 for 67% high school graduation figure, October 2007, at

http://www.all4ed.org/about_the_crisis/schools/state_information/Washington.
Office of the Superintendent of Public Instruction reports 70.1% graduation rate in
2007. U.S. Department of Education reports 74.6% graduation rate for Washington
state in 2007.

[52] "Washington State Card," Alliance for Excellent Education, February 2008, at
www.all4ed.org/files/Washington.pdf.

[53] "Role of Pre-college (Developmental and Remedial) Education for Recent High
School Graduates Attending Washington Community and Technical Colleges,"
Research Report No. 07-2, Washington State Board for Community and Technical
Colleges, December 2007.

[54] "Key facts about higher education in Washington – 2007," Washington Higher
Education Coordinating Board, February, 2007, page 38, at
www.hecb.wa.gov/news/newsfacts/documents/IntroductionforWeb.pdf.

[55] "2005 Skills Gap Report – A Survey of the American Workforce," by Phyllis
Eisen, Jerry J. Jasinowski and Richard Kleinert, Deloitte, National Association of
Manufacturers, The Manufacturing Institute, Spring 2005, pages 16 and 17.

[56] "Wimping out on standards?" by Chester Finn and Liam Julian, Fordham
Foundation, *Weekly Bulletin*, May 22, 2008, at
www.edexcellence.net/institute/publication/publication.cfm?id=358&pubsubid=13
68#1368.

[57] "Early Learning Proposals in Washington State," by Liv Finne, Washington
Policy Center, December 2007, page 2, at
www.washingtonpolicy.org/Centers/education/policybrief/07_finne_earlylearningp
rop.html.

[58] "2006 Overview," Thrive by Five, page 4, at www.thrivebyfivewa.org.

[59] For Georgia see, "Georgia Pre-K Longitudinal Study: Final Report 1996-2001,"
by Gary T. Henry et al., Andrew Young School of Policy Studies, Georgia State
University, May 2003, at www.aysps.gsu.edu/publications /2003/pre-k.htm. For
Oklahoma see, "Preschool For All? Don't Feed the Beast; Claims that preschool
boosts reading scores later are at odds with history," by Lisa Snell, *Orange County
Register*, May 25, 2006. For New Jersey see, "Preschool reality check in New
Jersey," by Lisa Snell, The Reason Foundation, July 30, 2007, at
www.reason.org/commentaries/snell_20070809.shtml.

[60] "Early Learning Proposals in Washington State," by Liv Finne, Washington
Policy Center, December 2007, page 9, at
www.washingtonpolicy.org/Centers/education/policybrief/07_finne_earlylearningp
rop.html.

[61] "How Much is Too Much? The Influence of Preschool Centers on Children's
Development Nationwide," by Susanna Loeb, Margaret Bridges, Bruce Fuller, Russ
Rumberger, Daphna Bassok, Stanford University, University of California, Berkeley,
November 2005. See also National Bureau of Economic Research, NBER Working
Paper No. 11812, issued December 2005, at www.nber.org/papers/w11812.

[62] "Early Childhood Education May Harm Children, by Cathy Gulli, *Macleans
Magazine*, September 11, 2006.

[63] Ibid., page 3.

[64] "School Readiness, Full-Day Kindergarten, and Student Achievement, An
Empirical Investigation," by Vi-Nhuan Le, Sheila Nataraj Kirby, Heather Barney,
Claude Messan Setodji, Daniel Gershwin, the RAND Corporation, with support
from the Rockefeller and Ford Foundations, 2006, at
www.rand.org/pubs/monographs/2006/RAND_MG558.pdf.

---

[65] Ibid.

[66] Washington Administrative Code, 392-121-182 and "Program Implementation Guidelines for Alternative Learning Experiences," Office of the Superintendent of Public Instruction, November 1, 2005, page 2.

[67] Author interview with Karla Pollich, Marketing Director for Insight Schools of Washington, January 4, 2008.

[68] "Online Curriculum Information and Resources," Online Curriculum Overview of the Education Technology Support Center (ETSC) program, Office of the Superintendent of Public Instruction, at www.k12.wa.us/EdTech/OnlineCurriculum.aspx.

[69] "Selected Findings, Distance Education Courses for Public Elementary and Secondary School Students: 2002-03," National Center for Education Statistics, 2005, Table 5.

[70] "K-12 Online Learning: A Survey of U.S. School District Administrators," by Anthony Picciano and Jeff Seaman, The Sloan Consortium, 2007, page 17.

[71] "Distance Education Courses for Public Elementary and Secondary School Students: 2002-03, Selected Findings," National Center for Education Statistics, 2005, page 7.

[72] "Public Elementary and Secondary School Student Enrollment, High School Completions, and Staff from the Common Core of Data: School Year 2005-06," National Center for Education Statistics, 2007, Table 2.

CHAPTER 6

1. Improving the Business Climate

Recommendations

1. Amend or repeal laws and regulations that impede business innovation and entrepreneurship.

2. Repeal laws and regulations that no longer serve a public purpose and only work to keep competitors out of the marketplace.

3. Require the governor to review and approve new agency regulations.

Background

While the United States has experienced a troubled economy recently, Washington state seems largely immune to the national trend. The smaller impact of a national downturn on our region, however, can lead to a deceptive impression about the state's long-term economic prospects. Not everything is rosy for business in Washington – particularly for small businesses. Fewer small businesses (those with fewer than 50 employees) are able to afford health insurance for their workers.

There is a lack of qualified employees willing to work in certain industries. The state-imposed regulatory environment is more complex and difficult than ever. Washington has a relatively hostile business climate, which limits job creation and imposes a drag on general economic prosperity.

While the overall business climate is important to the economic vitality of the state, policymakers should pay special attention to smaller firms.[1]

- Of the state's 198,200 employer firms, 98 percent (194,600) are small businesses;

- In addition, about 387,500 people in Washington are self-employed;

- Small firms employed 55.8 percent of the non-farm private workforce in 2004 (the latest data available);

- About 1.3 million people work for small businesses in Washington;

- Washington has the highest business start up rate and the highest business failure rate in the country;

- Washington's recovery from the 2000–2001 recession was led by a surge of new jobs created by small businesses, and they contribute significantly to annual job creation today.

While larger businesses play an important role in creating and sustaining a viable economic climate, small businesses are a major catalyst for job growth and revitalization.

Policy Analysis

Entrepreneurs and businesses face numerous challenges every day. Some of the strongest threats to their economic survival come not from competitors, but from the confusing tangle of state, county and municipal regulations.

State and local regulators place significant barriers between entrepreneurs and their dreams. The staggering amount of regulatory red tape amounts to more than 100,000 requirements that a small business owner must know, understand and follow in order to run a business legally. The regulatory structure strangles small businesses, drives up the cost of entering the market and increases the cost of living for consumers.

Washington Policy Center's Center for Small Business and Entrepreneurship has identified several issues small business owners say are the primary barriers to their success. Those issues are:

- the rising cost of health insurance;
- a clogged transportation system;
- the high business tax burden;
- high-cost unemployment insurance;
- the state workers' compensation monopoly;
- confusing and complex regulations;
- tort and liability expenses;
- access to affordable water and energy.

Many of these issues are discussed in other chapters of this policy guide. Other sections in this chapter provide recommendations regarding the overall business climate, affordable health care for small businesses, unemployment insurance, regulatory reform and estate tax repeal.

State and local policymakers should reduce government-imposed barriers for Washington entrepreneurs, which would expand economic opportunity for all citizens, and promote a vibrant business climate today and for future generations.

Recommendations

1) Amend or repeal laws and regulations that impede business innovation and entrepreneurship. During the state's 119 year history, literally thousands of laws have been enacted that make it more difficult to start and run a small business in Washington. Policymakers should initiate a systematic review process to identify outdated laws in need of amendment or repeal.

2) Repeal laws and regulations that no longer serve a public purpose, and only work to keep competitors out of the marketplace. Such laws harm consumers by keeping competitors out of the marketplace. The for-hire vehicle, taxicab, hair care and moving industries provide examples of antiquated or overly-strict regulations that work against the public interest by reducing price competition and consumer choice.

3) Require the governor to review and approve new agency regulations. New agency laws hugely affect the business community. Submitting any new significant rule to review and approval by the governor would help slow the incessant flow of new regulations from state bureaucrats, and would create clear accountability when new business restrictions are put in place.

2. Small Business Access to Health Insurance

Recommendations

1. Legalize the sale of basic health insurance plans to small businesses.

2. Allow small business owners to purchase health plans in any state, just like other types of insurance.

3. Freeze health care mandates until the cost and benefit of current mandates are studied.

4. Encourage affordable access to Health Savings Accounts.

Background

The steadily-rising cost of health insurance is a major problem for the business community. Small business owners who participated in Washington Policy Center's Small Business Project identified the cost and availability of health care as their number one concern. Business owners voiced particular concern about the way state imposed mandates drive up health insurance costs for small firms.

The sale of health insurance in Washington is governed by an amazingly complex combination of state laws, rules and regulations, and small businesses have few resources for dealing with the confusing web of red tape. Increases in health insurance costs are forcing many small business owners to reduce or eliminate health care coverage for their workers.

According to a National Federation of Independent Business (NFIB) survey of small business owners throughout Washington, the number of employers who offer health care coverage for all employees has dropped from 65 percent in 1993 to less than 50 percent today.

Policy Analysis

Health insurers in Washington are required by law to obey 53 state imposed mandates covering a broad range of providers, illnesses and treatments.[2] A mandated benefit is a requirement that an insurance company cover (or offer coverage for) common health care providers, benefits and patient populations.

Employers must often pay for coverage their employees do not want or need. Each mandate may only add one-quarter or one-half a percent to the cost of buying health coverage, but added together their impact is enormous. Conservative estimates show mandates add at least 15 to 20 percent to the price of a health insurance policy.[3]

The large number of mandates, combined with the heavy taxes and regulations placed on all insurance policies, means economical low-cost health coverage is not available in Washington. It is like a hotel market with all Hiltons and Sheratons, but no Motel 6.

Because they are forced to buy expensive "Cadillac" insurance plan or no plan at all, plus yearly double-digit premium increases, the business community is scrambling for health plan alternatives.

Business owners deal with competition every day. They understand that reducing barriers to entry for new health insurance products would increase competition in the marketplace. Small business owners support a package of reforms that would streamline state regulations, reduce mandates, increase competition among insurers and encourage low cost Health Savings Accounts (HSAs).

HSAs offer small employers a cost-effective way to provide health coverage to their employees when traditional coverage is too expensive. Money placed in HSAs is tax free and belongs to individual workers. The money is theirs to keep if they switch jobs, are unemployed for a time or decide to retire. HSA funds can be used tax free to pay any qualified medical expense. An accompanying catastrophic insurance policy covers medical costs in case of major illness or injury.

Recommendations

1) Legalize the sale of basic health insurance to small businesses. In recent years, the legislature has considered a number of bills trimming mandates and regulations that would open new opportunities for small businesses to obtain health insurance. The Senate in particular has made progress in this direction. Though none of these bills became law, lawmakers should allow insurers to again offer low-cost, economical health plans to Washington residents.

2) Allow small business owners to purchase health plans in any state, just like other types of insurance. Health insurance is less heavily regulated in most other states, and coverage is often less expensive in those states than in Washington. Allowing small business owners to shop for coverage across state lines would lower costs and create more options for small business employees and their families. In addition, the resulting competition would lower prices and improve service for all businesses and citizens in Washington.

3) Freeze health care mandates until the cost and benefit of current mandates are studied. Health care plans offered by insurance companies in Washington must include 53 mandated benefits in order to be legally offered in the market. Health care mandates in Washington include options such as mental health, acupuncture and massage therapy. Together, these mandates add 15 to 20 percent to the cost of health insurance in Washington.

4) Encourage affordable access to Health Savings Accounts. Reducing state imposed mandates and streamlining insurance regulations would reduce the cost of insurance plans that must accompany Health Savings Accounts. Lowering the cost of HSAs would allow many small business owners to offer affordable health benefits to their workers.

3. Regulatory Reform

Recommendations

1. Regulate for results, not for process.

2. Reorganize the Office of Regulatory Assistance into an Office of Regulatory Reform that would identify regulations that duplicate or contradict each other, are outdated or do more harm than good.

3. Include a regulatory sunset provision for new regulations, and submit all existing regulations to review by the legislature every five years.

4. Create a regulatory fast track for companies and individuals with a good record of complying with regulations.

Background

The right to live where we choose, the right to own property, the right to make a living and the right to enter into voluntary agreements are all fundamental aspects of a free society. Respect for our natural rights is essential to maintaining civil life, and the central function and purpose of government is to protect the basic freedoms of its citizens.

Yet government itself often poses a grave and immediate threat to these rights. One of the most pressing public issues today is the ever-expanding scope and burden of government regulations, and the implications of this trend for people's economic liberties.

The overall problem is summarized by a statement in an editorial from *The Seattle Times*, "Sometimes, the government simply doesn't know when to leave the marketplace alone."[4] Today, Washington citizens, small businesses and major industries face an expanding array of regulations at all levels of government.

The burden of regulation

Very small firms, that is, those with fewer than 20 employees, spend 45 percent more per employee than larger firms in order to comply with just federal regulations. A firm with fewer than 20 employees might spend $7,647 per employee to comply with federal regulations, whereas a firm with over 500 employees would spend only $5,282 per employee.[5]

Total state regulation has expanded to fill 32 phonebook-sized volumes, which together form a stack of paper over five feet high. These rules have the force of law, and they strictly control and limit the day-to-day activities of every person in the state.

The fundamental policy question facing the people of Washington and their elected representatives is: What is the right balance of government intervention versus economic freedom? The answer is that government power should be limited to the rules needed to assure public health and safety, help the needy and protect consumers, so that over-regulation does not choke off the oxygen the economy needs to thrive.

The drafters of Washington's constitution provided guidance by recommending "a frequent recurrence to fundamental principles," which is "essential to the security of individual rights and the perpetuity of free government."[6]

Within the limits of ordered liberty it is the right of citizens to live their lives as they see fit, not as the government directs. When state government oversteps its bounds by regulating the smallest details of lawful activities, it hinders the vibrant economic and social life of the community.

Government is the largest employer

Government as a whole is now one of the largest industry classifications in the state. Washington ranks among the highest states in the per capita tax burden, and is among the highest in the overall cost of government it places on its citizens. One national study ranked Washington as one of the most regulated state.[7] Another study ranked Washington at only 31st in economic freedom, well below top-ranked Kansas.[8]

Policy Analysis

The numbers provide ample warning that state government is becoming too large and expensive, and is moving too slowly to adapt to the changing world around it. In combination with the burgeoning cost and size of government, the regulatory burden on Washington residents has increased substantially. As small business owners, non-profit groups, homeowners, farmers and other ordinary citizens work to realize their dreams, they find they are increasingly frustrated by government regulators.

One builder of affordable housing calls the detailed permit reviews required by the Growth Management Act "ridiculous," and says the process plods slowly and adds significant costs. Added costs include inventory carrying charges, fees for sophisticated engineering and extensive legal fees.

In the end, costs must be passed along to homebuyers in the form of higher prices, pushing many low-income families out of the housing market. One Vancouver builder found that government taxes and regulations added 22 percent to the sale price of his homes.[9]

A recent study by the University of Washington found that state and local land use restrictions add $200,000 to the cost of a home in Seattle, helping push the median inflation-adjusted home price in the city to $447,800.[10] The study's author noted that, "The state is intervening to restrict supply. It's not that there's no land at all.[11]

Examples of easing regulations

In New York, the governor created a Governor's Office of Regulatory Reform (GORR) to work with all agencies to reduce the number and complexity of state regulations. The Office's message to citizens is explicit: "If you're getting the runaround or being unnecessarily hounded by one of our state agencies call us."[12] GORR officials say they will intervene and take care of the problem – fast. The Office's goal is to make New York more attractive to business growth, and it has been credited with helping to create thousands of new jobs.

Another idea taking root among several states is the creation of a small business ombudsman for state government. The idea is based on the U.S. Small Business Administration's Office of the National Ombudsman (ONO). Like the federal office, a state-level ombudsman would be someone who is empowered to represent business owners as they navigate the confusing maze of state agencies and their thousands of pages of requirements.

The state ombudsman could listen to citizen complaints and investigate regulatory problems on their behalf. The federal office has saved small businesses across the country thousands of dollars. A state ombudsman would provide a similar benefit to Washington businesses.[13]

In streamlining regulations, Washington leaders do not need to reinvent the wheel. By following the successful example of New York, or similar efforts in states such as Texas, Massachusetts and New Jersey, policymakers can reform and modernize the state's Byzantine regulatory system.

Recommendations

1) Regulate for results, not for process. Measuring the results of the regulatory process, rather than the process itself, would enable policymakers to know whether state agencies are accomplishing their core mission, or simply spending their budgets. Focusing on measurable outcomes would free agencies, businesses and individual citizens to find the best way to achieve desired public goods.

2) Reorganize the Office of Regulatory Assistance into an Office of Regulatory Reform that would identify regulations which duplicate or contradict each other, are outdated or do more harm than good. Currently, the Office of Regulatory Assistance only tries to help citizens through the complex maze of existing state regulations. It does not ask whether those requirements are in any way useful or needed. Reorganized as an Office of Regulatory Reform, it could actively review all state regulations and determine which ones duplicate or contradict each other, are no longer needed, or do more harm than good to the public interest.

3) Include a regulatory sunset provision for new regulations, and submit all existing regulations to review by the legislature every

five years. Under the current system most state regulations are written to last forever. Policymakers should require all agency rules and regulations to carry a sunset provision, every five years be reviewed and, if still needed, reauthorized by the legislature.

4) Create a regulatory fast track for companies and individuals with a good record of complying with regulations. To focus enforcement where it is needed, state regulatory agencies should authorize companies and individuals who have a good record of following environmental and regulatory rules to approve their own applications and permits. The results would be periodically audited by state oversight agencies. Companies and individuals that did not follow regulations voluntarily would be penalized and their self-monitoring authorization would be revoked.

4. Unemployment Insurance Reform

Recommendations

1. Bring state benefits more in line with the national average.

2. Allow workers to have personal unemployment accounts.

3. Increase benefit compliance audits.

4. Require training or community service as a condition of receiving benefits.

Background

Washington's unemployment insurance system imposes the second-highest per employee cost in the nation.[14] While the tax *rate* is not higher than most states, businesses in Washington must pay that rate on the first $31,400 of salary for each employee.[15] In contrast, businesses in most other states only pay unemployment taxes on the first $7,000 to $10,000 of salary.

Generous benefits

A primary cost-driver of Washington's state-run system is the high level of benefits it pays out. The maximum unemployment benefit, a generous $515 per week, is close to the highest in the nation. Washington's average weekly benefit payout is $325, 12 percent higher than the nationwide average of $290.

Lawmakers make it easy for workers to receive tax-funded unemployment benefits. Among the ten reasons a person can use to get state unemployment benefits are, "to accept other work," a pay reduction of 25 percent, or a reduction in work hours of 25 percent.[16]

A person must work just 17 weeks to qualify for benefits. Employers, especially in the arts and seasonal businesses, often specifically design temporary employment positions so that a worker will receive unemployment payments once the employer has no further need of the employee. The level of benefits paid out is not based on financial need.[17]

In 2008 the legislature further expanded the unemployment insurance program. Lawmakers made employees who voluntarily leave their current work to join an apprenticeship program eligible to receive tax-funded benefits.[18]

Effort at reform

In an effort to slow cost increases and promote job creation, the legislature passed major reforms to the system in 2003, most of which went into effect January 2004. The reforms included holding the maximum weekly benefit at $496, reducing the maximum time an employee can collect unemployment benefits from 30 to 26 weeks, and changing the benefit calculation to reflect a full year of work, not just the two highest-paid quarters.

In 2005, however, the legislature reversed itself and repealed several key improvements from 2003 – just when many of these reforms were beginning to have an effect. The legislature's sudden repeal of unemployment insurance reforms added an unexpected burden to the business climate and angered many small business owners.

In 2006, the state legislature enacted a broad unemployment insurance package, making permanent the 2005 changes, key among them:

- Businesses would be taxed according to a four-quarter scale while worker benefits would be paid out by the two-quarter scale, therefore, most businesses would get some tax relief in their unemployment insurance premiums.

- The general unemployment insurance trust fund would pay the difference between the taxes collected from individual businesses and the benefits paid out to workers.

Policy Analysis

Today, Washington's unemployment benefits are among the most generous in the nation, and the average unemployment payroll tax imposed on workers is the second-highest in the nation, at $803 per worker.

High unemployment benefits increase unemployment because the incentive to collect unemployment is often greater than the incentive to work. Many people will try to collect the maximum they can from the system, waiting until their benefits are almost exhausted before seriously seeking new employment.

In addition to discouraging work, the current employment tax system is fundamentally unfair. Despite a lifetime of paying in, workers receive no refund when they retire, and workers who have not been unemployed never receive any benefit.

Washington's high unemployment tax burden has four primary negative effects on the state economy:

1. It discourages job growth and deprives the people of Washington of new work opportunities;

2. It encourages existing businesses to outsource jobs to other states;

3. It has a smothering effect on start-up businesses, and punishes successful businesses that attempt to hire more workers;

4. It discourages businesses in other states from relocating or expanding their operations to Washington.

Given the high costs of Washington's unemployment benefits system, policymakers should consider an alternative system based on personal, portable worker benefit accounts.

Such an approach has worked in other countries. In 1981, Chile pioneered a new system in which workers pay 10 percent of their wages into a personal account administered by a private fund. Employers contribute an additional 2.4 percent. A portion of the funds go into the general fund to cover young workers and those who cannot contribute enough into their account to meet the minimum level of benefits.[19]

Key to the success of Chile's program is individual control of personal benefits. In contrast to the Washington system, unemployed workers in Chile can collect benefits whenever they are out of work for any reason, whether they are laid-off, fired or choose to leave their job. Strict qualification limits and punitive enforcement are not required because workers control their own benefits.

One of the best features of Chile's system is the built-in incentive for saving long-term. At retirement, workers keep all the money in their unemployment account. Washington's system has no such provision – employees here receive nothing from the system at retirement.

Recommendations

1) Bring state benefits more in line with the national average. When carried too far, high unemployment benefits increase unemployment. At a certain point, the incentive to remain on subsidized unemployment is greater than the incentive to work. Studies show that job-finding activities and formal job placement rises dramatically in the final few weeks of benefit eligibility. Bringing benefits in line with the national average would reduce the cost of unemployment taxes and help ensure a competitive business climate, while maintaining worker protections.

2) Allow workers to have personal unemployment accounts. Under the current system, Washington workers receive no refund or benefit when they retire, and workers who have not been unemployed receive no benefits at all. A system based on individual accounts returns fairness and equity to the system. Personal accounts promote individual responsibility, provide workers with a financial asset, encourage saving for retirement, and would relieve the state of most of the administrative cost and complication of the current system.

3) Increase benefit compliance audits. In a recent performance audit, the State Auditor praised the Employment Security Department for its fraud protection practices, pointing to the Department's automated claims management system as a model of efficiency. Ironically, many employers feel it is this system that encourages workers to avoid seeking a job. Increasing audits of people who are on unemployment would help ensure that they are really complying with job search requirements, rather than simply waiting for their benefits to run out.

4) Require training or community service as a condition of receiving benefits. Many people view unemployment benefits as a kind of paid vacation from the state. Job search requirements are minimal and unenforced, so people often pursue personal interests while receiving unemployment checks. Weekly training and community service would help prepare unemployed people for a return to work, and would provide a reasonable incentive to accept a job when one is available.

5. Estate Tax Repeal

> ## Recommendation
>
> 1. Repeal the Washington estate, gift and inheritance tax.

Background

In 1981, Washington voters approved Initiative 402 to repeal the state estate tax. It passed by a greater than two-to-one margin.[20] State lawmakers then instituted a "pick-up tax" by taking a portion of federal estate taxes levied on deceased Washington residents.

In 2001, Congress enacted a ten-year phase out of the federal estate tax. However, the Washington state legislature did not take action to conform state law to that change. As the federal tax was reduced year by year, the state Department of Revenue began collecting estate tax revenues at a rate higher than the legally allowed tax rate.

Currently, the federal estate tax rate is scheduled to fall to zero in 2010, but will skyrocket to 55 percent in 2011, unless Congress acts to make the phase out of the federal tax permanent. Legislation to accomplish this is pending in Congress.

The Washington Supreme Court ruled in February 2005 that, because of Initiative 402, the Department of Revenue is only entitled to a portion of federal estate taxes due, and that Congress' action in 2001 eliminated the ability of Washington to collect a portion of the soon-to-expire federal tax. The court's decision meant that, if the legislature did nothing, Washington's estate tax would end in 2010 when the federal tax expired.

In 2005, however, state legislators enacted a new estate tax. The new tax law "de-couples" Washington's estate tax law from the federal government's tax laws.[21] The 2005 law repeals Initiative 402 and re-instates a stand-alone Washington estate tax law. Washington's estate tax will continue unchanged after the federal tax ends in 2010.[22]

Policy Analysis

The rate at which an estate is taxed varies from 10 percent to 19 percent, depending on the size of the estate. Estates in Washington are taxed if the assessed value exceeds $2 million. Family farms are exempt, but there is no exemption for family owned small businesses.

The impact of the 2005 estate tax law is growing. The Washington Department of Revenue estimates it will collect tax from just over 200 estates in 2006, 220 in 2007, and 240 in 2008. The Department estimates the estate tax will bring about $235 million to state coffers during the 2007-09 budget cycle, more than double what the state collected in 2005-07.[23]

Tax officials expect the amount of revenue they collect to increase even more over time, as more families are affected. Total revenue from estate tax collection equals about four percent of Washington's operating budget.

Recommendation

1) Repeal the Washington estate, gift and inheritance tax. The estate tax is counterproductive because it impedes economic growth and discourages family businesses from remaining in or relocating to this state. Most importantly, it is unfair, because it targets family-owned businesses that can least afford to pay it, while their larger, incorporated competitors are exempt.

6. Business and Occupation Tax Reform

Recommendations

1. Reduce the harmful effects of B&O tax pyramiding.

2. Reduce taxes for all businesses; do not just shift the tax burden among businesses.

3. Increase the transparency of the B&O tax.

4. Provide B&O tax relief for new and small businesses.

Background

The Business and Occupation (B&O) tax is Washington's second-largest source of tax revenue; only the general sales and use tax generates more money for state government. The B&O tax is a gross receipts tax, which means that the tax is levied on businesses' gross income, gross sales, or value of products. There are no deductions allowed for the cost of doing business, such as payments for raw materials, rent, or wages paid to employees.[24]

As a gross receipts tax, even business owners who lose money must pay the tax, based on the total volume of their annual sales.

The B&O tax was first imposed in 1935 and today consists of ten major tax rate categories. The rates themselves are relatively low in comparison to most other states' corporate income taxes. For example, Washington's manufacturing and wholesaling tax rate is 0.484 percent; the retailing tax rate is 0.471 percent.

Business owners are taxed according to their commercial activities, and one company may be subject to more than one tax rate.

The first $28,000 in yearly gross income is not taxed. Firms that do this amount of business or less pay no B&O tax and are not required to file.

The legislature has also enacted several small business tax credits that relieve a portion of B&O tax liability. The Tax Reference Manual states, "a [small business] subject to the 0.484 percent tax rate would incur no B&O tax liability until annual income exceeds $86,777."[25] SB 6407, introduced in the 2008 session, would have increased the small business tax credit by seven percent, thus providing greater tax relief for small firms, but this bill did not pass.

Washington is one of the few states in the nation that relies so heavily on a gross receipts tax. The pros and cons of the tax are often debated, and while policymakers recognize the harmful effect the tax has on small, new and unprofitable businesses, they disagree about whether and how to alleviate the tax burden they impose on those businesses.

Policy Analysis

Pyramiding tax system

The B&O tax is a broad-based tax system. The tax base to which the tax is applied is much larger than the gross state product (GSP). This means that the economic activity that state leaders are taxing is much greater than the value of what businesses are actually producing. The GSP is the total value of all goods and services produced by Washington businesses in a single year. Washington's B&O tax base is approximately 177 percent of the GSP.

The B&O tax base is broader than the GSP because lawmakers apply the tax to every transaction for any single product, from the time of production until final sale to the consumer. Each time a transaction takes place, say, between a wholesaler and a distributor, the product is subject to taxation, even though the inherent value of the product remains the same.

This broad base explains why very low B&O tax rates bring in so much money for the state. However, taxing the many stages of production and distribution creates unique problems for high volume, low profit margin businesses.

A high volume, low profit margin business (for example, a retailer) generates a high number of transactions, each involving a small amount of profit. Therefore the B&O tax system imposes a higher effective tax rate. This is in contrast to a low volume, high profit margin business that handles few transactions, but makes more profit per transaction. Washington's B&O tax system ends up favoring this second type of business, while financially punishing the first kind.

This problem is inherent in what are called "pyramiding" or "turnover" tax systems. A large business that has centralized and vertically integrated its operations has a tax advantage over a competitor, often a small business, that must contract out to help produce its product. The state taxes work that is contracted out, but not work that is moved from one company division to another.

The B&O tax system rewards big companies that do most production in-house, and makes it much harder for small, innovative competitors to break into markets already dominated by large firms.

Tax exemptions increasing

A Department of Revenue (DOR) report on tax exemptions lists 567 "exclusions, deductions, preferential tax rates, deferrals and credits," and runs over 300 pages.[26] The number of different tax breaks changes every year during the legislative session. Not all 567 exemptions are geared towards industry and commerce. Many of them apply to property taxes.

However, as described by DOR, 246 exemptions are aimed at "business incentive," "other business," and "agriculture." If the "commerce" and "services" categories are included, that number rises to 272. Forty-eight percent of the total tax exemptions target the business community, whereas the other exemptions focus on individuals and property owners.

Since 2001, the legislature passed 147 exemptions, deductions or credits to the tax code. This is an average of 21 per year. Over the previous 25-year period, 1975-2000, the legislature averaged just over nine exemptions per year. In the period 1950-1974, there were fewer than four averaged exemptions per year.[27]

This situation creates a system in which state lawmakers pick winners and losers in particular industries. Each year, more exemptions, deductions or credits are enacted into the state's tax code. Most of them give a benefit to certain industries, or even subsets of industries. This practice, while perhaps well-intentioned, becomes a game of "What industry can finagle the most tax exemptions?" Lawmakers respond to special interest requests, instead of providing broadly-applied tax relief for all Washington businesses and industries.

Lack of transparency

The B&O tax is a stealth tax. Consumers are not aware of the role the gross receipts tax plays in increasing the cost of a product. Sales taxes are always displayed as a line item on a bill of sale, but the B&O tax portion is not reported to consumers; it is built into the purchase price.

Tax relief for new and small businesses

Washington state ranks seventh in the nation for business start ups (after ranking first and second earlier this decade), but still ranks worst in the nation in business terminations. The state does not keep track of why Washington firms fail, but businesses owners routinely cite the state's burdensome tax structure as one major cause.[28]

In 2007, legislation was introduced to exempt new businesses from the first year of B&O tax, and to reduce B&O taxes for a firm's first few years.[29] However, the bill failed to gain enough votes for passage.

Recommendations

1) Reduce the harmful effects of B&O tax pyramiding. The pyramiding effect, taxing every transaction in the production process, is a major source of the economic problems caused by the state's B&O system. The system's lack of transparency rewards large, high profit margin companies and disproportionately harms high volume, low profit margin businesses.

2) Reduce taxes for all businesses; do not just shift the tax burden among businesses. Policymakers should enact broad tax relief for all businesses, instead of continuing to increase the hundreds of tax exemptions, credits and deductions that benefit favored industries.

3) Increase the transparency of the B&O tax. Consumers are paying a stealth tax they rarely see. This creates a sense that consumers do not play a role in B&O transactions when, in reality, they end up footing most of the cost of the tax. Like the sales tax, consumer tax receipts should show the estimated cost of the B&O tax and how it contributes to the final purchase price.

4) Provide B&O tax relief for new and small businesses. Policymakers should exempt new businesses, regardless of industry, from B&O tax liabilities for an introductory period of one year. After getting established, a new business' B&O tax liability could steadily increase until it is paying the full amount within a few years of startup.

Additional Resources from Washington Policy Center

"24 Ways to Improve the State's Small Business Climate," by Carl Gipson, January 2008.

"Lawmakers Have Time to Fix Feel-Good, Do Nothing Legislation," by Carl Gipson, January 2008.

"Washington Policy Center Comments on WAC 296-62-095 – Heat-related Illness Rule," by Carl Gipson, April 2008.

"The Streamlined Sales and Use Tax Agreement: A Primer on the New Law," by Hallie Hostetter and Carl Gibson, Policy Note 2007-03.

"An Overview of Washington's Emergency Heat Stress Rule," by Carl Gipson, Policy Note 2007-21.

"2007 Legislative Session: Some Problem-Solving Legislation Tends to Create Further Headaches for Small Businesses," by Carl Gipson, May 2007.

"Proposed State-Mandated Warranty Would Increase Costs to Homebuyers," by Paul Guppy and Christopher Fox, March 2007.

"Small Business May Need a Good Defense this Legislative Session," by Carl Gipson, January 2007.

"A Citizens' Guide to Initiative 920: A Measure to Repeal the Estate Tax," by Carl Gipson, October 2006.

"Punishing Targeted Businesses Hurts Us All," by Carl Gipson, September 6, 2006.

"Small Business Needs to be Heard in Order for Our Economy to Prosper," by Carl Gipson, August 2006.

"Legislative Session Largely a Let-Down for Small Business," by Carl Gipson, April 2006.

"House Strips Away Senate's Plan to Help Small Businesses Afford Health Insurance," by Carl Gipson, March 2006.

"Reviving Washington's Small Business Climate: Policy Recommendations from the 2005 Small Business Conferences," by Carl Gipson, January 2006.

"Mandatory Paid Sick Leave - Another Ailment for the Small Business Climate," by Carl Gipson, January 2006.

"'Fair Share' Bill is Unfair and Impractical," by Paul Guppy, January 2006.

"An Honor Washington Could Do Without -- Highest Minimum Wage in the Nation," by Carl Gipson, January 2005.

"When the Union Really Isn't Working for the Worker: New Collective Bargaining Agreement Includes Increase in Union Dues," by Daniel Mead Smith, January 2005.

"Entrepreneurship in The Emerald City: Regulations Cloud the Sparkle of Small Businesses," by Jeanette Peterson, August 2004.

"Agenda for Reform: Priority Solutions for Improving Washington's Small Business Climate," by Eric Montague, January 2004.

"The Small Business Climate in Washington State," by Eric Montague, March 2002.

"An Overview of Initiative 841: Repeal of State Ergonomics Regulations," by Paul Guppy, October 2003.

"Reforming Washington's Workers' Compensation System," by Allison Demeritt, May 2004.

---

[1] "2007 Small Business and Territorial Profiles - Washington," State Economic Profiles, United States Small Business Administration, at www.sba.gov/advo/research/profiles/07wa.pdf.

[2] "Health Insurance Mandates in the State 2008," by Victoria Craig Bunce, Director of Research and Policy, and J.P. Wieske, Director of State Affairs, Council for Affordable Health Insurance, May 2008, at www.cahi.org/cahi_contents/resources/pdf/HealthInsuranceMandates2008.pdf.

[3] "How Mandates Increase Costs and Reduce Access to Health Care Coverage," by Paul Guppy, Research Director, Washington Policy Center, June 2002, at www.washingtonpolicy.org/Centers/healthcare/policybrief/02_guppy_mandates.html.

4 "Restaurant Smoking Ban is Needless Regulation," editorial, *The Seattle Times*, January 27, 1997.

5 "The Impact of Regulatory Costs on Small Firms," by Mark W. Crain, Lafayette College, Easton, Pennsylvania, 2005. Research done under contract for the United States Small Business Administration.

6 Constitution of the State of Washington, Article I, Section 23.

7 "Economic Freedom in America's 50 States: A 1999 Analysis," by John Byars, Robert McCormick and Bruce Yandle, Clemson University, January 2000. According to "A Regional Economic Vitality Agenda," published by the Washington Research Council, Washington businesses carry 54 percent of the tax burden, highest of any of the seven nearest western states.

8 "U.S. Economic Freedom Index: 2004," by Ying Huang, Robert E. McCormick and Lawrence J. McQuillan, Pacific Research Institute, 2004, at www.special.pacificresearch.org/pub/sab/entrep/2004/econ_freedom/00_summary.html#table1.

9 "Government Regulations Add 'Sticker Shock' to New Home Prices," by Paul Guppy, Policy Note 99-14, Washington Policy Center at www.washingtonpolicy.org/Centers/government/policynotes/99_guppy_stickershock.html.

10 "U.W. study: Rules add $200,000 to Seattle house price," by Elizabeth Rhodes, *The Seattle Times*, February 14, 2008.

11 Ibid.

12 Governor's Office of Regulatory Reform, State of New York, at www.gorr.state.ny.us/gorr/.

13 See, "Small Business Ombudsman Model for State and Local Governments," U.S. Small Business Administration, at www.sba.gov/idc/groups/public/documents/sba_program_office/omb_model_08.pdf.

14 "2008 Competitiveness Redbook," Table 23, Unemployment Insurance Taxes (3rd quarter 2006), Association of Washington Business and WashACE, 2008.

15 "Significant Measures of State UI Tax Systems," Program Statistics, Employment and Training Administration, U.S. Department of Labor, page 58, at www.ows.doleta.gov/unemploy/finance.asp.

16 Revised Code of Washington 50.20.050 and "Final Bill Report, SSB 6751," Washington State Legislature, 2008 session, at www.apps.leg.wa.gov/documents/billdocs/2007-08/Pdf/Bill%20Reports/Senate%20Final/6751-S.FBR.pdf.

17 "Are you eligible for benefits?" Washington State Employment Security Department, Unemployment Benefits, at www.esd.wa.gov/uibenefits/apply/cligibility/am-i-eligible.php, accesses May 28, 2008.

18 "SSB 6751, Allowing individuals who left work to enter certain apprenticeship programs to receive unemployment insurance benefits," Washington State Legislature, 2008 session. The new law was effective June 12, 2008.

19 Data about the Chilean system from, "Chile Will Privatize a New Span of Its Noted Social Safety Net," by Larry Rohter, *The New York Times*, June 24, 2002, available at www.nytimes.com.

20 Initiative Measure No. 402, passed November 3, 1981, Initiatives to the People 1914 through 2005, Office of the Secretary of State, at http://www.secstate.wa.gov/elections/initiatives/statistics_initiatives.aspx.

[21] ESB 6096, "Creating an estate tax," introduced by Senator Eric Poulsen, March 24, 2005, signed by Governor Gregoire, May 17, 2005, WashingtonVotes.org, at http://www.washingtonvotes.org/Legislation.aspx?ID=37972.

[22] "Estate Tax, Deaths on or after May 17, 2005," Washington State Department of Revenue, at www.dor.wa.gov/content/FindTaxesAndRates/OtherTaxes/tax_estateOnAfter051705.aspx.

[23] "Inheritance/Estate Taxes," All Budgeted Funds – Budget Totals, Table 1, Revenue by Source, Washington State Department of Revenue budget summary, 2007-09, at http://www.ofm.wa.gov/budget07/summary/table01.pdf.

[24] More information on the history of the B&O tax can be found in "Tax Reference Manual, Information on State and Local Taxes in Washington State," Department of Revenue, State of Washington, January 2007, at www.dor.wa.gov.

[25] Ibid., pages 103 – 111.

[26] "2008 Tax Exemption Report, A Study of Tax Exemptions, Exclusions, Deductions, Deferrals, Differential Tax Rates and Credits for Major Washington State and Local Taxes," Research Division, Department of Revenue, January 2008, at www.dor.wa.gov/docs/reports/2008/tax_exemptions_2008/tax_exemptions_2008.pdf.

[27] Ibid.

[28] See "Tax Burden" chapter of *Reviving Washington's Small Business Climate*, Washington Policy Center Policy Brief, January 2006.

[29] HB 1516, Washington State Legislature, introduced January 2007.

CHAPTER 7
GOVERNMENT ACCOUNTABILITY

1. Abuse of the Emergency Clause

<table>
<tr><td align="center">Recommendation</td></tr>
<tr><td>1. Restrict use of the emergency clause to genuine emergencies and adopt constitutional limitations on its use.</td></tr>
</table>

Background

In 1912, Washington amended its constitution to allow initiatives and referenda, which allow voters directly to pass or repeal state laws. Through these processes, citizens can draft and approve legislation or recall legislation passed by the legislature. Article 2, Section 1, of the state constitution says:

> "The second power [after initiatives] reserved by the people is the referendum, and it may be ordered on any act, bill, law, or any part thereof passed by the legislature."

Lawmakers can, however, attach an emergency clause to any bill or section of a bill, because the legislation is supposedly needed to protect the government or public safety. Bills or bill sections that contain an emergency clause cannot be repealed by the people through a popular referendum. The emergency clause appears in the same part of the constitution, Article 2, Section 1, and requires that the bill or section with the clause is

> "...necessary for immediate preservation of the public peace, health or safety, support of the state government and its existing public institutions."

The emergency clause not only immunizes a bill from repeal by referendum, it also gives the bill's provisions immediate legal effect, bypassing the normal waiting period of 90 days after the legislature adjourns.

In order to repeal a bill that includes an emergency clause, citizens must file an initiative, which is a much more difficult process than a referendum. The number of valid signatures needed to put a referendum on the ballot is four percent of the votes cast for the office of governor in the most recent election, or 112,440 signatures. The threshold for initiatives is eight percent, or 224,880 signatures.[1] By adding one sentence to a bill, lawmakers make it twice has hard for the people to repeal it.

Policy Analysis

During the 2005 session, lawmakers inserted the emergency clause in 98 bills, or about 19 percent of all bills passed.[2] The governor vetoed the emergency clauses out of two bills. In a few bills the emergency clause was used for its true purpose, such as in the state budget, which must take effect sooner than 90 days after adjournment.

In the vast majority of cases, though, the emergency clause is used in low-priority legislation, like regulating horseracing or off-road vehicles.[3] One lawmaker even attached an emergency clause to his bill creating a state potato commission, although that bill did not ultimately pass.[4]

In 2006, during a shorter session, the emergency clause was inserted in 34 bills.[5] Apparently, lawmakers and the governor thought the, "immediate preservation of the public peace, health or safety" was needed when they added the emergency clause to the bill allowing the lieutenant governor to raise money to pay for the 2006 meeting of the National Lieutenant Governors Association.[6]

The most serious misuse of the emergency clause occurs when lawmakers use it to pass controversial and unpopular legislation. In 2006, the emergency clause was inserted into SB 6896, which canceled Initiative 601's budget limits to allow for a large increase in spending.[7]

Lawmakers did the same thing in 2005 with SB 6078, which enacted a large tax increase and boosted state spending sharply.[8]

These two bills together comprised the largest spending measures in state history – a total two-year increase of 17 percent. By attaching emergency clauses to these bills, lawmakers denied citizens the right to challenge the dismantling of voter-approved Initiative 601.

Lawmakers have routinely abused the exemption by attaching an emergency clause to 764 bills since 1997, including 24 times during the 2008 legislative session.[9] In recent sessions, the governor has reduced abuse of the emergency clause by using her line item veto power to remove them from bills before signing them. A typical example is her partial veto of SB 6310:

> "This bill makes technical corrections to existing law by deleting obsolete terms and correcting references. I do not believe that an emergency clause is warranted."[10]

Some lawmakers acknowledge the emergency clause is tapped as a regular strategy to provide political cover against popular referendums.[11] Legislators would show greater respect for the state constitution, and for the people of Washington, by limiting the use of this important legal power to genuine public emergencies.

The most effective way to end the legislature's abuse of the emergency clause is with a constitutional amendment creating a supermajority vote requirement for its use. This means that the legislature would be prohibited from attaching an emergency clause unless a bill is approved by a 60 percent vote. Budget bills, however, would be exempt from the supermajority vote requirement, allowing them to pass with a simple majority and not be subject to referendum.

If a true public emergency occurs that warrants denying the people their right of referendum, a 60 percent vote requirement in the legislature should not be difficult to achieve. In the case of a true emergency, the public would most likely welcome the use of the emergency clause by the legislature, recognizing that it is intended to be used at just such a time to protect public safety or the normal functioning of state government. Political convenience, however, should no longer qualify as an exemption to the people's right of referendum.

Recommendation

1) Restrict use of the emergency clause to genuine emergencies and adopt constitutional limitations on its use. Lawmakers should refrain from using the emergency clause to deny people their constitutional right of referendum. If an emergency clause is attached to a bill, it should contain a specific description of the public emergency being addressed, and why special legislation is needed to address the problem.

A constitutional amendment should be adopted prohibiting the use of an emergency clause on a bill unless it is approved by a 60 percent vote. Appropriation bills, however, should be exempt from the supermajority vote requirement, allowing them to pass with a simple majority and not be subject to referendum, because they are necessary to fund normal government functions.

2. Open-Government Reforms

Recommendations

1. Create a Public Records Ombudsman authorized to enforce the Public Records Act.

2. Clarify the use of the attorney client-privilege exemption.

3. Create criminal penalties for willful violation of the Public Records Act.

4. Require audio taping of executive sessions.

5. The legislature should make itself subject to the Public Records Act and Open Public Meetings Act.

6. Adopt a constitutional amendment placing the preamble of the Public Records Act into the constitution, and require a 60 percent vote of lawmakers to enact a new exemption from disclosure to take effect.

Background

In 1972, voters overwhelming enacted Initiative 276, providing citizens with access to most records maintained by state and local government.[12] The new law created the Public Records Act (PRA). The preamble to the PRA says:

> "The people of this state do not yield their sovereignty to the agencies that serve them. The people, in delegating authority, do not give their public servants the right to decide what is good for the people to know and what is not good for them to know. The people insist on remaining informed so that they may maintain control over the instruments that they have created.
>
> This chapter shall be liberally construed and its exemptions narrowly construed to promote this public policy and to

assure that the public interest will be fully protected. In the event of conflict between the provisions of this chapter and any other act, the provisions of this chapter shall govern."[13]

When approved by the voters in 1972, the Public Records Act granted government only 10 exemptions from public disclosure. Since then, more than 300 exemptions have been added. State courts have further weakened the public's access to information with various legal rulings.

On May 19, 2008, the State Auditor released a performance audit of government officials' compliance with the Public Records Act. The audit noted:

> "In recent years, court cases in which state agencies and local governments have been assessed fines and penalties have been specifically related to the entities' improperly withholding public records and/or delaying release of the records. We did not identify litigation that was based on entities' practices other than improper denials or excessive delays.

> In addition to penalties, attorneys' fees, and costs awarded by the court, the entity also bears it own legal costs of the litigation. Accordingly, minor court awards can be expensive if the legal costs associated with the litigation are considered as well.

> In addition to the financial expense of being involved in a legal dispute involving public records, failing to respond properly to public records requests can erode the public's overall trust and regard for the entity and government in general."[14]

The Auditor's report gives recent examples of costly lawsuits that agencies and officials have lost for violating public records laws:[15]

- The Department of Corrections settled a lawsuit for $65,000 in late 2007;

- The Department of Corrections settled another public records lawsuit earlier in 2007 for $541,000;

- In 2006, the City of Spokane settled a case for $299,000, involving its refusal to release public records regarding financing of a parking garage. At the time, it was thought to be the largest public records related settlement in the history of the 1972 Public Records Act;

- A state Court of Appeals judge in 2007 fined King County Executive Ron Sims $123,000 for failing to comply with the state's Public Disclosure Act.

Along with the Public Records Act, citizens are provided access to the activities of government via the state Open Public Meetings Act (OPMA). Created by the legislature in 1971, the intent section of this law states:

> "The legislature finds and declares that all public commissions, boards, councils, committees, subcommittees, departments, divisions, offices, and all other public agencies of this state and subdivisions thereof exist to aid in the conduct of the people's business. It is the intent of this chapter that their actions be taken openly and that their deliberations be conducted openly." [16]

Despite the clear directive of the open meetings law, the State Auditor has identified more than 400 violations of this law by governmental entities over the past few years.

Policy Analysis

Due to the massive expansion in the number of exemptions from public disclosure and numerous violations of the Public Records Act and Open Public Meetings Act, meaningful open-government reforms are needed to restore the people's power to remain "informed so that they may maintain control over the instruments that they have created."

Public records ombudsman

Currently, when government officials violate the Public Records Act, citizens are forced to file a lawsuit to receive the public records improperly withheld. This means an individual must take on the full force and legal resources of the government agency being sued. To level the playing field, the legislature should authorize an independent, open-government ombudsman to be an advocate for citizens.

This independent public records advocate would be able to provide information on public records and open public meetings to state and local agencies and the public, while also representing the public in obtaining public records from state and local agencies.

Although the Attorney General has appointed an assistant attorney general to provide advice on open-government issues, this "ombudsman" is not truly independent. The primary mission of the Attorney General is to represent state agencies in legal actions, including defending agency officials who claim exemption of public records from disclosure.

This creates a conflict of interest that can prevent an ombudsman in the Attorney General's office from acting independently and in the interest of protecting the public's right to know. Several other states have created an independent ombudsman to assist the public. Washington lawmakers should follow their example.

Attorney-client privilege abuse

One of the most egregious examples of judicial weakening of the state Public Records Act occurred in 2004. That year, the state Supreme Court issued a decision in *Hangartner v. City of Seattle*. In its ruling, the justices declared that attorney-client privilege must be considered an exemption from the Public Records Act. This exemption is in addition to the limited exemption already in the law, which allows only attorney-client communications associated with an active lawsuit to be withheld from disclosure.

The irony of this ruling is that the ultimate clients of government are the citizens, yet under the guise of attorney-client privilege, government records can be withheld from the public.

The result of this decision is that virtually all communication between government agencies and their attorneys can be kept secret, even routine communication not related to any actual or threatened lawsuit. This ruling has the potential to block disclosure of a substantial amount of information necessary to hold government accountable. This ruling should be reversed, so the law retains only the original, narrow exemption based on ongoing litigation.

Criminal penalties for violations

If a government official violates the Public Records Act, their agency must pay monetary penalties. Unfortunately, that means that the penalties are either paid by taxpayers or taken through cuts in the agency's programs. There are no individual penalties for those who willfully decide to withhold public documents, or who engage in a deliberate cover-up, even if they know the documents should be disclosed.

Many states hold a government employee who criminally and willfully withholds public records liable for that failure. Penalties for the law-breaking employee include dismissal, fines or jail time. In fact, even in Washington state it is a gross misdemeanor, punishable by up to a $5,000 fine and a year in jail, to willfully destroy a public record that should have been preserved.[17]

To ensure that public records are not willfully withheld, violations for doing so should be criminally enforced against the guilty individual, instead of punishing the taxpayer for the individual's illegal activity.

Audio taping of executive sessions

The Open Public Meetings Act requires all meetings of state and local government governing bodies to be open to the public and announced in advance. However, the law allows the governing officials to meet behind closed doors in an executive session for certain limited purposes, such as consulting with their attorney on litigation, or discussing the maximum price they are willing to pay for a parcel of land.

Closed executive sessions are allowed only if the purpose of the meeting is announced in advance, and the secret discussion is limited to the announced allowed topic.

As previously mentioned, the state auditor has identified over 400 instances when state and local officials have abused this ability to meet behind closed doors. To ensure executive sessions are not being used to evade public disclosure, the sessions should be audio recorded. The recordings could be made exempt from disclosure under the Public Records Act and from subpoena or discovery in a lawsuit.

If a lawsuit is filed under the Open Public Meetings Act challenging the propriety of the executive session, and the person filing the lawsuit presents evidence sufficient to convince a judge that a violation had likely occurred, the audio recordings could be used to settle the question.

If a judge finds the challenged executive session included improper discussions and violated the law, the audio recording of only the portions of the meeting that should not have occurred in executive session could then be publicly disclosed.

Legislative privilege from transparency

Although all state and local governmental agencies are subject to the Public Records Act and the Open Public Meetings Act, the legislature is exempt from full disclosure under the claim of "legislative privilege." This is why state lawmakers are able to go into an executive session to plan strategy and discuss the reasons why legislators do or do not support a bill, while local governments are prohibited from using executive sessions to discuss policy decisions.

While all local government records and internal communications not subject to another exemption are subject to public disclosure, the legislature and state and local agencies have often claimed legislative privilege to block the release of emails and other internal policy-related records.

This double standard is an understandable irritant to local government officials, who must operate under a different, stricter standard of disclosure. It is also a disservice to citizens who are denied the fullest disclosure of the records and activities of their state lawmakers. To lead by example, and to further the public's right to know, the legislature should make itself subject to all the requirements of the Public Records Act and Open Public Meetings Act.

Recommendations

1) Create a Public Records Ombudsman authorized to enforce the Public Records Act. An independent public records advocate should be created to provide information on public records and open public meetings to state and local agencies and the public, and to represent the public in obtaining public records from state and local agencies.

2) Clarify the use of the attorney client-privilege exemption. The use of attorney-client privilege by government officials to deny access to public records should be limited to situations where actual litigation is pending or threatened. Officials should not use it to block public disclosure simply because an attorney has participated in a discussion of government policy, attended a meeting, or has seen a particular document.

3) Create criminal penalties for willful violation of the Public Records Act. To ensure that government records are not willfully and improperly withheld from the public, violations for doing so should be criminally enforced against the lawbreaking individual, instead of financially punishing the taxpayer for the official's illegal activity.

4) Require audio taping of executive sessions. To ensure executive sessions are not being used to evade public disclosure requirements, these sessions should be audio taped. If a lawsuit is filed under the Open Public Meetings Act challenging the legality of the closed executive session, a judge could use the audio recordings to determine if a violation of the law has occurred.

5) The legislature should make itself subject to the Public Records Act and Open Public Meetings Act. There should be no distinction or favoritism between state lawmakers and any other local or state government officials when it comes to the state's open-government laws. To lead by example, and to further the public interest, the legislature should make itself subject to all the requirements of the Public Record Act and Open Public Meetings Act.

6) Adopt a constitutional amendment placing the preamble of the Public Records Act into the constitution, and require a 60 percent vote of lawmakers to enact a new exemption from disclosure to take effect. The intent section of the Public Records Act is clear: "The people of this state do not yield their sovereignty to the agencies that serve them. The people, in delegating authority, do not give their public servants the right to decide what is good for the people to know and what is not good for them to know."

Despite this clear statement, state judges have added hundreds of new exemptions from public disclosure and have weakened citizens' ability to see important public information. To reverse this trend toward secrecy in government, the statutory protections of the Public Records Act should be enhanced and placed in the state constitution.

3. Protecting Voter-Approved Initiatives

Recommendation

1. Adopt constitutional reform that requires a two-thirds vote of the legislature to amend a voter-approved initiative.

Background

Article 1, Section 1 of the state constitution says,

"All political power is inherent in the people, and governments derive their just powers from the consent of the governed, and are established to protect and maintain individual rights."

It is because of this clear authority of power of the people over their government that before any legislative powers are granted, the people reserve for themselves co-equal lawmaking authority. This power is explained in Article 2, Section 1 of the state constitution:

"The legislative authority of the state of Washington shall be vested in the legislature, consisting of a senate and house of representatives, which shall be called the legislature of the state of Washington, but the people reserve to themselves the power to propose bills, laws, and to enact or reject the same at the polls, independent of the legislature, and also reserve power, at their own option, to approve or reject at the polls any act, item, section, or part of any bill, act, or law passed by the legislature. (a) Initiative: The first power reserved by the people is the initiative."

Despite reserving this power to enact laws, it is very difficult for citizens to qualify an initiative for voter consideration. The number of valid signatures needed to put an initiative on the ballot is eight percent of the votes cast for governor in the most recent election, or 224,880.[18]

The high threshold required for an initiative to get on the ballot, and then the majority vote required for it to become law, ensures that such laws reflect the will of the people and should be respected by state lawmakers.

Reflecting this principle, the state constitution, in Article 2, Section 41, requires the legislature to muster a two-thirds affirmative vote in order to amend an initiative within two years of its becoming law. After two years have passed, however, the legislature needs only a simple majority vote to amend a voter-approved initiative. In fact, lawmakers have done this many times.

Policy Analysis

While the protection given to voter-approved initiatives by Article 2, Section 41 may appear to be sufficient, lawmakers' habit of routinely amending initiatives, along with their practice of attaching emergency clauses to their changes, denies the people the ability to stop a majority of the legislature from meddling with voter-passed laws.

For example, in 2005, lawmakers amended three voter-approved initiatives and attached referendum-denying emergency clauses to each change. The three initiatives that were amended were:

- **Initiative 402** – passed by voters in 1981, this initiative eliminated the state death tax and tied the state tax rate to the federal IRS code. Later, when Congress phased out the federal death tax, the state tax was phased out too. The state treasury, however, continued to collect the tax. A state supreme court ruling upheld Initiative 402, meaning the state death tax would no longer exist. In response, the legislature instead repealed Initiative 402 by a simple majority vote, and enacted a stand-alone state death tax, which is in place today. [19]

- **Initiative 134** – passed by voters in 1992, this initiative created rules for corporate and union political campaign contributions. The legislature amended Initiative 134 to overturn a state supreme court ruling upholding the law as written instead of as interpreted by state agencies. The effect was that the voters' original intent was changed by state agency officials, supported by a simple majority vote in the legislature. [20]

- **Initiative 601** – passed by voters in 1993, this initiative created state tax and spending restrictions to restrain the growth of government and to limit tax increases. To accommodate a massive increase in state spending and to pass a $500 million tax increase, lawmakers, in 2005, by a simple majority vote, suspended Initiative 601's requirements for a two-thirds vote to raise taxes. They also enacted a permanent new spending calculation that allows the legislature to spend at a faster rate than originally allowed by Initiative 601.[21]

The legislature amended all these initiatives after the protective two-year window provided by the constitution had expired. By adding an emergency clause to each of their changes, lawmakers prevented voters from holding a referendum on the changes being made to the laws they had enacted.

Because of this, Article 2, Section 1 of the state constitution should be amended to remove the two-year time limit and require a two-thirds vote whenever lawmakers seek to change laws enacted by the people.

Alternatively, if lawmakers cannot secure a two-thirds vote to amend an initiative, they should create a procedure that allows them to send the proposed changes to voters for approval. This would allow voters final say over whether the legislature's desired changes should be adopted, and would show that legislators respect the people's constitutional power as co-equal lawmakers.

Recommendation

1) Adopt constitutional reform that requires a two-thirds vote of the legislature to amend a voter-approved initiative. The two-year limitation on requiring a two-thirds vote of lawmakers to amend an initiative should be eliminated, so that the two-thirds requirement applies whenever the legislature seeks to change a voter-approved law. The only time legislators should be allowed to amend an initiative with a simple majority vote is when they first send the proposed changes to the voters for approval.

4. Reducing the Number of Statewide Elected Offices

Recommendations

1. Reduce the number of elections for statewide offices from nine to four, by making the Secretary of State, Superintendent of Public Instruction, Commissioner of Public Lands and Insurance Commissioner governor-appointed positions.

2. Have candidates for governor and Lieutenant Governor run on one ticket, like the U.S. President and Vice President.

Background

Every four years Washington voters are asked to elect officials for nine separate statewide offices (not counting the state supreme court). These offices are:

1. Governor;
2. Lieutenant Governor;
3. Secretary of State;
4. Treasurer;
5. State Auditor;
6. Attorney General;
7. Superintendent of Public Instruction;
8. Commissioner of Public Lands and;
9. Insurance Commissioner.

Since voters can only realistically focus on a few high-level offices, there has been a debate about whether this is the most effective way to structure our state government.

One view holds that voters should use the "long ballot" to institute the greatest amount of direct democracy, by requiring election of a large number of statewide officials.

Others argue that a "short ballot" approach is better because the people choose a limited number of top officials, who are then held uniquely responsible for the proper functioning of government. Proponents of this view say elected officials are then subject to greater public scrutiny because there are fewer of them.

All of these statewide elected offices, except Insurance Commissioner, are established by the state constitution. Insurance Commissioner is unique since the legislature, not the constitution, established the elective nature of the office.

Other than the nine elected positions, all other senior officials in the executive branch are appointed by the governor. They make up the governor's cabinet and include many key positions, many as important as some elected offices.

State officials appointed by the governor include (in-part):

- Secretary of Social and Health Services;
- Director of Ecology;
- Director of Labor and Industries;
- Director of Agriculture;
- Director of Financial Management;
- Secretary of Transportation
- Director of Licensing;
- Director of General Administration
- Director of Community Trade & Economic Development;
- Director of Veterans Affairs, Director of Revenue,
- Secretary of Corrections;
- Secretary of Health, Director of Financial Institutions;
- Chief of the State Patrol.

The duties and responsibilities of some of these appointed officials are similar to, and in some cases carry more responsibility than, those of the Secretary of State, Superintendent of Public Instruction, Commissioner of Public Lands or Insurance Commissioner.

Policy Analysis

Today, eight of Washington's statewide elected officials are autonomous from the governor. In practice they can lobby the legislature independently, and even work against what the governor is trying to accomplish.

Any such conflict is resolved in those parts of government that are administered by appointees. If a policy disagreement arises among cabinet officers, the governor settles it by forming a single, unified policy for the administration.

Similarly, if the legislature is unable to reach agreement with a cabinet official over important legislation, the dispute can be taken "over his head" to the governor. The governor may or may not agree with the position the cabinet appointee has taken, but at least the legislature will get a final answer. The legislature knows that, through the governor, the executive branch speaks with one policy voice.

The reason this works is because the governor has direct authority over the appointed officials. They serve at the governor's pleasure and can be dismissed at any time. The governor is accountable to the voters for the overall performance of the administration.

Accountability offices

The Secretary of State, Superintendent of Public Instruction, Commissioner of Public Lands and Insurance Commissioner are policy offices, much like those currently in the governor's appointed cabinet. Direct election of these offices does not necessarily create greater public accountability, because most Washingtonians don't know the names of these officials.

The Treasurer, Auditor and Attorney General, however, carry out an oversight role, working to ensure government agencies are following the law. It is because of this distinction that independent election of these offices makes sense.

Since there would be just three of these "watchdog" offices, it would be easy for voters to remember what function these offices perform in state government. Voters would then clearly understand what they are voting on when selecting among candidates running for these positions.

Office of Lieutenant Governor

To ensure the successful transition of power in the event the governor is unable to fulfill his duties, it makes sense to have an elected Lieutenant Governor ready to step into the top office. That does not mean, however, that the Lieutenant Governor needs to be independently elected from the governor. Instead, Washington should model the office of Lieutenant Governor after that of the Vice President of the United States. This would mean that candidates for governor and Lieutenant Governor would run on the same ticket.

Maryland structures its election of governor and Lieutenant Governor this way. Article 2, Section 1B of the Maryland constitution states:

> "Each candidate who shall seek a nomination for Governor, under any method provided by law for such nomination, including primary elections, shall at the time of filing for said office designate a candidate for Lieutenant Governor, and the names of the said candidate for Governor and Lieutenant Governor shall be listed on the primary election ballot, or otherwise considered for nomination jointly with each other.

> "In any election, including a primary election, candidates for Governor and Lieutenant Governor shall be listed jointly on the ballot, and a vote cast for the candidate for Governor shall also be cast for Lieutenant Governor jointly listed on the ballot with him..."[22]

Shorter ballot and greater accountability

With fewer statewide elected offices, voters would choose the five highest state officials in four elections, as follows:

1. Governor and Lieutenant Governor
2. Attorney General
3. State Treasurer
4. State Auditor

If problems arise with public education, insurance regulation, or management of public lands, voters would know that the solution lies with the governor, who could change the top managers of these policy areas at any time. If the governor fails to use his appointment powers to improve the management of these departments, voters could take that failure into account at election time.

Reducing the number of statewide elected offices would shorten the length of the ballot and focus public accountability in a way that people can understand and remember, both during a governor's term and in election years when voters are assessing candidates for the state's top offices.

Recommendations

1) Reduce the number of statewide elected offices from nine to four, by making the Secretary of State, Superintendent of Public Instruction, Commissioner of Public Lands and Insurance Commissioner governor-appointed positions. The state constitution should be amended to change these offices from elected to appointed positions. The office of Insurance Commissioner can be changed by statute. The offices should then be restructured as cabinet agencies putting the governor fully in charge and responsible for the actions of the policy offices in the executive branch.

2) Have candidates for governor and Lieutenant Governor run on one ticket, like the U.S. President and Vice President. The constitution should be amended to provide for the governor and Lieutenant Governor to run together on the same ticket. This would allow for an orderly transition of power if the governor is unable to fulfill the responsibilities of the office, and would bring the Lieutenant Governor into the cabinet.

Additional Resources from Washington Policy Center

"Emergency Clause Usage Drops, Constitutional Reforms Still Needed," by Jason Mercier, April 2008.

"Bringing Sunshine to State Spending," by Jason Mercier, January 2008.

"Restoring Our Right of Referendum," by Jason Mercier, January 2008.

"Transparency and Accountability Reforms: Searchable State Budget Website and Emergency Clause Reform," by Jason Mercier, January 2008.

"Ending Abuse of the Emergency Clause," by Jason Mercier, 2007.

"Creating a Free, Searchable Website of State Spending," by Jason Mercier, 2007.

"Time to Shine Light on Government Spending," by Jason Mercier, October 2007.

"Five Principles of Responsible Government," by Paul Guppy, January 2007.

"Performance Audits Seek to Improve How Government Spends Our Money," by John Barnes, October 2005.

---

[1] Washington Secretary of State Office, "Filing Initiatives and Referenda in Washington State," page 11, at www.secstate.wa.gov/elections, accessed May 23, 2008.

[2] See www.WashingtonVotes.org and www.leg.wa.gov for more information on bills.

[3] SB 5951 and HB 1003, Washington State Legislature, 2005 legislative session, introduced by Sen. Marilyn Rasmussen (D-Eatonville), and Representative Bill Hinkle (R-Cle Elum), respectively.

[4] HB 1608, Washington State Legislature, 2005 legislative session, introduced by Representative Bill Grant (D-Walla Walla).

[5] See www.WashingtonVotes.org and www.leg.wa.gov.

[6] HB 2419, Washington State Legislature, 2006 legislative session, introduced by Representative Kathy Haigh (D-Shelton).

[7] SB 6896, Washington State Legislature, 2006 legislative session, introduced by Senator Margarita Prentice (D-Renton).

[8] SB 6078, Washington State Legislature, 2005 legislative session, introduced by Senator Debbie Regala (D-Tacoma).

[9] "Emergency Clause Usage Drops, Constitutional Reforms Still Needed," by Jason Mercier, Washington Policy Center, April 2008, at www.washingtonpolicy.org/Centers/government/policynotes/08_mercier_emergen cyclauseusuage.html.

[10] Governor's message for partial veto of SB 6310, March 27, 2008.

[11] In November 2005, the Evergreen Freedom Foundation released a survey of legislators on the use of the emergency clause. Several lawmakers insisted that the clause is used for purely political purposes, and one claimed to have heard a colleague say the clause was being attached to specific legislation to shield the bill from repeal by referendum. See, "Emergency Clause Reform Survey Results," Evergreen Freedom Foundation, November 28, 2005, at http://www.effwa.org/pdfs/ecr.pdf.

[12] The initiative passed by a yes vote of 72%, "Initiative to the People – 1914 through 2007," Initiative Measure No. 276, Office of the Secretary of State, at www.secstate.wa.gov/elections/initiatives/statistics_initiatives.aspx.

[13] Revised Code of Washington, 42.56.030.

[14] "Open Public Records Practices at 30 Government Entities," Washington State Auditor, Performance Audit Report, Report No. 1000011, May 19, 2008, at www.sao.wa.gov/Reports/AuditReports/AuditReportFiles/ar1000011.pdf.

[15] Ibid, pages 2 and 3.

[16] Revised Code of Washington, 42.30.010.

[17] Revised Code of Washington 40.14.16 and 42.20.

[18] Washington Secretary of State's Office, "Filing Initiatives and Referenda in Washington State," page 11, at www.secstate.wa.gov/elections, accessed May 23, 2008.

[19] SB 6096, House vote April 22, 2005, 50 to 48; Senate vote April 19, 2005, 26 to 20; signed into law May 17, 2005; Bill Information, History of Bill, Washington State Legislature at www.apps.leg.wa.gov/billinfo/summary.aspx?bill=6096&year=2005.

[20] SB 5034, House vote April 13, 2005, 56 to 40; Senate vote April 20, 2005, 26 to 20; signed into law May 13, 2005; Bill Information, History of Bill, Washington State Legislature at www.apps.leg.wa.gov/billinfo/summary.aspx?bill=5034&year=2005.

[21] SB 6078, House vote April 15, 2005, 56 to 40; Senate vote April 16, 2005, 26 to 20; signed into law April 18, 2005; Bill Information, History of Bill, Washington State Legislature at www.apps.leg.wa.gov/billinfo/summary.aspx?bill=6078&year=2005.

[22] "Executive Department," Article II, Section 1B, Constitution of Maryland, at www.msa.md.gov/msa/mdmanual/43const/html/02art2.html.

CHAPTER 8

1. Improving Workers' Compensation

Recommendations

1. Legalize private workers' compensation insurance and move the system towards greater choice and competition.

2. Allow small groups and associations to self-insure.

3. Increase fraud prevention efforts.

4. Clarify the calculation of benefits.

5. Bring benefit levels more in line with those in other states.

Background

The phrase "workers' compensation insurance" often elicits vacant stares and furrowed brows from those who hear it. This complex and important social program, which replaces employer liability for workplace injured workers, is often confusing and tedious for employers, workers, policymakers and the public alike.

The Department of Labor and Industries (L&I), which administers the state's workers' compensation program, is one of the largest agencies in state government, with more than 2,700 full-time staff and a biennial budget of $537 million.[1]

By law, only L&I is permitted to sell workers' compensation insurance in Washington, and virtually all businesses in the state are required to have such insurance. The program provides insurance that covers over 168,000 employers and 2.5 million workers, and it collects more than $1.55 billion in premiums each year. In 2007, premium collections became so high the Department declared a partial rate holiday, allowing employers to keep $346 million of their money until the rate L&I charged for premiums more accurately reflected the true costs of the program.[2]

L&I also oversees almost 400 employers who self-insure and provide coverage for 830,000 workers, about one-third of all workers in the state. The L&I program and self-insured companies provide coverage for the more than 140,000 industrial injuries that are reported annually.[3]

Policy Analysis

The original purpose of workers' compensation was to provide sure and certain relief for workers in the event of an on-the-job injury. In return for joining a legally-mandated program, employers gained protection against the uncertainty of individual lawsuits brought against them by injured employees. For employers and workers, the system is intended to provide security, financial predictability and fair treatment.

Yet over the years the "exclusive remedy" aspect of workers' compensation has eroded. Workers routinely sue the Department in court to gain a higher level of benefits, and, while they are not suing employers directly, employers must bear the full cost of lawsuits and any resulting awards through higher workers' compensation taxes. In addition, employers must pay the long-term cost of litigation when court decisions result in a permanent higher level of benefits for all claimants.

In the past few years, businesses have become increasingly frustrated with the Department's rate increases. Every rate increase is essentially a tax increase on business, which is passed on to consumers in the form of higher prices.

The 2007 rate holiday afforded employers and workers a period of partial tax relief. From July 1st through the end of the year, L&I officials suspended the Medical Aid portion of the workers' comp premiums – the Accident Fund premium was not affected. The rate holiday expired at the end of 2007 and Department officials then permanently increased rates an average of 3.2 percent.

Washington has one of the highest rates of workers' compensation benefits paid out by any state in the nation. Washington's benefit payments increased 12 percent from 2001 to 2004, and today the average weekly benefit is almost $700 per covered worker – about 57 percent higher than the U.S. worker's compensation average.[4]

High insurance costs are a significant contributor to job loss, layoffs and wage cuts, and have a detrimental effect on the economic vitality and business climate of the state. In recent years L&I has greatly varied the premium adjustments, resulting in cost swings between whopping rate increases of up to 30 percent and brief rate holidays. In 2008, employers pay 4.5 percent more on average in L&I accident fund premiums, 10.5 percent more on the Medical Aid fund premiums, and 17.1 percent more in the Supplemental Pension Fund.[5]

Much of the financial strain in the system is the result of structural weaknesses and lack of competition. Washington is one of only five states where buying private workers compensation insurance is illegal. Except for the few companies that self-insure, all employers are forced to purchase insurance from the sole provider: the state. Bringing competition to workers' compensation insurance in Washington would create more choices, reduce prices and improve service for both workers and employers.

The system has also been weakened by a series of lawsuits. Injured workers and their lawyers who sue and win realize an immediate economic gain. But the system as a whole is undermined and risks become fiscally unsustainable, to the ultimate detriment of all employers and workers.

Major reforms are needed to bring the workers' compensation system back to its original purpose: a true insurance plan which mitigates risk for employers, provides fair and reliable benefits for injured workers, and contributes to a stable business environment for all Washington citizens.

Recommendations

1) Legalize private workers' compensation insurance and move the system towards greater choice and competition. Washington is one of only five states nationwide that makes it illegal for companies to purchase private workers' compensation insurance. Large companies may have sufficient cash flow to self-insure, but all others must purchase insurance from one source at a non-negotiable price – the state government.

2) Allow small groups and associations to self-insure. Washington law currently bans groups of small employers from joining together to self-insure, reserving that choice only to large companies and a few public entities. Allowing groups and associations to self-insure would bring greater choice and price competition to the system. Standards for coverage would still be set by the state, so basic protections for workers would not be compromised.

3) Increase fraud prevention efforts. Fraud has cost L&I and taxpayers millions of dollars over the years. The Department is starting to crack down on fraudulent claims. In 2007, L&I recovered more than $139 million in unpaid premiums and overpayments. Passage of Initiative 900 in 2006, directing the State Auditor to conduct audits of L&I, will help keep the focus of the Department on accountability.

4) Clarify the calculation of benefits. No-fault insurance is supposed to keep costs low by eliminating the need for lawsuits. Yet this approach is not working. Lawsuits have built new fixed costs into the system. Policymakers should make the way benefits are calculated clearer and simpler to avoid legal disputes.

5) Bring benefit levels more in line with those in other states. Reducing the maximum benefit cap to match the national average would save money and establish a more reasonable level of benefits.

2. Minimum Wage and Living Wage

Recommendations

1. Decouple automatic minimum wage increases from the Puget Sound Consumer Price Index to reflect the true cost of living across the state.

2. Delay automatic increases in years when state unemployment is higher than the national average.

3. Allow restaurants to count tip income as part of normal minimum wage earnings, so employment costs in one industry are not artificially inflated.

4. Refrain from imposing mandatory "living wage" controls, whether or not directed at a particular industry.

Background

Washington has the highest state minimum wage in the nation. At $8.07 an hour it is fully 38 percent higher than the current federal minimum wage of $5.85. However, the federal minimum wage is scheduled to rise to $6.55 on July 24, 2008 and $7.25 per hour on July 24, 2009.

Because a high minimum wage decreases job opportunities, Washington law allows 14- and 15-year-olds to be paid 85 percent of the state minimum wage, or $6.86 an hour, in order to mitigate some of the job losses for people in this age group.[6]

Washington's unemployment rate has declined to about 4.3 percent for the first time in several years, but that was not always the case. During the recession years of 2000-2001 and in 2002-2005, Washington's unemployment rate topped out at 7.7 percent, a period when the state's minimum wage and its unemployment rate were respectively the highest or second highest in the nation.[7]

Washington's present minimum wage law was enacted by voters with passage of Initiative 688 in 1998. The measure enacted a two-step boost in the state minimum wage from $4.90 to $6.50, and for the first time created regular yearly increases tied to inflation.[8]

The state minimum wage now automatically increases every January 1st and is pegged to the Puget Sound cost of living, the highest in the state. Previously, the legislature had increased the minimum only ten times since the first state-mandated wage was enacted in 1959.

Under the current policy of automatic increases, the state minimum wage has increased 65 percent in ten years. Inflation over the same period was 32 percent.

Washington has some 74,000 minimum wage jobs, or about 3.5 percent of all industry jobs. They tend to be concentrated in certain industries: food services, retail sales, health care, agriculture, forestry and fishing. The majority of minimum wage workers are employed by small businesses.

Minimum wage jobs usually supplement other income; very rarely are they the sole financial support for a family. Eighty-five percent of those earning the minimum wage either live with a parent or relative, are part of a two-income couple or are single and have no children.[9] The chart below shows the rise in Washington's minimum wage compared to the federal minimum.

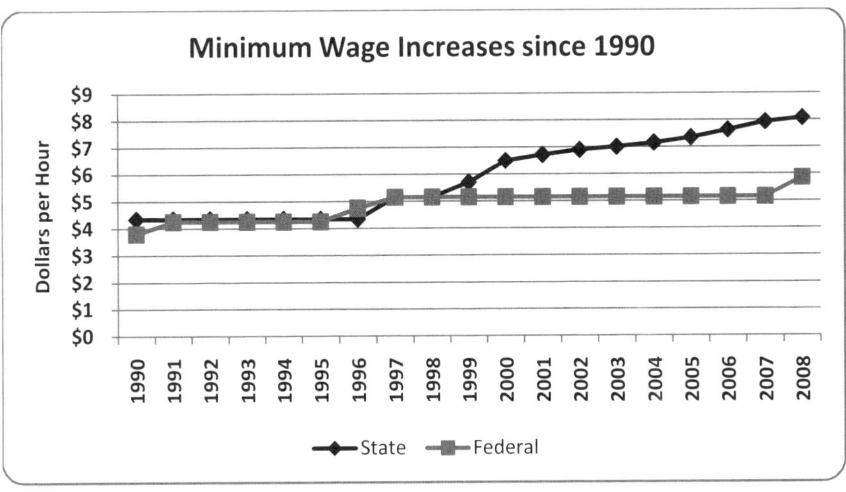

In Washington, the minimum wage increases automatically every January 1st, regardless of economic conditions. Sources: Department of Labor and Industries and U.S. Department of Labor

Among minimum wage supporters is an activist subset that endorses the idea of a mandatory "living wage." A living wage is a hyper minimum wage, where the mandated wages paid to employees are based on the worker being able to afford a certain theoretical standard of living.

Living wage ordinances throughout the nation have primarily been enacted within local government limits. Bellingham is the only city in Washington that has imposed a living wage ordinance, and even there the law only applies to a limited number of government contractors. Bellingham officials are concerned the hyper-minimum would drive businesses and jobs out of the city if it was broadly applied.

Supporters of the living wage, however, are beginning to target private industries and mandate living wage requirements. For instance, in 2007, living wage proponents came within a few hundred signatures of putting a hyper-minimum wage initiative on the ballot in the city of Spokane.

The initiative would have mandated that large retail stores of over 95,000 square feet pay their employees a minimum wage of 135 percent of the state's minimum wage, if the employee received a pre-set level of health care benefits, or 165 percent of the minimum wage if the employee did not receive the approved level of health care benefits.[10]

If Spokane voters had passed the living wage ordinance, the impact of the policy would have been detrimental to the very working people the law was intended to help. But its effects would have been felt city-wide. The unintended consequences of a city-wide living wage ordinance would have resulted in fewer jobs, fewer working hours for those in the retail industry who would have fallen under the new law, and a trickle-down effect on smaller retailers who are unable to pay the higher wage and would have lost employees.

Policy Analysis

During the difficult economic recovery, Washington's small businesses were particularly harmed by the state's high minimum wage requirement. The burden of job loss falls disproportionately on low-skilled and minority workers. A study by labor policy researchers at Cornell University concludes that, "A 10 percent increase in the minimum wage causes four times more employment loss for employees without a high school diploma and African American young adults than it does for more educated and non-black employees."[11]

Workers priced out of the labor market

Washington's high minimum wage law falls hardest on those who can least afford it. The poor, homeless, teenagers and other young workers trying to enter the workforce are the first to be impacted by a rising unemployment rate. When state law artificially increases the cost of creating jobs, fewer jobs are created. Low-skill, low-income workers are the first to be priced out of the job market.

The high minimum wage creates a ripple effect through the economy by pushing up all wages, which is one reason powerful unions always support minimum wage increases. Supporters of an ever-higher minimum wage grew weary of the public debate needed to argue for increases. They included a provision in Initiative 688 that linked the wage to inflation, insuring it would go up automatically every January 1st, with no debate, no additional vote and no discussion.

Politically the strategy is brilliant. It avoids all that messy public discussion about the harmful effects of raising the minimum wage – increases just happen, and most people do not notice the broader effect on the job market.

The result is a higher cost of living for everyone. While most people can pay a little more for a hamburger or a house, the burden again falls heaviest on those who can least afford it: the poor and the unemployed.

The high minimum wage is not the only reason Washington is less competitive nationally than other states, but it is a strong contributing factor. Washington suffers deeper economic down-turns and slower recoveries than other states. Policymakers should recognize that putting state labor policy on auto-pilot does not improve job opportunities or the business climate, but actually makes them worse.

The arguments made against the minimum wage are even stronger against the mandated living wage. Backers of the living wage are basing an employee's earning on the perceived need of the employee and not on productivity or labor demand or supply. Ignoring fundamental economic principles in the course of determining worker remuneration is a form of price control and will result in increased labor costs, higher prices for consumers, or perhaps even the loss of jobs.

Tip income and the minimum wage

Washington state is one of only seven states where food servers receive the state minimum wage *in addition* to their tips. This puts an undue burden on small restaurants, many of which are family-owned, by artificially inflating their wage costs in comparison to other types of businesses. In states without this restriction, hourly and tip income may be counted together, and the law specifies that from these two sources no employee may ever be paid less than the minimum wage.

Restaurant servers in Washington average almost $19 an hour in tips plus wages, meaning on average they earn over $11 an hour in tips.[12] One proposal would allow employers in the restaurant industry to pay 50 percent of the minimum wage ($4.04 in 2008) to tipped employees, with the legal guarantee that no worker would earn less than the legal minimum wage. This reform would not fully equalize treatment among industries, but it would spur job creation and help level the playing field by treating employment costs in restaurants like those in other businesses.

Recommendations

1) Decouple automatic minimum wage increases from the Puget Sound Consumer Price Index to reflect the true cost of living across the state. Forcing all labor costs to match the most expensive region creates a particular burden for businesses in the eastern and rural parts of the state. Using regional measures of inflation is fair and would more accurately reflect price changes in the local economy.

2) Delay automatic increases in years when state unemployment is higher than the national average. If full control over minimum wage policy cannot be returned to the legislature, a mechanism should be created which suspends automatic increases when the unemployment rate is high and people are most in need of work opportunities.

3) Allow restaurants to count tip income as part of normal minimum wage earnings, so employment costs in one industry are not artificially inflated. Allowing tips to be counted as income would expand job opportunities and lower wage costs, especially for smaller, family-owned restaurants.

4) Refrain from imposing mandatory "living wage" controls, whether or not directed at a particular industry. Arbitrarily raising the cost of labor among a specific industry based solely on workers' perceived need is bad economic policy and bad public policy, and it leads to higher prices for consumers and job losses or cutbacks for workers.

3. The Temporary Labor Market

Recommendation

1. Minimize state regulation of the temporary labor market to promote job opportunities for low-income and part-time workers.

Background

Policymakers and the public tend to place much emphasis on the economy producing permanent, full-time jobs, yet one valuable segment of our state's workforce is often overlooked: temporary workers. They are students and homemakers, recent immigrants and new citizens, people between jobs and permanent part-timers.

For many laid off workers, a temporary job is the best path back to full-time employment. For others, a temporary position frees up time for other interests. The temporary labor market is a reflection of how free citizens pursue their own goals in life. Everyone has the right to work, not work, or work less, as they choose. The temporary labor market makes these highly personal economic choices possible.

Integral to the temporary labor market are the job-finding agencies that bring workers and employers together for the benefit of both. As requests from employers come in, workers are matched with specific jobs and sent to the business or jobsite. Typical jobs include construction, homebuilding, food packing, landscaping and light manufacturing. Increasingly, temporary employees are highly paid technical, computer and health care workers seeking flexible schedules. At the end of the day, workers return to the placement company's office and receive a paycheck.

Private temporary placement companies make this efficient labor market possible because they handle all the paperwork, make sure workers follow federal and state regulations, and make the required payroll deductions.

People seeking quick employment need only show up on time and be willing to work. Employers get reliable workers with a minimum of red tape. Workers get the chance to work where they want and when they want.

In 2007, the services of temporary staffing agencies across the country benefited three million workers on an average day, and over the course of the year helped 11.4 million people find gainful work.[13]

The temporary labor market is not only good for individuals, it is an essential part of reducing unemployment in society. It makes up a little over two percent of non-agricultural employment, and growth in the number of temporary jobs is a leading indicator that the economy is emerging from an economic downturn.[14]

The temporary labor system is entirely voluntary and, like most good ideas, is elegantly simple: people can work and get paid the same day.

Policy Analysis

The temporary labor market, however, has its detractors. Traditional labor unions, in particular, do not like flexible work arrangements, because these jobs exist outside the conventional union structure. Their ideal is that every employer should use unionized workers and no others. Rather than accept a vibrant temporary workforce that serves the needs of individuals and employers, unions try to use the force of government to foreclose what they see as inconvenient labor competition.

Opponents of voluntary temporary labor seek to burden this market with as many regulatory barriers as possible. One lawsuit in another state sought to bar workers from paying a minimal fee to cash their paychecks in the dispatch office at the end of the day. The result of the lawsuit was to force workers to wait a day and go to a bank or to a costly check-cashing store. Many temporary workers, however, are low-income and do not have bank accounts. Many of them would prefer to pay a small fee and cash their paychecks right away.

Temporary labor opponents have also sought to force closure of heated waiting rooms where workers gather to seek work. They claim that workers should be paid while they wait for job assignments. Since few businesses can afford to pay people for not working, temporary labor offices would have to close their waiting rooms, and job seekers would be left to congregate on street corners.

Temporary placement companies often provide workers with hard hats, work boots, dust-masks and eye-protection for free. Temporary labor opponents say workers should not be held responsible for lost or broken equipment, meaning that workers would have to provide important safety gear themselves.

Opponents support legislation to force temporary companies to provide mandated paid health benefits, even though such top-down requirements defeat the purpose of providing flexible and voluntary job opportunities for temporary workers.

Many local governments have tried to set up day labor centers, using tax dollars to compete directly against their own citizens. Local officials intend tax-subsidized day labor centers to act as cover for people who are in the country illegally. In contrast, a local private employer can be punished under federal law for hiring illegal workers. Also, the employer, through local taxes, is subsidizing a government program that finds work for undocumented workers.

Together these hostile efforts add up to a coordinated assault on the temporary labor market. Adverse rulings by the courts or onerous regulations imposed by government come with a high cost. Employers lose information about where to find able and willing workers and thousands of job opportunities disappear. Washington's economy would become even more difficult for struggling small businesses and innovative start-ups.

Worst of all, the most vulnerable in our communities would lose vital job opportunities, forcing them onto public assistance or leaving them vulnerable to the underground labor market.

Recommendation

1) Minimize state regulation of the temporary labor market, to maximize job opportunities for low-income and part-time workers. Letting the temporary labor market operate as freely and efficiently as possible is an effective way to stimulate our state economy, while creating choice and opportunity for thousands of hard-working men and women. For example, placement agencies should be able to offer paycheck cashing services for a minimal fee, so low-income workers are not forced to open bank accounts as a condition of finding work. In addition, local governments should not set up day labor placement centers that compete against their own citizens.

4. Mandatory Paid Sick Leave and Paid Family Leave

Recommendations

1. Avoid imposing a mandatory, one-size-fits all sick leave policy on Washington business owners and their employees. Allow employers to retain flexibility in setting compensation and benefits.

2. Repeal the Paid Family Leave Insurance program until sufficient long-term funding can be identified, or transform the mandate into a voluntary program.

Background

In the 2006 session, lawmakers considered a bill that would have made every employer provide a minimum amount of paid sick leave for each employee.[15] There was no exemption for small businesses. Under the proposal, all businesses would have been mandated to give 10 days of paid sick leave based on the following requirements:

- An employee would be granted at least 40 hours of paid sick leave for each six months of full-time work;

- An employee would be entitled to take paid sick leave after completing six months of consecutive employment;

- Part-time employees would receive paid sick leave in proportion to the hours they work.

The bill did not pass, but proponents have made it clear they intend to continue to push in future legislative sessions for a law that would impose a single, paid sick leave policy on every employer in the state.

Currently, forty-four percent of Washington employers voluntarily offer full-time workers a paid sick leave benefit.[16] Nationally, no state requires paid sick leave as a matter of law.

Proponents of mandatory paid sick leave say that it is needed for employees to supplement income for days lost at work when caring for themselves or their children, and to avoid bringing contagious diseases to the workplace.

Employers cite several reasons why they do not always offer paid sick leave. Many jobs are temporary, or are jobs where an employee's absence is covered by a fellow co-worker. Some employees prefer to receive other forms of compensation, rather than be eligible for paid sick days they may never use. Some jobs are based on tips and gratuities, thus paying an employee full compensation to stay at home undermines businesses' economic viability.[17]

Impact on small businesses

Small businesses would be disproportionately impacted by a mandatory paid sick leave policy. As the following chart shows, every business category is affected, but employers with fewer than 100 employees would be disproportionately impacted.

Percentage of Washington businesses affected by proposed paid sick leave mandate	
All firms	56%
100+ employees	33%
50-99 employees	47%
25-49 employees	54%
10-24 employees	58%
2-9 employees	58%

Many small firms already offer some level of paid sick leave, but if that level were less than ten days, the mandated benefit bill considered by the legislature would automatically increase these business' costs.

Seventy-three percent of Washington firms offer paid time off to full-time workers, without distinguishing between sick leave and vacation time.[18] In addition, 23 percent of firms report offering undesignated paid leave, often accumulated for workers in personal "time banks," on top of the yearly paid holidays the employer already provides.[19]

Undesignated leave and personal time banks allow workers to use their paid time off as they see fit, without losing an earned benefit if they don't happen to take sick days. Mandating paid sick leave by law would end this flexibility, since paid time off does not meet the proposed definition of sick leave.

Estimates vary of how much work productivity would be lost due to a new mandatory benefit imposed upon employers. According to some surveys, employees often use paid sick days in proportion to how much leave is available. If an employee has 12 sick days a year he or she will typically use about seven days per year, and an employee with five sick days will use about three days a year.

A study by the U.S. Small Business Administration shows that employees of small businesses have, by-and-large, access to fewer benefits than do the employees of large businesses.[20] The smallest firms are often forced to make substantially higher contributions per participant for benefits than the largest firms. Smaller businesses face a much higher marginal cost in implementing any new mandated benefit, placing them at a marked disadvantage compared to their larger competitors.

Paid family leave insurance program

In April 2007, the legislature enacted a paid family leave insurance program. This program would pay qualified applicants – those with newborn children or newborn adopted children – up to $250 per week for five weeks in order for the parent(s) to remain at home with the new child.

The program is unusual, since only California had a similar system in place when the legislation passed (New Jersey has since passed a similar program as well). Funding the program became problematic when state agency managers expressed their hesitation about administering the program. Washington's program is scheduled to begin reviewing applications and paying out benefits on October 1, 2009.

The problems with this mandatory program are diverse. First, the state would need to set up, from scratch, a new entitlement program. Such an effort is unlikely to take place in the short amount of time between passage of the legislation and October 1, 2009.

Second, legislators failed to identify a permanent source of funding. A line-item in the 2007-2009 supplemental budget sets aside $6.2 million for set-up costs and an initial start-up phase of operation. However, proposals on the necessary permanent funding have ranged from a new employee payroll tax, to using general fund dollars, to taxing candy and gum.

The special Paid Family Leave Task Force failed to produce a funding recommendation, and in 2008 the legislature, perhaps concerned about imposing more taxes in an election year, did not identify a funding source. Instead, finding money for the program has been left to a future legislature.

Third, there is almost no flexibility in the program. Just about every worker in the state would have to pay into the system, even people who are self-employed. There are no exemptions for small businesses, even though a small business is much less likely to be able to handle an extended leave for an employee. Larger firms are better able to switch personnel around to cover employees out on leave. Smaller firms tend to take a flexible approach in times of employees' need.

A National Federation of Independent Business study shows that 66 percent of small businesses provide some sort of paid leave and that the remaining one-third of small businesses deal with employee leaves on a case-by-case basis, thereby meeting the same standard that backers of the new family leave insurance program are advocating.[21]

Policy Analysis

In the modern economy, most companies have adopted voluntary and flexible ways of compensating their employees, based on the demands of workers and the need of firms to stay competitive in their particular market. Many companies give their employees three, five or seven days of paid leave per year. Arbitrarily increasing the number of paid sick days from seven to ten through a state-imposed mandate, for example, may help a few employees, but will contribute to unemployment and increase the cost of living for all citizens.

Likewise, a new state entitlement program – one that, as yet, has no funding source – will only further negatively affect the business climate, particularly for small business owners who are less able to cover for employees on leave.

Smaller businesses are often forced to adjust to a new employment mandate by raising prices, reducing paid vacation, cutting other non-cash benefits, hiring fewer workers or a combination of all four. In forcing employers to provide a new benefit, policymakers would end up making things worse for workers, not better.

The cumulative effect of top-down regulations, such as numerous health insurance mandates and the automatically increasing minimum wage, already inhibit the ability of Washington businesses to create jobs. The proposed mandatory sick leave requirement, added to existing regulations, would significantly increase costs, especially for local small businesses, and make our business climate even less attractive to out-of-state companies.

Recommendations

1) Avoid imposing a mandatory, one-size-fits all sick leave policy on Washington business owners and their employees. Allow employers to retain flexibility in setting compensation and benefits. Blanket regulations that apply one rule to every business are harmful to the economy as a whole. Most businesses have some sort of paid sick leave or paid time off policy, but business owners should not have a single, one-size-fits-all rule forced upon them by the state.

2) Repeal the Paid Family Leave Insurance program until sufficient long-term funding can be identified, or transform the mandate into a voluntary program. The program should be suspended until a permanent source of funding can be identified. The program could also be revamped to make it a voluntary system or provide for an opt-out for small businesses that already offer paid leave to their employees.

5. Mandatory Paid Health Benefits

Recommendation

1. Do not impose a restrictive "Fair Share" health benefit mandate on the Washington labor market.

Background

In 2006, the legislature debated a bill proponents refer to as the "Fair Share Act," which would require all companies in Washington with 5,000 or more employees to provide a certain level of health care benefits, or pay a new nine percent payroll tax to the state treasury.[22]

Proponents say the proposal would reduce the number of uninsured by increasing access to health coverage for Washington workers. They say owners of large companies have a responsibility to provide a minimum standard of health coverage to their workers and that if they do not do so voluntarily the state should require it by law.

Proponents also say companies shift their health coverage costs to the taxpayers when their workers enroll in publicly-funded health programs. The nine percent payroll tax is intended to reimburse the government for this perceived corporate subsidy.

Policy Analysis

A close analysis of the proposal finds it to be bad public policy for two primary reasons: it is wrong in principle and wrong in practice.

Wrong in principle

The idea is wrong in principle because it unfairly targets a narrow group of companies. Citizens should always be concerned when certain groups or businesses are singled out as the target of government power.

The proposal is unfair to workers who choose to access health coverage in other ways, such as through a spouse or individual-based coverage that puts workers in charge of their own health care. Mandating a one-size-fits-all, employer-based health care system deprives workers of choices in one of the most important areas of life.

It is particularly unfair to temporary and part-time workers. If a temporary employee works just *one day,* he could be counted toward the employer's quota of 5,000 workers. Increasing the regulatory burden on jobs in Washington will encourage outsourcing to other states and countries.

The bill is unfair to business owners who should have the right to run their business free from micro-management by the state. If the largest companies can be hit with a costly and inflexible mandate, then no business in Washington is immune to similar treatment. Supporters of "Fair Share" have said they view the requirement as a basic employment standard and that it should eventually be applied to all companies.

The proposal discourages new jobs. It creates a strong incentive for companies to maintain no more than 4,999 employees in Washington, and severely punishes successful companies that attempt to hire more workers.

Public health programs are not "corporate welfare"

Proponents of the "Fair Share" proposal say employers are receiving corporate welfare when their workers sign up for public health programs for which they are eligible.

Yet the state itself encourages people to participate in public health programs. For example, since the inception of the Basic Health Plan 20 years ago, it has been the express policy of Washington state to sign up as many working people as possible. It is illogical and contradictory to criticize employers when workers actually join a state plan for which they are legally eligible.

It is equally wrong to say that public health programs for working people are "corporate welfare." Corporate welfare is a special economic benefit or market protection that policymakers give directly to favored companies. Many working people live in public housing, receive food assistance and use subsidized transportation. These important social programs are not "corporate welfare" to the companies that give these workers jobs, and neither is broad-based subsidized health care.

Part of national labor union strategy

In January 2006, the Maryland legislature passed a "Fair Share" bill over Governor Ehrlich's veto. The Maryland bill applies to companies with 10,000 employees and imposes an eight percent payroll tax. A year later, the federal courts struck down the Maryland law as violating the Employee Retirement Income Security Act (ERISA).

The Washington "Fair Share" bill was similar to the Maryland bill, except that the payroll tax is higher and it applies to companies with half as many in-state employees. It is also similar to the "Pay or Play" legislation that died in the Washington legislature in 2005. That bill applied to companies with as few as fifty employees. Proponents say they plan to re-introduce both bills in future legislative sessions.

Proponents say they will continue to push the "Fair Share" bill in Olympia. Even if the bill is passed in Washington, however, it is likely that, like the similar proposal in Maryland, it would ultimately be struck down in federal court as a violation of the ERISA law.

Reducing artificial costs imposed by government

The "Fair Share" proposal's mandatory approach ignores the large artificial costs the state already imposes on the provision of health care coverage. The greatest barrier to health insurance is cost. State policies contribute significantly to the cost of health insurance. Such policies include state-imposed mandates, lack of basic health coverage and disincentives for purchasing Health Savings Accounts. Specific recommendations for reducing government-imposed health costs are presented in Chapter 4.

Recommendation

1) Do not impose a restrictive "Fair Share" health benefit mandate on the Washington labor market. The "Fair Share" approach does nothing to make health coverage more affordable, personal or portable. It is not only unfair to workers and employers, it moves our state in exactly the wrong direction in efforts to make health care more affordable.

Additional Resources from Washington Policy Center

"This Session, There's a Little Something for Everyone," by Carl Gipson, March 2008.

"24 Ways to Improve the State's Small Business Climate," by Carl Gipson, January 2008.

"Proposed Bill Would Unionize Foster Parents," by Paul Guppy, February 2008.

"Bill to Unionize Daycare Workers Violates the National Labor Relations Act," by Liv Finne, February 2008.

"Unionizing Daycare, Requiring Union Membership and Collective Bargaining in the Provision of State Subsidized Daycare Services," by Liv Finne, February 2008.

"A National Movement Hits Close to Home," by Carl Gipson, November 2007.

"The Living Wage Movement Comes to Washington State," by Carl Gipson, Policy Note 2007-23.

"An Overview of Washington's Emergency Heat Stress Rule," by Carl Gipson, Policy Note 2007-21.

"Limited Benefit Plans: A Proven Way to Help the Uninsured in Washington," by Dann Mead Smith, March 2007.

"Living Wage Proposals: Imposing Price Controls on Labor," by Carl Gipson, Legislative Memo, March 2007.

"The Revamped 'Fair Share Act' is Still Wrong in Principle and Practice," by Carl Gipson, Legislative Memo, February 2007.

"New Payroll Tax Proposed to Pay for New Entitlement: Paid Medical Leave Insurance Plan Would Tax All Workers for the Benefit of a Few," by Carl Gipson, January 2007.

"Legislature Poised to Roll Back Unemployment Reforms," by Carl Gipson, February 2006.

"Reviving Washington's Small Business Climate: Policy Recommendations from the 2005 Small Business Conferences," by Carl Gipson, January 2006.

"Mandatory Paid Sick Leave - Another Ailment for the Small Business Climate," by Carl Gipson, January 2006.

"'Fair Share' Bill is Unfair and Impractical," by Paul Guppy, January 2006.

"Small Business Owners Have Their Say," by Carl Gipson, January 2006.

"An Honor Washington Could Do Without -- Highest Minimum Wage in the Nation," by Carl Gipson, January 2005.

"When the Union Really Isn't Working for the Worker: New Collective Bargaining Agreement Includes Increase in Union Dues," by Daniel Mead Smith, January 2005.

"Reforming Washington's Workers' Compensation System," by Allison Demeritt, May 2004.

"Consumer, Not Corporate, 'Greed' is Ultimately Behind Layoffs," by Mark J. Perry, 2002.

---

[1] "2007-2009 Operating Budget Proposal – As Enacted," Office of Financial Management, http://www.leg.wa.gov/pub/billinfo/2007-08/Pdf/Bills/Session%20Law%202007/1128-S.SL.pdf.

[2] "2007 Year in Review, Statistics at a Glance," Washington State Workers' Compensation State Fund, Department of Labor and Industries, at http://www.lni.wa.gov/IPUB/200-013-000.pdf.

[3] Ibid.

[4] "Workers' Compensation – Benefits Paid," 2008 Competitiveness Redbook, WashACE, 2008.

[5] Data from Independent Business Association based on L&I payroll tax rate increases, December 2007.

[6] "Washington's 2008 minimum wage is $8.07 an hour," Workplace Rights, Department of Labor and Industries, January 2008, at www.lni.wa.gov/workplacerights/wages/minimum/default.asp.

[7] Regional Resources – Washington state, Labor Force Data, Bureau of Labor Statistics, United States Department of Labor, at http://www.bls.gov/ro9/ro9_wa.htm.

[8] Office of the Secretary of State, Index to Initiative History and Statistics, 1914 – 2003, Initiative No. 688, passed November 3, 1998, http://www.secstate.wa.gov/elections/initiatives/statistics_initiatives.aspx.

[9] "Distribution of Workers Affected by Proposed $7.00 [national] Minimum Wage," Minimum Wage Statistics, Employment Policies Institute, http://www.epionline.org/mw_statistics_state.cfm.

[10] See "A National Movement Hits Close to Home: The Living Wage Proposal in Washington State," by Carl Gipson, Washington Policy Center, November 2007.

[11] "Why Raising the Minimum Wage is a Poor Way to Help the Poor," by Dr. Richard Burkhauser and Dr. Joseph Sabia, (both of Cornell University), published by the Employment Policies Institute, July 2004, http://www.epionline.org/study_detail.cfm?sid=71.

[12] "Tips as Wages," Issue Brief 12/05, Washington Restaurant Association, December 2005, at www.wrahome.com/PDF%20files/12_05_Issues_Brief_tip_Credit.pdf.

[13] "Staffing Industry's Positive Role in U.S. Economy, Economic Benefits of Flexible Labor," by Edward A. Lenz, Issue Paper, American Staffing Association, March 4, 2008.

[14] Ibid.

[15] HB 2777, introduced by Rep. Mary Lou Dickerson, January 13, 2006. The companion bill in the Senate was SB 6592.

[16] "Washington State Employee Benefits Report," Washington State Employment Security Department, March 2008.

[17] See "Mandatory Paid Sick Leave – Another Ailment for the Small Business Climate," by Carl Gipson, Legislative Memo, Washington Policy Center, January 2006, at www.washingtonpolicy.org/SmallBusiness/LegMemoMandatorypaidsickleave.

[18] "Percent of Firms Offering Paid Leave to Full-Time Employees by Leave Type," Washington State Employee Benefits Report, Washington State Employment Security Department, Labor Market and Economic Analysis Branch, March 2008, page 10, at www.workforceexplorer.com/admin/uploadedPublications/8836_EB_2007_Report.pdf.

[19] Ibid.

[20] "Cost of Employee Benefits in Small and Large Business," United States Small Business Administration, Washington, D.C., August 2005.

[21] "National Small Business Poll: Family and Medical Leave," National Federation of Independent Business, Volume 4, Issue 2, 2004.

[22] HB 2517, "Requiring large businesses to pay a certain amount in health care coverage," sponsored by Representative Eileen Cody. The companion bill in the Senate was SB 6356.

CHAPTER 9

1. Cyber-Security and Identity Theft

Recommendations

1. Enhance privacy laws, based on consumer notice, consent and security, to limit how companies share sensitive customer information with outside organizations.

2. Keep burden on government, not citizens, to justify when private information must be shared.

3. More public education – state agencies should continue to work with federal agencies to identify areas of need for increased data security.

Background

As fast as electronic technology develops for legitimate and legal purposes, so too does technology intended for malicious reasons. As quickly as code writers produce software designed to enhance security, someone with criminal motives is seeking a way around it.

As the electronic economy develops, particularly in Washington, an increasing number of individuals and organizations rely on electronic and web-based means of storing and exchanging information. The privacy and security of this information is more important than ever.

Cyber-security affects virtually everyone in modern society, since sensitive financial and medical records are often stored in potentially vulnerable computer systems, and an increasing amount of shopping and other routine business takes place over the internet.

There are several types of cyber-threats that consumers face every time they turn on their computers, surf the internet or read their e-mail. The two most common are "phishing" and spyware (or adware).

"Phishing" is a type of computer fraud designed to steal a person's identity and other information by imitating legitimate organizations like banks or government agencies. Spyware is software secretly downloaded onto a computer for the purpose of tracking a user's passwords or account numbers as he or she navigates the internet.

Both "phishing" and "spyware" are symptoms of the broader crime of identity theft. Identity theft is quickly becoming a much larger threat to society in general, not just computer users. Information in our porous electronic and physical mail systems is not secure enough to defend against high-tech 21st century threats.

Washington ranked 8th in the nation in 2004 for identity theft – more than 5,600 residents reported they were victims, an increase of almost 20 percent from 2003. Fortunately, through increased awareness in the private and public sector, Washington, in 2008, now ranked 13th for identity theft.

Nationally, identity theft crimes cost U.S. consumers more than $49 billion a year.[1] More than eight million people were victimized, with financial losses averaging $5,720 per person.[2] While these losses are down compared to past years, the financial industry warns that careful vigilance by consumers is still needed.

Having ones identity and credit stolen goes beyond mere financial repercussions. Victims may be rejected for jobs, home mortgages, insurance policies or credit cards because someone else is using their personal information maliciously.

Guarding against identity theft is the focus of new state laws as well as recent criminal task forces. The state Attorney General's office formed an Identity Theft Advisory Panel in 2005 to ask citizens, businesses and government agencies about the best ways to fight identity crimes.

In 2005, the legislature passed a bill to strengthen law enforcement tools against spyware, phishing and identity theft.[3] This was followed up in the same year with two bills dealing with computer crime: House Bill 1966 and Senate Substitute Bill 5939. The first laid out general guidelines for prosecuting cases of identity theft. The second required that policy reports be given by request to victims of identity theft in order to facilitate fraud alerts and to clear fraudulent activity from victims' records.

The legislature felt more checks were needed on the consumer side and, in 2008, the legislature enacted Substitute Senate Bill 5826. This legislation dealt with a consumer's right to place a freeze on his personal credit information in order to prohibit a credit agency from furnishing the consumer's credit to a third-party, without prior authorization from the consumer.

The legislature also passed Second Substitute House Bill 1273, creating the Financial Fraud and Identity Theft Crimes Investigation and Prosecution Program as a part of the Department of Community, Trade and Economic Development. This unit will help monitor trends in identity theft and financial fraud crimes and will help coordinate investigatory and prosecutorial personnel dedicated to cracking down on these crimes.

Policy Analysis

In addition to tougher enforcement by the Attorney General's office and state law enforcement agencies, consumers themselves should become educated about changing security threats. Current defensive software can only do so much because new threats constantly emerge to subvert existing protections. A mix of public and private cooperation is necessary to address ever-present threats and to reduce the incidence of cyber-crime.

While steps have been taken to help curb identity theft over the past two years, most identity crime takes place off-line. People are much more likely to be victimized through what they throw into their trash cans or leave in an unsecured mailbox than through the internet. According to the Better Business Bureau, only 11 percent of known identity theft cases occurs online.[4] Low-tech dumpster diving and telephone fraud account for more thefts than internet-based fraud.

However, it is still important that private companies be encouraged to develop products that respond to today's threats. Consumer education is also important. A well-informed consumer is better equipped to avoid identity victimization than a consumer who relies solely on government regulation for protection.

Recommendations

1) Enhance privacy laws, based on consumer notice, consent and security, to limit how companies share sensitive customer information with outside organizations. Individual consumers who voluntarily give their private information to a company need to be informed about that company's policies regarding use of that information, and whether it will be given or sold to a third party.

2) Keep burden on government, not citizens, to justify when private information must be shared. Government has legitimate reasons to have limited and carefully defined access to information about private citizens, especially for law enforcement purposes. But the burden must remain on the government to show when such access is justified, not on citizens to explain why sensitive personal information should remain private.

3) More public education – state agencies should continue to work with federal agencies to identify areas of need for increased data security. Increasing the public's knowledge (both consumers and businesses) of the most vulnerable areas susceptible to identity theft will help stem crime. This also has the potential to save taxpayer money.

2. Access to Broadband

Recommendations

1. Freeze any increases in telecommunications and wireless taxes, or reduce taxes as necessary to foster growth.

2. City, state and local governments should refrain from operating a municipal broadband network – either wired or wireless.

3. Encourage market forces to expand broadband service wired or wireless, into rural areas.

4. Adopt a "hands-off" approach to regulating and taxing advances in the telecommunications and technology industries.

Background

The world marketplace is quickly evolving into a digitally-connected web of business and consumer communication. The technological infrastructure necessary to support and advance the emerging e-commerce engine is complex and expensive. Private companies that risk capital on expanding the reach of broadband technology will only do so if it makes economic sense.

Policymakers should be aware that heavily taxing and regulating an industry that depends on rapid innovation stifles the research and development high-tech companies are using to extend broadband access to more people. A heavy-handed taxation policy on e-commerce also drives away consumers – or causes them to seek services from alternative (and not always legal) vendors.

While the number of broadband internet connections grew rapidly from 2005 to 2006, the United States overall ranks low on broadband penetration compared to other industrialized nations. The U.S. led the world in broadband penetration as recently as 2000, but since then we have fallen to 15th place worldwide.

A broadband connection provides a computer user with convenient high-speed service when using the internet, usually through a dedicated line. This is opposed to a much slower dial-up connection, which uses an existing telephone line to connect the user to the internet.

The U.S. also runs behind in the speed of the average broadband connection. Despite this slower relative growth, 84 million Americans, or 47 percent of the population, have broadband at home. Large numbers of households skipped the dial-up modem age and went straight to a high-speed internet connection.[5]

Policy Analysis

Counterproductive federal, state and local tax and regulatory policies hamper new investment in broadband and wireless infrastructure.[6] In some parts of Washington, publicly-subsidized ventures, like Tacoma's Click! Network, are undercutting private service providers and driving away future investment. Click! received millions of dollars in public subsidies, and yet it has never fulfilled its original promises to the taxpayers of Tacoma.[7]

Overall, communication services in Washington face a higher level of taxation than the purchase of most other goods or services. By one estimate, telecommunication companies pay an average of 39 percent more in taxes than other industries.[8] In Washington, for example, telecommunication consumers pay well over half a billion dollars a year in taxes.[9]

The Beacon Hill Institute and the Tax Foundation found that Washington's average wireless tax rate is just over 18 percent, more than twice the highest combined state and local sales tax rate in any U.S. city or county.[10] Similarly, the tax analysts of the journal *State Tax Notes* rank Washington as having the second highest combined wireless taxes and fees in the nation – or about 150 percent higher than the national average.[11]

Reducing the tax burden on telecommunications customers would lower a major barrier to broadband access for rural residents and smaller businesses. It would result in greater consumer fairness. Currently, when a customer signs up for a wireless or broadband connection, a large number of state and local taxes are imposed through monthly billing.

Unlike state and local sales taxes, these fees are not widely known and therefore consumers are generally unable to take into account these added costs prior to purchasing the service.

Expanding broadband to rural areas

Rural Washington lags behind the rest of the state in access to broadband internet connections, largely because of the higher cost of outlying networks. Building fiber optic pipelines from urban or suburban transmission stations to rural communities is extremely expensive and time consuming, compared to the number of new customers reached.

Several telecommunication companies are undertaking extensive broadband buildouts, but other companies are circumnavigating the physical limitations of laying new pipe or using existing telephone and power lines by using the emerging technology of Wireless Fidelity Internet protocol (Wi-Fi).

Wi-Fi connections already exist in thousands of homes and businesses in Washington, but they are mostly short-range connections. A Wi-Fi user has to be within at least 150 to 300 feet of the nearest wired connection.

Some cities have tried establishing public, city-wide Wi-Fi systems to provide free wireless broadband service for residents. Large cities such as San Francisco and Philadelphia, and smaller ones such as St. Cloud, Florida, and Spokane have tried these systems with limited success. Many times the government's feasibility studies on subscription rates and capital costs turn out to be wrong, predicting much rosier results than the actual outcome, and causing entire networks to shut down or be sold at a loss to a private operator.

Two policy considerations are key to establishing workable rural Wi-Fi connections for citizens. First, as seen time and again with new technology, it is essential that private companies initiate Wi-Fi service instead of a government-run, taxpayer subsidized system. The discipline of the market prevents private companies from becoming entrenched, or a politically-protected agency which continues spending public money whether or not it is accomplishing its purpose. Once a public agency gets established, it quickly focuses more on preserving government jobs than on serving the public.

Several companies are marketing themselves as Wireless Internet Service Providers (WISPs) and buying up available spectrum to carry wireless internet signals. Private companies are also using a newer technology, Worldwide Interoperability for Microwave Access (WiMAX), which will cover a much larger area that a Wi-Fi signal.

A WiMax signal can cover about 20 square miles. Wireless companies are also tapping into radio spectrum to roll out mobile internet devices on their growing system – technologies such as 3G, 4G, LTE (Long Term Evolution), HSDPA (High-Speed Downlink Packet Access) or UMTS (Universal Mobile Telecommunications System).

Policymakers should recognize that there exists sufficient competition among private companies to provide ample and affordable internet access. Municipal governments should resist the urge to jump into the market. History is strewn with examples of governments investing in outdated technology, or blowing project budgets and taking from the taxpayers' pockets to cover cost overruns, as Tacoma's Click! Network has done.

There is no lack of adoption by the general public of these new improvements in telecommunications. It took more than 90 years for landline service to reach 100 million consumers. It took over 21 years for 100 million consumers to buy a color television. But it took less than 17 years for wireless phones to reach 100 million consumers.

As new technological improvements, such as VoIP, which allows affordable phone service over the internet, bolster the telecommunications industry, government should approach the technology with a light regulatory hand. The immense proliferation of wireless technology is testament to the landmark 1996 federal Telecommunications Act, which left the wireless industry largely unregulated.

The benefits of this wise policy can be seen in the fact that the U.S. has over 255 million wireless subscribers, with an 84 percent penetration rate, and that wireless-only households (homes that do not have a traditional wireline telephone) jumped from 8.4 percent in 2005 to almost 14 percent in 2007.[12]

Recommendations

1) Freeze or reduce taxes on telecommunication services. Telecommunications services are highly taxed, and often the taxes are passed off as "fees," because over the years state and federal legislators have found this to be a convenient revenue source. In an era of rapidly-growing technology, however, the high tax burden runs the risk of stifling innovation and slowing affordable access to broadband for citizens.

Freezing or lowering the telecommunication tax burden would directly benefit current and future broadband users, and would contribute to the prosperity of Washington and the nation.

2) City, state and local governments should refrain from operating a municipal broadband network – either wired or wireless. Government can play an important, indeed a vital, role in fostering an effective local telecommunications market, but owner and market competitor is not one of them. Running a sophisticated telecommunications and cable service is simply not a core function of government, and policymakers should allow private companies to build and operate these services.

3) Encourage market forces to expand broadband service, wired or wireless into rural areas. Advanced technology and communications systems continue to expand the ability of rural small businesses to compete with businesses located in urban areas. Integral to the continued growth of rural businesses is the further expansion of affordable broadband access—wired and/or wireless. Policymakers, both state and federal, should take steps to reduce the regulatory barriers to building broadband access to rural communities.

4) Adopt a "hands-off" approach to regulating and taxing advances in the telecommunications and technology industries. The state government should adopt a policy of limiting regulations on communication technologies, like Voice over Internet Protocol (VoIP), which evolve at breakneck speed and offer numerous benefits to consumers and businesses.

3. Teleworking and Telecommuting

Recommendation

1. State government should evaluate the need for increased telework options for state workers thereby establishing a "best practices" approach to teleworking.

Background

The internet age has transformed many parts of our state's economy. As companies continue to improve the data speeds of networks that reach beyond a business or government, such as homes and schools, employees are increasingly able to seek out new and improved ways of doing their work from remote locations, while relying on broadband internet networks to stay connected to their co-workers and managers.

Teleworking, also referred to as telecommuting, is not new. However, employees of both the public and private sector have new and improved tools, like faster and less expensive laptops, wireless fidelity networks, broadband cellular systems, and virtual private network hookups, in order to work more efficiently from any place that has networking capability.

While teleworking is not for everyone – there will always be certain types of jobs that require an office presence – both businesses and government should re-evaluate their needs in regard to employee location and management practices, and consider the benefits of a teleworking policy.

State government has the opportunity to set a "best practices" approach by increasing teleworking for state employees as part of the Commute Trip Reduction Program, a program that emphasizes carpools and vanpools, and other methods of commuting.

Policy Analysis

There are many benefits to increasing both public and private sector teleworking, ranging from increased employee satisfaction and retention, to higher productivity levels. But human resources benefits aside, there are also important public policy benefits.

First is the potential for decreased traffic congestion. The Puget Sound region has notoriously bad traffic, and congestion relief is no longer a top priority for state transportation officials (see Chapter 10 for more details).

As commutes get longer in both duration and distance, teleworking can provide an important alternative. A 2006 University of Maryland study found that nearly half of all commuters travel more than 20 miles a day to and from work, 22 percent travel more than 40 miles, and 10 percent travel more than 60 miles.[13]

The other area where increased teleworking can have an important impact is on the environment. Removing thousands of Washington commuters from the highways would conserve fuel and reduce CO2 emissions.

The same University of Maryland study found that 1.35 billion gallons of fuel worth $4.5 billion (at $3.33 a gallon) could be saved if everyone with the potential to telework did so just 1.6 days per week (as of this writing, the AAA estimates a gallon of gas for Washington drivers is approximately $3.86). Similarly, the Environmental Protection Agency calculates that this much saved fuel would prevent 26 billion pounds of carbon dioxide from being released.

The federal government took up the issue of increasing teleworking options for its workers a number of years ago. Several bills have been introduced to implement programs in federal agencies in order to facilitate increased teleworking. In the wake of the attacks on September 11, 2001, the federal government recognized that teleworking has an added security benefit. It helps the government continue to function if it has to resort to its contingency plans.

The state of Washington employs approximately 110,000 workers, and while it is not possible for all state workers to telecommute, state government should set up systems that allow for more public employees to telework. In addition to its own merits, this policy would set an important example for private employers.

Recommendation

1) State government should evaluate the need for increased telework options for state workers; thereby establishing a "best practices" approach to teleworking. The state government has an opportunity to implement programs that private sector businesses could emulate in order to increase telework options for their employees – thereby helping reduce traffic congestion and encourage energy savings.

4. High-Tech Education

Recommendations

1. Encourage scholastic achievement in the areas of science, technology and mathematics.

2. Retool the education system to better prepare students for careers in engineering, science and technology.

3. Increase infrastructure investment in higher education geared toward science, engineering and mathematics.

Background

Advanced technological innovations and inventions throughout the 20th century established America, and particularly Washington, as a key leader in high-tech industries. Rising to the top of the technology industry was difficult, but remaining at the top is equally so.

Other countries have greatly increased the number of their students graduating with degrees in science, technology, engineering and mathematics. These countries are already attracting a significant number of jobs from multinational corporations. Certain sectors in high-tech industry are beginning to move from the United States to nations that have a more readily available and highly educated workforce. In the process they are taking valuable research and development investments away with them.

Policy Analysis

Our economy is based on a highly educated and productive workforce that is adaptable to emerging technological sectors and is motivated to spur technological innovations. But the innovation of our entrepreneurs can only be sustained to the extent that our private and public institutions invest in the infrastructure that produced such entrepreneurs in the first place.

Maintaining major technical innovation requires a sufficient number of graduates with Ph.D. level degrees in science, technology, engineering and math (called STEM). Yet each year fewer American students focus on STEM subjects at advanced levels.

In 1987, 4,700 Ph.D. degrees were awarded to American citizens, while 5,600 Asian citizens were awarded Ph.D. degrees. By 2001, only 4,400 Ph.D. degrees were awarded to Americans, while 24,900 Asian citizens received Ph.D. degrees.[14] At a time when the number of American students receiving Ph.D. degrees declined, the number earned in Asian countries jumped by a factor of five.

The United States is also awarding fewer engineering degrees as a percentage of all undergraduate degrees than other countries. The following table shows the number of engineering degrees awarded in the United States compared to those awarded in other parts of the world.

Worldwide Engineering Degrees Awarded **Select Countries/Regions** *(in thousands)*		
	Engineering degrees	Engineering degrees as % of all degrees
China	351.5	28%
European Union	198.3	16%
Japan	98.4	8%
Russia	82.4	7%
India	82.1	7%
South Korea	64.9	5%
United States	60.6	5%
Mexico	44.7	4%
Taiwan	41.9	3%
Brazil	25.3	2%

Source: U.S. National Science Foundation

Most European countries also award a higher percentage of degrees in STEM subjects than the United States, led by Germany with 31 percent of bachelor degrees awarded in engineering and science.[15] The U.S. awarded only five percent of its bachelor degrees in engineering and science.

Recommendations

1) Encourage scholastic achievement in the areas of science, technology, and mathematics. Too many students enter college with an interest in engineering, science or technology but drop out or change the focus of their majors. Colleges and university leaders should use contracting out and other efficiencies to reduce tuition costs and increase academic opportunities for science and technology students.

2) Re-tool the education system to better prepare students for careers in engineering, science and technology. The average time to obtain a Ph.D. is at its greatest length ever, just over seven years. The higher education system should be re-tooled to help Ph.D. students in engineering, mathematics, science and technology leave school in a reasonable time and begin their professional careers.

3) Increase infrastructure investment in higher education geared towards science, engineering and mathematics. Policymakers should take steps to encourage our institutions of higher learning to attract more U.S. students to graduate in the areas of science, mathematics and engineering, as well as seek to retain the talents of non-U.S. citizens upon their graduation.

5. Ending Cable Monopolies

Recommendations

1. Deregulate cable franchises to increase choice and lower prices for local customers.

2. End outdated local cable monopolies in favor of statewide franchises that allow more choice for consumers.

Background

New telecommunication technology is making it possible for consumers to buy cable programming from alternate sources, like telecom companies and internet providers, but government regulators insist on maintaining outdated local cable monopolies.

In the 1970s, building a cable network from scratch was expensive and risky. It made sense for local governments to use the "natural monopoly" model to get the new technology established. Like mail delivery or early phone companies, the government offered cable providers insulation from competition in return for offering universal service.

The local cable company strung wires and installed a T.V. box for any homeowner who asked for it. The customer paid a set price and local officials collected taxes and franchise fees. As a result, cable service became widely available and cable companies earned a secure return on the huge capital investment they had made while building the network.

The cost of cable television and broadband internet access is also heavily influenced by local franchise fees. The fees are imposed on private cable operators by local governments in exchange for allowing the cable operators to service the city or county's cable customers. Between 1996 and 2007, nationwide franchise fees rose from $1.4 billion to $3 billion per year, leaving the average customer paying $46 per year just to cover the franchise fee.[16]

Cable companies are increasingly required to pay higher local taxes and franchise fees, and to give valuable channels to local governments for free. Sometimes cable companies are even made to deposit lump sum payments directly into city treasuries just to continue in business. Cable companies have no choice but to pass higher tax and franchise costs on to their customers. This is one reason cable prices have risen three times the rate of inflation for the past decade.

Policy Analysis

After nearly four decades, local monopoly cable no longer makes sense. Cable companies still provide universal service, but for municipal officials the original purpose of serving the customer has been lost. They now see the local cable company as just another lucrative revenue source, especially from high franchise fees. As the years pass, local government officials tend to squeeze this reliable money source harder.

In recent decades, the deregulation of airlines, trucking, railroads, banking and telecommunications has unleashed an explosion of innovation and choice for consumers that has made the U.S. economy the most dynamic in the world. The internet has succeeded spectacularly because government officials avoided smothering it with arbitrary rules and red tape. The government's hands-off approach means that ideas and investment flow where they are needed most, and because of it America is at the forefront of an unprecedented digital revolution.

The same dynamic will work for cable. New technologies make possible a range of programs, services and low prices that were unimagined in the past.

If full deregulation is too radical a change, policymakers should at least allow cable providers to compete within a statewide franchise, as several other states have done, so local customers would have a greater range of affordable services choices.

Recommendations

1) Deregulate cable franchises to increase choice and lower prices for local customers. Policymakers should build on the success of freeing up other business sectors and similarly deregulate local franchises, to allow cable businesses to set prices and compete against other communications providers in a normally-functioning marketplace. As a mature technology, cable has much to offer homeowners and business, and it is in a good position to compete in the telecommunications market.

2) End outdated local cable monopolies in favor of statewide franchises that allow more choice for consumers. Short of full deregulation, policymakers should allow a statewide franchise in cable services. Several states have already taken steps to implement a statewide franchise system.　 Washington should take the same approach, so consumers can more easily gain access to emerging technologies.

6. Technology and Government Transparency

Recommendation

1. County and local officials should follow the state government's example and create a free, searchable website of pubic spending.

Background

At some point most citizens wonder, "Just how, when and where does government spend our tax dollars? What do our elected representatives want to accomplish when they spend public money, and what results are actually achieved?"

Citizens of Washington will soon have the opportunity to answer these questions. In 2008, Washington lawmakers passed SB 6818, which was based on Washington Policy Center's recommendation that the state create a free, searchable budget website.[17] Governor Gregoire signed the "Promoting Transparency in State Expenditures" act into law in April 2008.[18]

The new law creates a free, easy-to-use, search-engine-type website that allows citizens to track the recipients of all state funds. The privacy of individuals is protected. Already, the state's Department of General Administration has created a searchable website showing its public contracts. The new statewide version will build upon the existing General Administration website. The expanded website is scheduled to begin service on January 1, 2009.

The provisions of SB 6818 are modeled on federal legislation passed by Congress in 2006. The "Federal Funding Accountability and Transparency Act" (FFATA) directs the Office of Management and Budget to lead the development of a single searchable website of federal spending that is accessible by the public for free.[19] In addition, Texas, Missouri and a number of other states have created websites showing the public how state money is spent.

Policy Analysis

The purpose of both the federal website and the new Washington site is to provide the public with information about how lawmakers distribute money. Citizens have a right and need to understand where their tax dollars go and who is benefiting from public spending. Collecting data about the various types of government contracts, grants and loans provides a broad picture and much needed transparency about the government spending process.

The ability to review contracts, grants, loans and other types of spending across many agencies, in great detail, would help build public trust in local government. As at the state level, it would help local officials explain not only how money is spent, but when they feel additional revenue is needed to fund public services.

When local officials say they are facing a budget shortfall and that new taxes are needed, the public and the news media could use the transparency website to confirm that officials are presenting an accurate financial picture. The website would also allow independent researchers to identify and highlight to policymakers where overspending and waste is in the budget, so that in many cases no tax increase would be necessary.

Lawmakers in county and local government have the opportunity to tap into the wealth of information created by these searchable websites. The software technology already exists and the added cost of setting up such a website is minimal, while the cost of daily operation is close to zero. High-tech companies like Microsoft and Google have expressed interest in helping set up such sites, at little or no cost to the public.

The benefit of using internet technology to communicate with the public is a win-win for everyone concerned with improving the budget process and increasing spending transparency at all levels of government.

Recommendation

1) County and local officials should follow the state government's example and create a free, searchable website of pubic spending. A free, searchable budget transparency website would not cure all local budget problems, but it would go a long way toward preventing waste and improving government performance. State lawmakers have the opportunity to help publicize the merits of such a program to local governments within the state.

Additional Resources from Washington Policy Center

"Communications Policy Guide, Release 2.0," by Washington Policy Center and Institute for Policy Innovation, December 2007.

"RFID (Radio Frequency Identification): Balancing Technology and Privacy," by Carl Gipson, February 2008.

"Leaving Well Enough Alone: State Wireless Regulations Could Harm Consumers," by Carl Gipson, December 2007.

"It's Time to Modernize Our State's Ma Bell-Era Telecom Laws," by Carl Gipson, February 2007.

"Better Prices and Better Services for More People; Assessing the Outcomes of Video Franchise Reform," by Steven Titch, January 2007.

"Reform Video Franchises for Cheaper, More Competitive TV Services," by Steven Titch and Carl Gipson, January 2007.

"Bring the Competition Revolution to Cable T.V.," by Paul Guppy, April 2006.

"We Won – So Let's Repeal the Spanish-American War Tax," by Paul Guppy, Policy Note 2006-03.

"A New Way to Make a Phone Call," by Paul Guppy, May 2004.

"It's Time for Consumer Choice in Local Phone Service," by Paul Guppy, 2002.

"When Government Enters the Telecommunications Market: An Assessment of Tacoma's Click! Network," by Paul Guppy, June 2001.

---

[1] "2007 Identity Fraud Survey Report, Identity Fraud Dropping, Continued Vigilance Necessary," by Mary T. Monahan, Javelin Research and Strategy, February 2007, at http://www.privacyrights.org/ar/idtheftsurveys.htm.
[2] Ibid.
[3] ESHB 1012, "Regulating computer software," sponsored by Representative Jeff Morris, enacted May 17, 2005, Title 19, Revised Code of Washington, text at www.apps.leg.wa.gov/billinfo/summary.aspx?bill=1012&year=2005.

[4] "ID theft: The real risk, Internet hackers stealing info make headlines, but most ID theft happens in the low-tech world, CNNMoney.com, March 22, 2005, data based on a Better Business Bureau telephone survey of 4,000 consumers, at www.money.cnn.com/2005/03/22/technology/personaltech/id_theft/index.htm.

[5] "Why it will Be Hard to Close the Broadband Divide," by John B. Horrigan, Pew Internet & American Life Project, August 2007, at www.pewinternet.org, accessed May 7, 2008.

[6] "Leaving Well Enough Alone: State Wireless Regulations Could Harm Consumers," by Carl Gipson and Trevor Cross, Washington Policy Center, Policy Note 2007-27, 2007.

[7] See "When Government Enters the Telecommunications Market, An Assessment of Tacoma's Click! Network," by Paul Guppy, Washington Policy Center Policy Brief, June 2001, at www.washingtonpolicy.org.

[8] "Telecommunications Taxes: 50-state Estimates of Excess State and Local Tax Burden," by Robert Cline, *State Tax Notes*, June 3, 2002, pages 931–47.

[9] Ibid.

[10] "Taxes and Fees on Communications Services," David Tuerck, Paul Bachman, Steven Titch, and John Rutledge, *Policy Studies*, The Heartland Institute and Beacon Hill Institute, May 31 2007, at www.heartland.org/article.cfm?artId=21102.

[11] Cited in "50-State Study and Report on Telecommunications Taxation," by Scott Mackey, Kimbell Sherman Ellis LLP, Committee on State Taxation, September 2007.

[12] "Wireless Quick Facts," CTIA, the International Association for the Wireless Telecommunications Industry, at www.ctia.org/advocacy/research/index.cfm/AID/10323, accessed May 20, 2008.

[13] "Telework in the Information Age: Building a More Flexible Workforce and a Cleaner Environment," by Matthew Kazmierczak and Josh James, The AeA Competitiveness Series, American Electronics Association, Volume 21, April 2008.

[14] "Sustaining the Nation's Innovation Ecosystem: Maintaining the Strength of Our Science and Engineering Capabilities," report of the President's Council of Advisors on Science and Technology, Washington, D.C., June 2004, available at www.ostp.gov/cs/home.

[15] Ibid.

[16] "Cable Industry Statistics," National Cable and Telecommunications Association, at www.ncta.com/Statistic/Statistic/Statistics.aspx, accessed May 12, 2008.

[17] See "Creating a Free, Searchable Website of State Spending," by Jason Mercier, Washington Policy Center, Policy Note 2007-25, December 2007, at www.washingtonpolicy.org/Centers/government/policynotes/07_mercier_statespe ndingwebsite.html.

[18] SB 6818, signed April 1, 2008, for details see www.washingtonvotes.org.

[19] See "Delivering Transparency in Government, Search Portal," FFATA Information Center, at www.ffata.org/ffata/.

CHAPTER 10

1. Transformation Spending

> **Recommendations**
>
> 1. Implement performance measures that tie spending to congestion relief.
>
> 2. Implement performance audit recommendations by State Auditor investigations.
>
> 3. End the practice of the state charging itself sales tax for transportation projects.
>
> 4. Save 15 percent on transportation projects by using market-based labor pricing, rather than the artificially-inflated prevailing wage system.

Background

Over the last 20 years, Washington's population has increased almost 40 percent, yet the state road network has not kept pace.

The basic highway system was planned in the 1950s and largely built in the 1960s. Since then, only parts of Interstate 90, the Tacoma Narrows Bridge and Interstate 405 serving Seattle and its suburbs have received large increases in carrying capacity.

Yet Washingtonians are paying more than ever to fund the transportation budget. The following bar chart shows that total transportation taxes and fees have risen significantly over the last ten years.

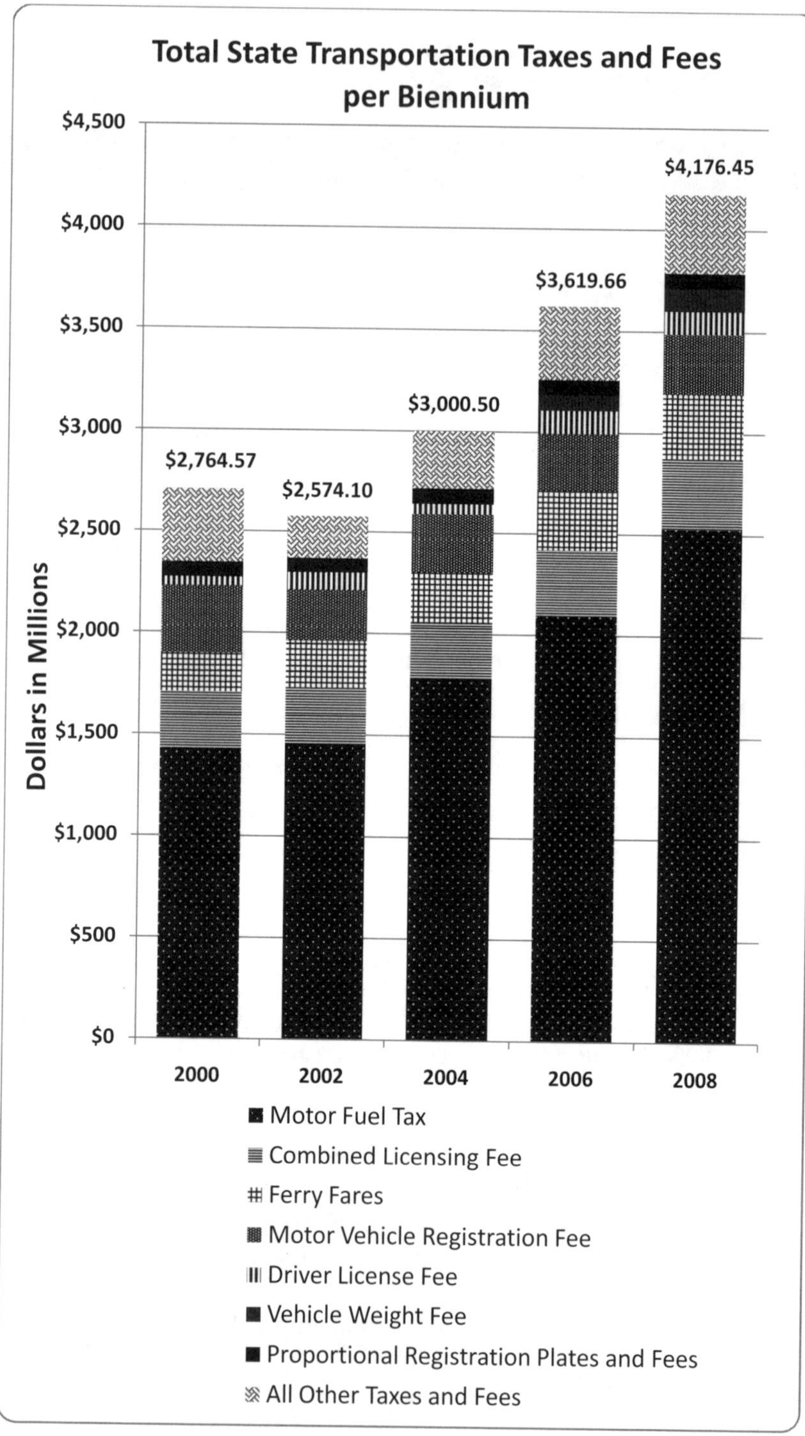

Total State Transportation Taxes and Fees per Biennium
Dollars in Millions
$4,500
$4,000
$3,500
$3,000
$2,500
$2,000
$1,500
$1,000
$500
$0
$2,764.57
$2,574.10
$3,000.50
$3,619.66
$4,176.45
2000
2002
2004
2006
2008
Motor Fuel Tax
Combined Licensing Fee
Ferry Fares
Motor Vehicle Registration Fee
Driver License Fee
Vehicle Weight Fee
Proportional Registration Plates and Fees
All Other Taxes and Fees

In the 1999-2001 biennium, Washington residents paid $2.65 billion in state taxes and fees to fund transportation.[1] In the current biennium residents paid about $4.18 billion, a 51.2 percent increase in the past ten years.[2] To put this in perspective, inflation over the same time period rose only 20 percent.[3]

These figures do not include local or special district transportation related taxes or fees. For example, families living in the Sound Transit taxing district in Pierce, King and Snohomish County pay substantially more.

Even so, the Puget Sound region has become one of the most congested metro areas in the nation. Other major traffic corridors around the state have received very slight capacity improvements at best, offering little relief to the state's 4.6 million drivers. Projections show the state population will grow by an additional 1.2 million people over the next twenty years, so under current transportation policies, traffic congestion can be expected to get significantly worse.

Policy Analysis

Congestion relief is the most basic tenet in any transportation program because it provides freedom of mobility for the public, yet most people are surprised to learn it is no longer a priority in Washington state.

In 2000, Washington's Blue Ribbon Commission on Transportation identified several benchmarks to measure the effectiveness of the state's transportation system. These performance measures were very specific and some of them were adopted into law. They include:

- Traffic congestion on urban state highways shall be significantly reduced and be no worse than the national mean;

- Delay per driver shall be significantly reduced and no worse than the national mean.

However, during the 2007 legislative session, lawmakers passed Senate Bill 5412, which repealed these precise benchmarks.

Instead, the legislature substituted five broader policy goals: Preservation, Safety, Mobility, Environment and Stewardship.[4]

Likewise, the spending strategy for transportation taxes is defined in the Washington Transportation Plan 2007-2026.[5] This document, created by the Washington State Transportation Commission (WTC) and the Washington State Department of Transportation (WSDOT), identifies five "Investment Guidelines" to help prioritize spending tax dollars in transportation.

The five priorities are nearly identical to the five goals set by Senate Bill 5412:

1. Preservation;
2. Safety;
3. Economic Vitality;
4. Mobility;
5. Environmental Quality and Health.

In both cases, Mobility should mean traffic congestion relief, but instead state officials define it as a strategy to move *people,* rather than improving vehicle flows. This means officials have shifted their spending priorities from actually fixing traffic congestion to trying to provide alternatives to congestion.

In other words, according to the Washington Transportation Plan, relieving traffic congestion is not an "Investment Guideline" in determining how transportation money is spent. Instead, the plan says policymakers should spend money on other forms of transportation, like buses or light rail operated by government agencies.

Ironically, this spending strategy will always lead to greater traffic congestion.

According to the Federal Highway Administration, private passenger vehicles account for about 85 percent of all forms of transportation in the Seattle region.[6] This means all other modes, like mass transit, bicycles and walking, serve only 15 percent of travelers.[7]

Adopting a policy that disproportionately spends public money on only 15 percent of the market will always lead to greater congestion, because the system that supports the remaining 85 percent is left to languish.

Initiative 900, which passed in November 2005, gave the State Auditor's Office authority to conduct performance audits of state agencies. Since then, the Auditor's office has conducted five audits of the Washington State Department of Transportation and identified nearly $300 million in redundant and inefficient services. In one audit, the Auditor concluded that

> "The Washington State Legislature should choose/identify projects based on congestion reduction rather than other agendas."[8]

Strengthening the tie between spending and traffic relief does not sacrifice public safety or preservation. These are not competing priorities. Traffic relief and safety/preservation can happen simultaneously, as long as regional leaders stop spending money in areas that do not relieve congestion. Washington policymakers should return to these specific performance measures and create a stronger link between spending and traffic relief.

Failed programs and cost overruns have severely harmed the Puget Sound region's transportation system, primarily by absorbing funding that would otherwise be available for improving road capacity. The defunct Seattle Monorail, which cost taxpayers over $100 million and served no purpose whatsoever, is an excellent example.

On an even larger scale, Sound Transit will spend more than $15 billion initially, to move a tiny fraction of the people who travel every day, yet all this money will do nothing to improve safety or relieve congestion on the region's existing highways.

Planning a transportation system that meets the needs of Washington residents requires strong leadership and a renewed insistence on results over process. Policymakers should recapture the vision of a transportation system based on freedom of movement. Key to realizing this vision is reducing structural barriers that artificially drive up the cost of building major transportation projects.

A prime example of high structural costs is the state's use of the expensive and antiquated prevailing wage system to pay for public construction. Prevailing wage is supposed to be the wage paid to the majority of workers in the applicable trade. In practice, though, the rate used is not the true market wage, but is the going union rate for the largest city in the region, usually Seattle. The effect of this interpretation is to reverse the meaning of the term "prevailing wage."

Currently the federal government and 33 states, including Washington, impose prevailing wage requirements on public construction projects. Ten states have abolished their prevailing wage laws, and reaped significant public benefits as a result.[9] To cite just one example, Florida lawmakers found they saved 15 percent on public projects once their state's inflationary prevailing wage law was repealed.[10]

Open market forces and transparent pricing determine the true prevailing price of labor, not a predetermined, government-fixed price. By interfering in the natural function of the labor market, the government artificially drives up how much it must pay to build and maintain the public road network.

Recommendations

1) Implement performance measures that tie spending to congestion relief. The legislature should require state and local transportation departments and special districts (like Sound Transit and the Regional Transportation Investment District) to reduce overall congestion by 50 percent in 25 years. Policymakers should also require annual audits from the State Auditor on the performance of state and local transportation officials to measure their progress, if any, in meeting the 50 percent reduction target.

2) Implement performance audit program improvements recommended by State Auditor investigations. Through the auditing process, the State Auditor has already identified about $300 million in cost savings by finding efficiencies and eliminating duplicitous services and waste. State Department of Transportation officials and the legislature should implement these money-saving recommendations.

3) End the practice of the state charging itself sales tax for transportation projects. The state's current practice of charging sales tax on transportation design and construction is simply a device for cycling money out of the transportation budget and into the General Fund budget. Ending this practice would increase the funding available for road improvements and traffic relief. The state's own projects should be tax exempt, so that all funds raised through dedicated transportation taxes can be used in the way they were intended: improving mobility for citizens.

4) Save 15 percent on transportation projects by using market-based labor pricing, rather than the artificially-inflated prevailing wage system. Built-in waste like the prevailing wage system makes it difficult for elected leaders to ask the public in good faith to pay more in taxes for needed transportation projects. Using competitive market wages would stretch limited transportation dollars and show respect for the financial sacrifice people make when paying for public roads.

2. Freedom of Mobility

Recommendations

1. Respect people's choices and allow for a greater freedom of mobility by actively working to *reduce* traffic congestion.

2. Reduce spending on costly and ineffective fixed-route mass transit.

3. Increase general purpose lane capacity and focus on relieving traffic chokepoints.

Background

Government serves society, not the other way around. Policies that force citizens to behave differently than they normally would disregard the natural marketplace and ultimately threaten to take away political freedom from citizens.

Similarly, government policies in transportation should be responsive to the market and improve the freedom of citizens to live, play and work where they choose.

Manipulating transportation policies to force a particular behavior coerces people into abandoning their individual liberties in favor of a socialistic benefit where supposedly a greater collective good is created.

These measures always fail because of what Milton Friedman called, "one of the strongest and most creative forces known to man," rational self interest; or people's desire to do what they believe is best for their own lives.

Instead, proponents of social change should work in the marketplace of ideas to persuade others to share their vision and work towards it. They should not use the power of government to force through their own ideas, but should seek to change policy, if that is needed, once reform is broadly supported by the public.

Trying to force people from their cars is not the proper role of government, and voters in the Puget Sound region confirmed this view with their firm rejection of the Roads and Transit measure (Proposition 1) in November 2007. The package favored spending on mass transit by a margin of three to one, and traffic congestion would still have doubled even if it passed. Wisely, voters decided to save their money for a plan that would actually reduce traffic congestion.

The state has a monopoly on our road system. As such, government leaders have agreed to provide its citizens with a certain level of service, or a freedom of mobility. Using traffic congestion as a tool rather than fixing it, is an attempt at social engineering that is sure to fail.

Policy Analysis

In a dual effort to manage congestion and reduce $CO2$ emission, the state's Climate Advisory Team (CAT) proposed reduction targets on the amount of per capita Vehicle Miles Traveled (VMT). The targets include a VMT reduction of 18 percent by 2020, 30 percent by 2035, and 50 percent by 2050.[11]

In 2004, each licensed driver in Washington drove his car about 12,555 miles. Transportation department officials project that, in 2020, each driver will drive about 13,500 miles annually. According to the CAT, an 18 percent reduction in VMT by 2020 means a Washington driver would be limited to only 11,070 miles per year, or about the same level that person drove in 1985.[12]

House Bill 2815 adopted these recommendations. It requires the Department of Ecology to report to the legislature by December 2008, after the general election, on recommended tools it needs to meet the targets. These recommendations will likely take a "carrot and stick" approach, by creating severe economic disincentives for drivers, while using their money to subsidize the use of public transit.

This type of policy strategy seeks to force drivers out of their cars and into transportation modes operated by public agencies. But restricting mobility in one mode for the benefit of another will always fail because it does not respect the choices of people to do what is best for them.

Instead of forcing behavior changes by limiting mobility through top-down social engineering, a more realistic way to reduce congestion and CO_2 emissions is to remove barriers to better technology that will improve fuel efficiency. Also, as mentioned, policymakers should make congestion relief a top priority, since cars sitting in traffic emit more CO_2. Ultimately, cars are part of the solution, not the problem.

Recommendations

1) Respect people's choices and allow for a greater freedom of mobility by actively working to *reduce* traffic congestion. Officials should adopt a policy that places congestion relief ahead of other spending considerations. Restrictions on Vehicle Miles Traveled (VMT) and deliberately or passively increasing traffic congestion to force people out of their cars should be avoided.

2) Reduce spending on costly, ineffective fixed-route mass transit. Policymakers should change spending priorities that heavily favor mass transit systems despite chronically low ridership. Riders of these expensive systems, like light rail and the Sounder Commuter Train, are being heavily subsidized by automobile commuters, yet research shows that fixed rail does nothing to reduce traffic congestion.

3) Increase general purpose lane capacity while focusing on fixing chokepoints. Focusing transportation funding on key chokepoints by adding general purpose lane miles will help move the most people at the least cost and least impact on the environment.

3. Transportation Spending Based on Market Demand

Recommendations

1. Use consumer demand to prioritize projects and spending.

2. Adopt a policy of fixing chokepoints and strategic increases in road capacity as the most effective ways to end traffic gridlock and allow citizens more freedom of movement.

Background

Transportation resources should be distributed based on natural market demand, rather than the current system of spending on services that are somehow meant to attract demand.

In economics, supply is a function of demand. This means a willingness to use a service must exist before a supply of that service is created. Boeing executives do not make 300 airplanes knowing they will only sell 100. Likewise, governments should not spend a disproportionate amount of taxes in low demand sectors, where the public's willingness to use the service does not justify the spending.

In any market, increasing the supply of a service or product before demand is available is wasteful and creates a large space between costs and benefits.

In the private sector, where benefits are measured by consumer choices, this type of inefficient behavior is unsustainable. A business will simply cease to exist once costs exceed the value of benefits to consumers.

But in the public sector normal economic laws do not apply. There is a higher tolerance for fiscal inefficiency because benefits are not always measured by consumer choices. There is also an element of public value.

Thirty years ago, mass transit accounted for six percent of daily trips in the Puget Sound region. After years of massive public subsidies, mass transit today accounts for less than four percent of daily trips.

The continued push for more mass transit and light rail funding in the face of a declining share of daily travel indicates that mass transit planning is based more on political ideology than on measurable results.

In transportation policy, public value should be measured by freedom of mobility and traffic relief for the public. Policymakers can keep the space between costs and benefits small by separating projects that provide these values from projects that do not.

Policy Analysis

European and U.S. transit systems provide good contrasting examples of how economic concepts apply in transportation.

Many people believe European countries have highly successful public transportation networks and one of the most-cited systems is in Switzerland. Switzerland lies in the center of Europe and is an important transportation hub for both freight and passenger traffic throughout the continent. The Swiss system is successful, not because of the amount of service or infrastructure, but primarily because it has certain demographic and economic characteristics that induce market demand.

In other words, there is an existing market with a natural customer base and Swiss policymakers respond with proportional public infrastructure spending. As a result, mode share, ridership and fare box recovery are high.

In the United States, transit resources are distributed in just the opposite way.

Under the "build it, and they will come" theory, many policymakers think that increasing the supply of transit will somehow automatically create more public demand. This speculative model fails because most U.S. cities do not posses the economic or demographic characteristics that create enough voluntary consumers for public transit.

Using the economic principles of supply and demand shows that building excess transit capacity before there is an equal amount of willingness to use it leads to an underperforming system. As a result, mode share, ridership and fare box recovery in U.S. mass transit systems are typically low.

Recommendations

1) Use consumer demand to prioritize projects and spending, proportionally. Until the 1970s, state leaders pursued a policy of increasing road capacity adequately to meet the growing mobility needs of Washington's drivers. Over the last three decades, however, policymakers have divided transportation funding between subsidized mass transit and public roads. This approach has not worked.

When prioritizing transportation projects, policymakers should use consumer demand to determine public spending, not the other way around. Applying these time-tested economic principles to transportation policy will improve people's mobility and reduce traffic congestion.

2) Adopt a policy of fixing chokepoints and strategic increases in road capacity as the most effective ways to end traffic gridlock and allow citizens more freedom of movement. Focusing on roadway chokepoints and interchange bottlenecks is the most cost-effective way to get traffic moving. This approach has less impact on the environment, and helps alleviate many people's concern that road building contributes to urban sprawl.

4. Freight Mobility

Recommendations

1. Create a freight budget account for freight-specific projects.

2. Increase heavy rail capacity to allow medium and long range freight distribution greater ability to shift from roads to rail.

3. Create freight-only lanes and corridors to support rapid pass-through for long range and local freight distribution.

Background

Freight mobility plays a significant economic role in any transportation policy but ironically, the current spending strategy used by policymakers is an obstacle to improving the efficiency of movement of goods around the state.

Most of the time, through various mechanisms, the freight industry pays a disproportionate share of taxes to fund transportation projects. Yet very little of the money goes to fund freight-specific infrastructure. The industry is forced to rely on projects that prioritize other transportation areas. The theory is, "what's good for one mode is good for all modes."

The problem is that transportation spending is based on other agendas rather than congestion relief. As a result, the cost of bringing goods to market rises and consumers end up paying more for products.

Sound Transit's East Link proposal is a good example. Reconfiguring the center lanes across Interstate 90 (I-90) for light rail, as agency officials propose, would not only fail to reduce traffic congestion, it would, according to the state Department of Transportation, worsen traffic congestion by 25 percent.[13]

Drivers of freight vehicles would suffer the most from this policy. During the morning peak drive, the number of truck drivers able to cross into Seattle would drop by 24 percent. Leaving Seattle during the afternoon peak drive, truck drivers would see a 19 percent reduction in capacity.[14]

A policy of linking public demand and traffic relief to spending would require Sound Transit officials to think in a different direction. The agency should keep the two center lanes as a reversible HOV and freight and transit corridor, and continue re-striping the outer roadway to create the additional lane in each direction, as already approved by the Federal Highway Administration. Because the center lanes are already a reversible HOV, freight and transit corridor, no light rail should be added to the bridge, and then the new lanes in the outer roadways would not need to be restricted.

Policy Analysis

Sound Transit could easily increase the I-90 bridge's freight and vehicle carrying capacity, and reduce congestion, without any additional infrastructure.

Instead, Sound Transit continues to plan for light rail across I-90 that would increase traffic congestion by 25 percent. Because I-90 is the only direct east/west corridor connecting Washington's ports to the rest of the country, this plan will result in negative economic impacts to the freight industry and ultimately to consumers.

According to the Federal Highway Administration, it costs the freight industry $32 dollars for every hour of delay. In 2004, that amounted to about $7.8 billion dollars nationally. That means the cost of getting goods to market adds nearly $8 billion dollars to consumer prices, all directly attributable to traffic congestion.

Combined with rising fuel prices and the potential of added congestion for passenger cars, the cost to consumers is even greater.

Recommendations

1) Create a freight budget account for freight-specific projects. In most cases this will not require new tax revenue because the freight industry already pays significant fees and taxes to fund transportation projects.

2) Increase heavy rail capacity to allow medium and long range freight distribution greater ability to shift from roads to rail. Improving the rail line through Stampede Pass and building more regional rail capacity will reduce shipping costs and incentivize the shift of freight movement from roads to rail.

3) Create freight-only lanes and corridors to support rapid pass-through for long range and local freight distribution. The new corridors would be tolled and the trucking industry would likely experience lower overall shipping costs, because of the reduced traffic delay in getting goods to consumers.

5. Public/Private Partnerships

Recommendations

1. Remove policy barriers that prevent private companies from contributing resources and entering into public partnerships.

2. End the public transit monopoly by allowing private companies to bid for services on existing and proposed transit routes.

3. Do not allow local transit agencies to use government subsidies to take business away from private citizens.

Background

Using the Public/Private Partnership concept (PPP), policymakers can find effective ways to fund new projects, and to maintain the current transportation infrastructure. Compared to the rest of the United States, however, Washington policymakers have been slow to embrace the PPP strategy.

These partnerships can take many forms. According to the National Council for Public-Private Partnerships, there are about a dozen types. They can range from mostly private to mostly public, and several types incorporate a balance of both characteristics.

There are many benefits to the public associated with a PPP. They leverage private dollars for public use, shift risk from taxpayers to the private sector, and lower overall project costs.

Other factors like public oversight, asset ownership, long-term maintenance, liability and labor, will determine what type of PPP fits best in a given situation. In Washington, these issues have been treated as obstacles and have been used by political opponents to prevent partnerships from forming. Yet these objections have been addressed by other states through their adoption of various types of partnerships. Undoubtedly, these concerns are important, but they should not deter policymakers from providing the public with the benefits of a Public/Private Partnership.

Using the PPP concept, a group of businesses in Pierce County have joined forces to pool financial and construction related resources to build and finance projects. Without the support of the partnership, it is unlikely there would be enough public money to build the projects for the benefit of Pierce County residents.

Partnering with the private sector is one way to increase financial resources and get roads built. Otherwise, funding problems become insurmountable, roads are not built and our road system continues to deteriorate. Public/Private Partnerships have a proven track record across the United States and should be embraced by public officials in Washington.

As mentioned earlier, 30 years ago mass transit accounted for six percent of daily trips in the Puget Sound region. After years of massive public subsidies (since 1960, federal, state and local governments have paid out more than $385 billion to transit systems nationwide[15]), mass transit today accounts for less than four percent of daily trips.

Even as the public funding devoted to mass transit increases in Washington, its share of total daily trips continues to fall each year. This is in line with national trends.[16] In spite of these trends, transit advocates continually push for new spending on government-operated buses and rail.

The continued push for more funding in the face of a declining share of daily travel indicates that mass transit planning is based more on political ideology than on measurable results.

A study by the American Enterprise Institute-Brookings Joint Center for Regulatory Studies sums up the situation well:

> "Transportation policy is largely shaped by entrenched political forces. The forces that have led to inefficient prices and service, excessive labor costs, bloated bureaucracies, and construction-cost overruns promise more of the same for the future."[17]

The primary reason mass transit in Washington is so inefficient is that it operates within a culture of monopoly. Insulated transit bureaucracies have little incentive to change and improve. No one in a position of responsibility loses his job when a transit agency's customer base shrinks. On the contrary, transit agency employment tends to increase as budgets grow and ridership share declines.

Privatization and public-private partnerships in transit can help alleviate the performance failures in the current system by introducing competition and price transparency. Hundreds of mass transit systems throughout the United States contract out some portion of their services.[18] More than one-third of the 500 state, regional and local government agencies that receive aid from the Federal Transit Administration contract out 25 percent or more of their transit services.[19]

Policy Analysis

Proponents of mass transit say it will relieve traffic congestion, save the environment and foster community values such as neighborliness and small-town charm.[20] Yet this is not happening. Congestion continues to worsen in America's large cities, and transportation spending continues to escalate.

The best solution is to allow private companies to bid for existing and proposed transit routes. Currently there are more than 100 private companies licensed to offer various auto transportation services in Washington, but they are barred by law from entering the public transit market.[21] Many of these companies have the ability and desire to provide high-quality transit services to the public in urban and rural areas, if local governments would allow them to do so.

Private companies available for transit services

Private companies are capable of offering improved service to transit riders in the region. For example, the owner of Airporter Shuttle/Bellair Charters, based in Ferndale, has expressed strong interest in providing three-county bus service.

His fleet of buses already serves the entire geographic area, reflecting a tremendous amount of experience and knowledge about commuting patterns and travel needs. Yet county transit agencies, not wishing to face competition, do not support private contracting under the legislature's expanded service program.

The service benefits available through competitive contracting are substantial. A national study by the Transportation Research Board of the National Research Council found that:

> "The main reasons transit systems contract for service, according to transit managers, are to reduce costs and increase flexibility to introduce new services… Half the general managers of transit systems that currently contract reported that reducing costs, increasing cost-efficiency, and introducing new services are the most important reasons for contracting. About one-third rated as important the desire to create a more competitive and flexible environment."[22]

A good example is the Federal Transit Administration's new rule requiring that special shuttle bus services to public events be provided by private contractors if they are available. In 2007, the University of Washington paid King County Metro $500,000 to carry fans to Husky home games. County bus drivers like the arrangement because it means guaranteed overtime and high pay. If allowed, however, a private company not bound by government unions, such as Seattle-based Starline Luxury Coaches, could provide the same service to football fans at much less cost to taxpayers.[23]

Local leaders ignore national evidence and experience by blocking private contracting from being part of their plan.

Contracting out transit services in other states

Other states show how market forces can be tapped to benefit the traveling public. In 2005, Michigan required local transportation authorities to allow private carriers to bid on services funded through regional transportation programs.[24]

The Michigan law also prohibits transit agencies from duplicating services and routes already provided by private carriers. Transit agencies cannot use government subsidies to take over the business of private carriers.

Washingtonians would directly benefit from private companies competing for mass transit routes and services. Often the expansion of public transit agency budgets is more about empire building and creating more public sector jobs than providing good service to the public at lower cost.

Recommendations

1) Remove barriers that prevent private companies from contributing resources and entering into public partnerships. Through public/private partnerships, the state can leverage private sector resources to build new infrastructure, reduce project costs and manage risk. These partnerships have a proven track record across the United States and should be embraced by public officials.

2) End the public transit monopoly by allowing private companies to bid for services on existing and proposed transit routes. Expanding competition, price transparency and public-private partnerships in transit in Washington would reduce cost and improve service to the traveling public.

3) Do not allow local transit agencies to use government subsidies to take business away from private citizens. Public transit agencies not only work to preserve their own monopolies, but often seek to take business away from private carriers. Washington should follow Michigan's example by prohibiting local transit agencies from using tax subsidies to duplicate routes served by private carriers.

6. Competitive Contracting

Recommendations

1. Establish clear oversight guidelines for managing any new competitive contracting system.

2. Encourage an atmosphere of healthy competition where private companies compete with state employees and other contractors to perform public work, like highway maintenance.

3. End state funding for research designed to derail the competitive contracting process.

Background

In 2002, the Washington legislature passed the Personnel System Reform Act which, among other things, allows state agencies to competitively contract for services historically provided by state employees.

The competitive contracting provision of the Act, which took effect July 2005, offers new flexibility to state transportation managers facing tight budgets and the urgent need to maintain service levels while reducing overall cost. In other states, competitive contracting is used routinely to boost the quality of services, while gaining the best value for taxpayers.

In Washington, highway maintenance is one area of government that would benefit greatly from competitive contracting.[25] An independent audit commissioned by the legislature in 1998 estimated that competitive contracting for highway maintenance would save state taxpayers up to $250 million a year, without reducing the high level of service expected by motorists.[26]

The state highway maintenance program covers nearly 18,000 lane miles of state highways, ten major mountain passes, 45 rest areas and dozens of other transportation-related systems. Basic maintenance operations include road repair, roadside and landscape maintenance, snow and ice control, rest area operations and many others.

Policy Analysis

The findings of the legislature's audit reflect the generally positive experiences other states have had with contracting out. These states use highway maintenance contracting to increase flexibility, ensure high quality and reduce cost in keeping up vital highway infrastructure. Similarly, competitive bidding would allow Washington policymakers to serve the public while getting the most out of scarce transportation dollars.

Competitive bidding does not mean privatization. In other states public employees compete for, and often win, competitions to perform government work. It is competition, not privatization, that achieves higher efficiency by allowing managers to choose the most cost-effective option while delivering improved services. Even when government workers provide a given public service, the very possibility of competition drives down costs and encourages excellence.

In a government agency the size and scope of the Department of Transportation – it is larger than most businesses in the state – one would reasonably expect there to be areas where its work could be done more efficiently.

Long-standing programs in states like Massachusetts, Texas, Florida and Virginia demonstrate that competition for highway maintenance can be effectively implemented with minimal impact on state workers and significant improvement in cost savings and work quality.[27]

Recommendations

1) Establish clear oversight guidelines for managing any new competitive contracting system. Key to the success of any competitive contracting program is strong oversight and a transparent contract award process. State managers can enhance public support by building on the practical experiences of other states in designing oversight and accountability into any contracting program.

2) Encourage an atmosphere of healthy competition where private companies compete with state employees and other contractors to perform public work like highway maintenance. By rewarding state employees for good work, and incorporating the best innovations of the private sector, competitive contracting would build morale and enhance the culture of excellence within the Department of Transportation. Based on the successful experiences of other states, highway maintenance is a good place for the Department to start a vigorous contracting program.

3) End state funding for research designed simply to derail the competitive contracting process. Efforts by Department of Transportation staff have attempted to cast a negative light on the competitive contracting process. Considering the proven success of competition and contracting across the nation, state managers should avoid wasting resources on research that has already been done elsewhere.

7. Sound Transit

Recommendations

1. Hold a public vote on whether Sound Transit should collect taxes beyond the ten year limit of its original plan, based on the agency's performance in fulfilling promises made to voters in 1996.

2. Require Sound Transit to maintain its promise to voters by rolling back phase one taxes.

3. Require that Phase One of Sound Transit Light Rail be completed and its effectiveness measured before more ambitious light rail projects are considered.

4. Adopt Bus Rapid Transit (BRT) as a more effective alternative to light rail.

Background

In 1996, voters in parts of King, Pierce and Snohomish counties created a new transit agency, Sound Transit, and entrusted it with new tax revenues based on a detailed ten year plan of what the agency would provide to the public in that timeframe. A comparison between what was proposed and the reality ten years later shows Sound Transit has failed to build the system it promised to voters.

Follow-up reports find that promoters of the ballot measure used planning assumptions that were overly optimistic, which made the project appear more acceptable to voters.[28] The ridership figures given to the public were inaccurate, and were based on unrealistic predictions that have not been realized.

The cost figures given to voters also turned out to be wrong. Today, the agency keeps its spending within its tax revenues only by drastically cutting back on promised services. In addition, operating costs for the system are much higher than voters were told they would be, and are higher than many transit services in other parts of the country.[29]

In 2007, the State Auditor's Office found that Sound Transit has substantially failed to deliver what voters authorized with the passage of Sound Move.[30]

Sound Transit also promised voters in 1996 that if a second phase was ever rejected, the agency would roll back phase one taxes to cover only debt and operations and maintenance costs.[31]

Since voters rejected ST2, through the defeat of Proposition 1 in November 2007, Sound Transit must roll back ST1 taxes to operation and maintenance levels. Sound Transit officials are planning to propose another ST2 program that will contain full ST1 taxes, so they are intending to violate the taxpayer protection clause voters approved for their agency in 1996.

Most importantly, Sound Transit leaders show little regard for what people think when they say they will not hold a vote on whether they should collect taxes beyond the ten-year limit of the original plan. Sound Transit lawyers assert that the agency's claim on tax revenue is not limited to ten years, as the 1996 ballot measure implied, but is permanent. According to their interpretation, Sound Transit can collect taxes forever.

Policy Analysis

Voters should have a say in how their transit taxes are used. The public's judgment should be based on what has been achieved since the project started. The following section compares the promises Sound Transit supporters made to voters during the 1996 campaign with the reality of what the agency achieved by 2008. Quotations are taken from official Sound Transit documents, the voters' pamphlet, and from "YES RTA" campaign material given to voters at the time.

Promise: "Implement a 10-year regional transit system plan."
Reality: Sound Transit is far short of providing the system plan promised in 1996. The agency has cut back on several service projects and unilaterally extended its program to at least 13 years.

Promise: "After 10 years, any addition to the system will have to be voter approved, assuring accountability and satisfaction."
Reality: Sound Transit has significantly reduced its original plans while collecting full tax revenues. The agency says it has no plans to seek voter approval for these changes.

Promise: "Cost of the plan is $3.9 billion."
Reality: The cost of Sound Transit today tops $15 billion and continues to rise, even after large cut-backs in service. Sound Transit supporters now say the costs they gave voters in 1996 were only "placeholder" figures.[32]

Promise: "Public transportation will have the capacity to move 40 percent of the region's commuters to their jobs."
Reality: Sound Transit and other forms of mass transit perform well below this capacity. Also, creating capacity is not the same as moving people. Today, over 95 percent of daily trips are in private automobiles.

Promise: "53,000 cars out of rush hour traffic everyday."
Reality: There are *more* cars in rush hour traffic today than in 1996. Annual data on traffic increases does not show a reduction of 53,000 cars a day.

Promised: "No one area will subsidize another."
Reality: Sound Transit is showing indications of reversing this policy. Its Citizen Oversight Committee says, "[Subarea equity] remains a serious impediment to the development of a regional system and requires an in-depth examination as to its continued usefulness."[33]

Promise: "Regional Express will swell ridership to 390,000 trips per day."
Reality: Sound Transit has not met the ridership figures promised in 1996. In 2007, Sound Transit averaged a total system ridership of only 49,300 trips per day, well below what was promised.

Promise: Nine round-trip Sound Transit trains between Seattle and Tacoma.
Reality: Sound Transit provides five round-trip rail trips between Seattle and Tacoma, nearly half of what voters were promised.

Promise: Upgrading existing Burlington Northern Santa Fe track for use by Sound Transit would be $470 million.
Reality: The true cost for upgrading the track turned out to be $942 million.[34]

Promise: A new 21-mile light rail line for $2.3 billion in ten years.
Reality: Sound Transit is building a 14-mile light rail for $2.7 billion, the last mile of which will cost $225 million.

Promise: Sound Transit light rail would be completed by 2006 and carry 42,000 daily riders.
Reality: Sound Transit light rail ridership in 2006 was zero, as it was in 2007, and will be in 2008. Light rail service will not be ready until 2009, at the earliest.

Promise: "40 percent of operating costs will be covered by fare revenues." "Fares will cover a growing share of the operating costs."
Reality: The opposite is happening. In 2007, fare revenues covered only 12.8 percent of operating costs, less than half of what Sound Transit officials promised.[35]

Promise: "Any second phase capital program which continues local taxes for financing will require voter approval within the RTA District. If voters decide not to extend the system, the RTA will roll back the tax rate to a level sufficient to pay off the outstanding bonds and operate and maintain the investments made as part of Sound Move."[36]
Reality: Despite the defeat of ST2, Sound Transit is already planning a second phase capital program using Sound Move taxes.

The data shows that Sound Transit has consistently failed to fulfill its commitments to the people of the region. The agency regularly and unilaterally changes its definition of success, usually by cutting services, while continuing to collect full taxes from the public. The agency's record over the last twelve years more than justifies a new vote.

In addition, Sound Transit should not move forward with new light rail plans until the present, shortened line is completed and evaluated. The Link Light Rail project broke ground in late 2003 and is scheduled to finish its initial phase in 2009, connecting downtown Seattle to SeaTac International Airport. Agency managers want to then extend light rail to Everett, Tacoma and the Seattle eastside suburbs. Such ambitious plans are not justified until the net benefits of the initial light rail segment, if any, are known.

Recommendations

1) Hold a public vote on whether Sound Transit should collect taxes beyond the ten year limit of its original plan, based on the agency's performance in fulfilling promises made to voters in 1996. Voters have not received what Sound Transit promised to them under the original ten-year plan. Instead, services have been cut back and costs have soared. The elected officials of Sound Transit's board should allow voters to have a say about whether the agency should continue collecting full taxes beyond the ten years authorized by the 1996 vote.

2) Require Sound Transit to maintain its promise to voters by rolling back phase one taxes. Sound Transit must maintain its promise to voters by rolling back its first phase tax rate. Voters rejected the agency's second phase capital program, which should have triggered the taxpayer protection clause the voters authorized in 1996.

3) Require that Phase One of Sound Transit Light Rail be completed and its effectiveness measured before more ambitious light rail projects are considered. Before more property is seized and torn up, and billions more of taxpayer dollars committed on extending the line, policymakers should perform an independent cost/benefit analysis on the 1996 plan's effectiveness and on any future expansion plans.

4) Adopt Bus Rapid Transit (BRT) as a more effective alternative to light rail. Buses operating in a dedicated travel lane provide frequent, flexible and high quality service at much less capital cost than building fixed light rail. BRT service creates less impact on the environment, less disruption to neighborhoods and functions at significantly lower operating cost than rail. Policymakers and transportation officials should adopt BRT services as a more cost-effective alternative to meeting Washington's mass transit needs.

8. Tolling Policy and HOT Lanes

Recommendations

1. Use toll roads and High Occupancy Toll (HOT) lanes to expand road capacity and reduce traffic congestion without increasing the general tax burden.

2. Tolls should only be implemented on new capacity or to replace an existing facility.

3. If the goal of placing a toll on a roadway is to manage demand, the tolled facility must provide drivers with a non-tolled alternative.

4. Toll revenue should be constitutionally protected from general fund spending.

5. Money from tolls should be spent only on the road where the tolls were collected.

Background

Pricing transportation infrastructure can help both policymakers and citizens in two ways. Implemented properly, tolls can provide revenue to expand the state's transportation system. This is the model Washington is most familiar with. Tolls have been used to pay for the Evergreen Floating Bridge and most recently, the expanded Tacoma Narrows Bridge. Typically, once the facility is paid for, the tolls are removed.

Pricing roadways has also been used to manage demand. Sometimes called "congestion pricing" or "demand management," tolls complete the economic equation between supply and demand by adding price.

Washington officials recently opened a form of congestion pricing through a pilot project on Highway 167 near Renton. For a fee, single occupant vehicles (SOV) can now choose to use the existing High Occupancy Vehicle (HOV) lane. Traffic volumes are monitored and, as congestion increases on Highway 167, the toll for a SOV driving in the HOV lane also rises. Likewise, as congestion decreases, the toll becomes cheaper.

These High Occupancy Toll (HOT) lanes are the best way to implement a congestion pricing system because it offers drivers a choice. They can either pay the premium to use the new capacity that was otherwise restricted, or they can choose the existing system.

Using tolls to manage congestion, however, is a major shift in the way tolls have been used in Washington and it raises significant philosophical, equity and fairness questions.

Policy Analysis

In a recent statewide Washington Policy Center poll, we asked citizens their thoughts on some of these issues. The following tables illustrate the results.[37]

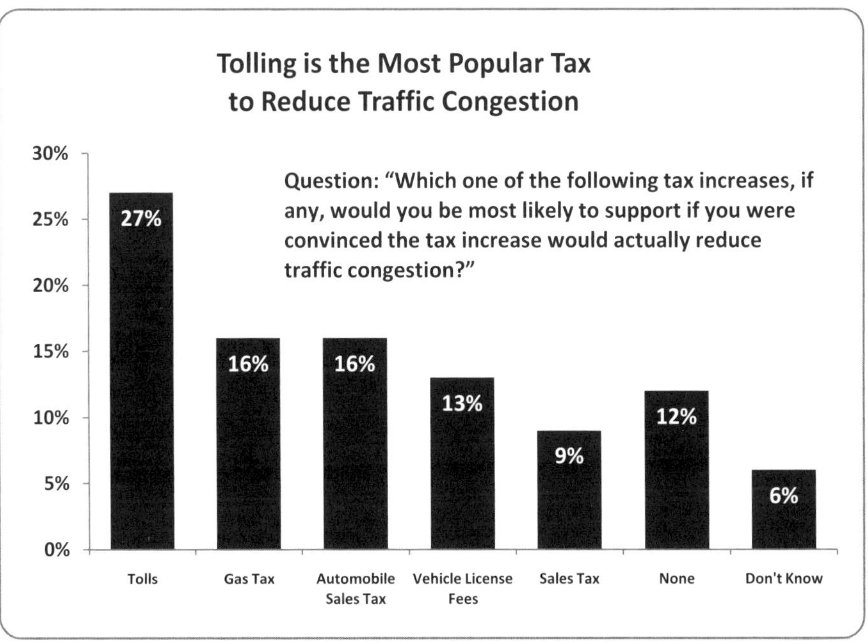

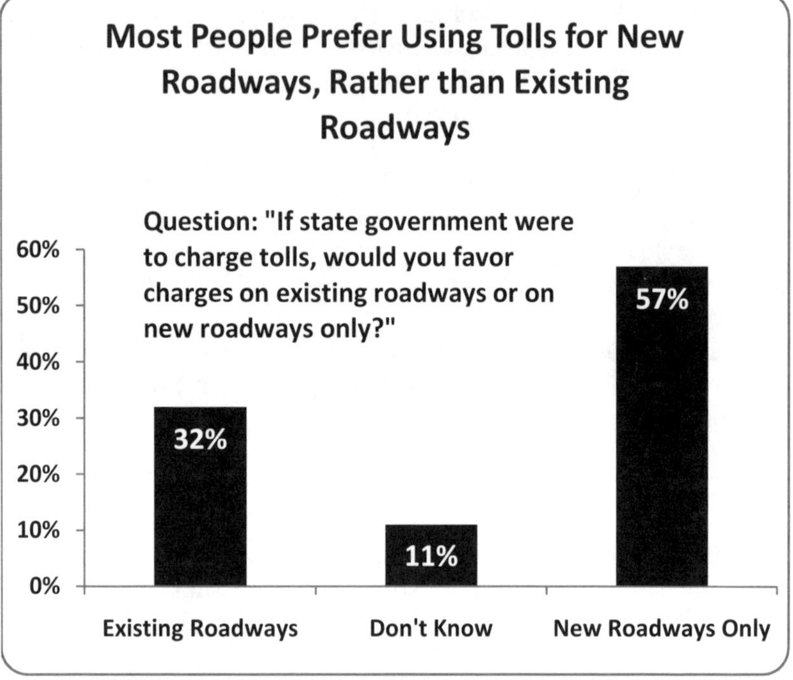

Most People Prefer Using Tolls for New Roadways, Rather than Existing Roadways
Question: "If state government were to charge tolls, would you favor charges on existing roadways or on new roadways only?"
60%
50%
40%
30%
20%
10%
0%
32%
11%
57%
Existing Roadways
Don't Know
New Roadways Only

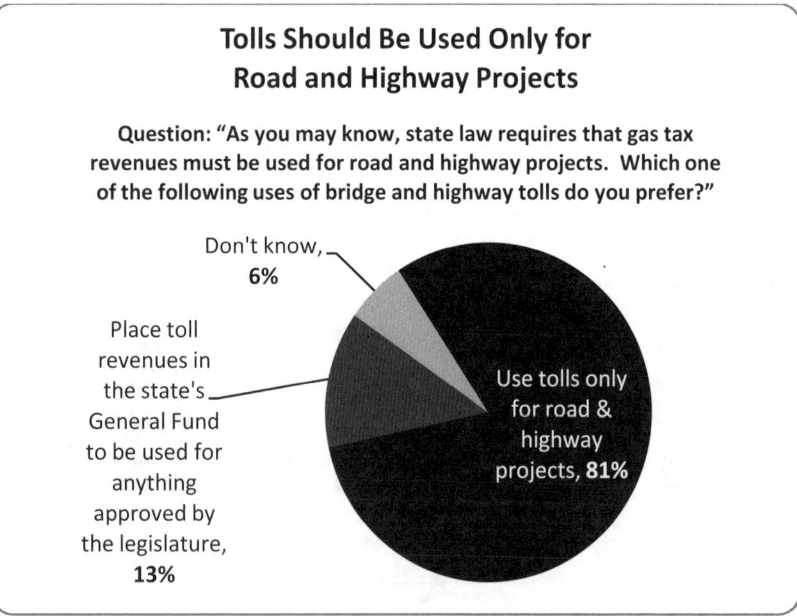

Tolls Should Be Used Only for Road and Highway Projects
Question: "As you may know, state law requires that gas tax revenues must be used for road and highway projects. Which one of the following uses of bridge and highway tolls do you prefer?"
Don't know, 6%
Place toll revenues in the state's General Fund to be used for anything approved by the legislature, 13%
Use tolls only for road & highway projects, 81%

According to the survey results, the public generally supports tolling over every other funding policy, as long as the toll has a measurable relationship with relieving traffic congestion.

It is not surprising that taxpayers favor tolls, since most people see them as the most direct type of user fee. But the public does have legitimate concerns about how these fees are implemented and how they are spent.

When compared with general fund spending, an overwhelming 81 percent of the public says that toll revenue should be used only for road and highway purposes. And a majority (57 percent) prefers tolls on *new* roadways only, rather than charges on existing lanes that have already been paid for with other taxes.

Toll roads and HOT lanes are not the universal solution to Washington's transportation needs, and when tolls are used they should be based on the principles recommended below.

Revenue from gasoline, licensing and similar taxes and fees will always make up the bulk of transportation funding. Revenue from toll and HOT lanes, however, offers an innovative and flexible way for transportation officials to increase road capacity and relieve congestion at key chokepoints around the state.

Recommendations

1) Use toll roads and High Occupancy Toll (HOT) lanes to expand road capacity and reduce traffic congestion without increasing the general tax burden. Recent research and the experience of other states and countries indicates that toll roads and HOT Lanes can provide an affordable, workable solution to traffic congestion. Washington state faces problems with congestion similar to those in California.

Close study of toll roads in San Diego, and the valuable experience gained from Washington's SR 167 pilot project, will provide policymakers with a good idea of how such highways can benefit drivers in Washington.

2) Tolls should only be implemented on new capacity or to replace an existing facility. Converting existing HOV lanes to HOT lanes qualifies because it adds new capacity for single occupant vehicles. HOT lanes also preserve the choice for drivers to pay the toll or use the existing system.

Tolling on existing roadways should be prohibited, since taxpayers already paid for the road. Tolling existing infrastructure should be prohibited for the same reason.

3) If the goal of placing a toll on a roadway is to manage demand, the tolled facility must provide drivers with a non-tolled alternative. Imposing tolls to limit how much people drive or to force people out of their cars restricts freedom of mobility. Providing a non-tolled alternative provides drivers a choice and prevents the state from using price as a punishment.

4) Toll revenue should be constitutionally protected from general fund spending. Approved in 1944, the 18th amendment to the Washington constitution ensures gas tax revenues are used only for highways. Toll revenue should be dedicated in the same way. If only drivers are paying the toll, then only drivers should receive the benefits.

5) Money from tolls should be spent only on the road where the tolls were collected. Only the new capacity or the replaced facility where a toll is collected should benefit from the revenue. Applying tolls to a broadly defined corridor is not fair to the drivers who paid the toll. The priority for using toll revenue should follow this order:

1. Debt on the new roadway;
2. Maintenance and operations of the new roadway;
3. Expansion of the new roadway.

9. Light Rail Transit

> ## Recommendation
>
> 1. Policymakers and the public should consider whether diverting significant transportation taxes toward light rail transit and away from other programs and services is worth the cost.

Background

Often, transportation officials try to estimate, with little success, how light rail transit would perform in Washington. Through unrealistic modeling and ambitious assumptions, they typically underestimate operating and capital costs and overestimate revenue and passenger demand.

For example, in 1996, Sound Transit officials in the Seattle area promised its first light rail segment would be completed by 2006 and would cost about $5 billion.[38] Today, Sound Transit says the total cost is about $15 billion and the segment will not be finished until around 2020.[39]

Analyzing the performance of existing light rail systems sidesteps these guesses and offers a factual picture.

There are six light rail systems on the West Coast that have been operating since at least 1995: in Los Angeles, Portland, Sacramento, San Jose, San Diego and San Francisco. Their performance over the last ten years results in the following key findings:

- Light rail systems on the West Coast serve only about 2 percent of the workforce in the service areas of the six systems.

- On average, these systems only remove between 0.39 percent and 1.1 percent of cars from the roadway.

- On average, West Coast light rail systems require taxpayer subsidies to pay for 73 percent of operations and 100 percent of capital improvements per year.

- The average cost to add one additional rider to the light rail systems on the West Coast is between $82,285 and $242,014 per rider.

- Attracting a new rider to light rail costs 16 to 47 times as much as attracting a new rider to a traditional bus system.

- When accounting for passenger demand, light rail on the West Coast is 12 percent more expensive to operate than bus service.

- In the ten years between 1996 and 2005, the public subsidy (operating costs only) for all light rail systems in the U.S. grew from $250 million to $729 million, an increase of 191 percent.

- The relationship between light rail and any environmental or economic development advantages is so slight that their use on influencing policy decisions should be proportionally small.

Policy Analysis

Examining the six existing light rail systems in major West Coast cities helps residents understand what they can expect from spending on similar systems in Washington.

The most relatively efficient systems on the West Coast are in San Francisco and Portland. They move the most people for the least cost and beat the six-city average in most cases.

By a large margin, the worst-performing system is in San Jose. In every category, its performance is worse than the six-city average.

Regardless of how each system ranks, however, the overall performance of all six light rail systems is poor. The experience of these systems reveals a very large gap between public costs and public benefits.

Even the best-performing light rail systems require a large taxpayer subsidy and have little or no effect on reducing traffic congestion. On average, light rail is more expensive to operate than normal bus service.

Recommendation

1) Policymakers and the public should consider whether diverting significant transportation taxes toward light rail transit and away from other programs and services is worth the cost. Based on the data, this analysis concludes that it is not. Spending significant amounts of transportation tax revenue on projects that have no effect in reducing congestion inevitably makes traffic worse.

Additional Resources from Washington Policy Center

"Transportation Taxes are up, but Traffic Congestion is Worse," by Michael Ennis, May 2008.

"The Facts on Light Rail: A Comparative Analysis of Light Rail Systems in Six West Coast Cities," by Michael Ennis, April 2008.

"Despite Claims, Gas Tax Projects Are Not on Track," by Michael Ennis, March 2008.

"Next Stop on Transportation," by Michael Ennis, January 2008.

"Five Principles of Responsible Transportation Policy," by Michael Ennis, January 2008.

"Washington Policy Center Poll Shows Nearly 70% of Voters are Unhappy with the State's Performance on Reducing Congestion," by Michael Ennis, January 2008.

"The Value of Public/Private Partnerships," by Michael Ennis, February, 2008.

"The Imbalance of Roads and Transit," by Michael Ennis, September 2007.

"Light Rail and Interstate 90," by Michael Ennis, July, 2007.

"Cost Exceeds Benefits in Sound Transit's Light Rail Expansion," by Michael Ennis, 2007.

"Your Transportation Tax Burden," by Michael Ennis, April 2007.

"The Cost of Sound Transit," by Michael Ennis, 2006.

"If the Roads and Transit Package Fails, What Next?" by Michael Ennis, 2007.

"More Bucks for Sound Transit Won't Mean Fewer Cars on the Road," by Michael Ennis, May 2007.

"The Case for Public/Private Partnerships in Transportation Planning," by Michael Ennis, January, 2007.

"Undermining Trust in Government: Sound Transit's Failed Promises," by Paul Guppy, June, 2006.

"A Guide to Transit Now," by Michael Ennis, September 2006.

"Tolls as a Tool - A Practical Way to Relieve Traffic Congestion in Washington," by Paul Guppy and Kelli Aitchison, March, 2005.

"DOT Should Adopt Reforms and Efficiencies Before We Give It More Tax Dollars," by Paul Guppy, April, 2005.

"Initiative 912 Fuels Debate over New Gas Tax," by John Barnes, October, 2005.

"Great Rail Disasters: American Cities Discover that Light Rail Reduces Transit Service," by Randal O'Toole, July, 2005.

"Great Rail Disasters: The Impact of Rail Transit on Urban Livability," by Randal O'Toole, February, 2004.

"Competitive Contracting for Highway Maintenance: Lessons Learned from National Experience," by Geoffrey F. Segal and Eric Montague, January, 2004.

"An Overview of Referendum 51," by Eric Montague, September 2002.

"Roads in the Right Places: A New Plan to Ease Congestion," by Eric Montague, 2001.

"Proven Ways to Pay for Transportation Without Raising Taxes," by Eric Montague, 2001.

"Traffic vs. Kids: How Puget Sound Gridlock Hurts Families," by Jeff Kemp and Paul Guppy, with Dawn Wilson and Kai Hirabayashi, October, 2000.

"Competing for Highway Maintenance: Lessons for Washington State, Parts I & II," by Dennis Lisk, September, 1998 and January, 1999.

---

[1] "1999-2001 Transportation Resource Manual," Joint Transportation Committee.
[2] "2007-2009 Transportation Resource Manual," Joint Transportation Committee.
[3] Inflation was calculated by using the Legislative Evaluation & Accountability Program's (LEAP) inflation calculator (Implicit Price Deflator).
[4] Senate Bill 5412, Washington State Legislature, at www.leg.wa.gov/pub/billinfo/2007-08/Pdf/Bills/Session%20Law%202007/5412-S.SL.pdf.
[5] "Washington Transportation Plan 2007-2026," at www.wsdot.wa.gov/NR/rdonlyres/083D185B-7B1F-49F5-B865-C0A21D0DCE32/0/FinalWTP111406_nomaps.pdf.
[6] Based on 2000 data, at www.fhwa.dot.gov/ctpp/jtw/jtw4.htm.
[7] Ibid.
[8] "Managing and Reducing Congestion in Puget Sound," Performance Audit Report of the Washington State Department of Transportation, Washington State Auditor, October, 2007, at www.sao.wa.gov/reports/auditreports/auditreportfiles/ar1000006.pdf.
[9] "Prevailing Wage Laws Mandate Excessive Costs," Policy Brief 99:33, Washington Research Council, November 29, 1999, at www.researchcouncil.org/Briefs/1999/PB99-33/PrevailingWagePB.htm.
[10] Ibid.
[11] "Leading the Way: A Comprehensive Approach to Reducing Greenhouse Gases in Washington State," Climate Advisory Team, February, 2008, at www.ecy.wa.gov/climatechange/CATdocs/020708_InterimCATreport_final.pdf.
[12] "Modes of Transportation, Vehicle Miles Traveled, 1980 – 2030 (projected)," Washington State Department of Transportation, at www.wsdot.wa.gov/planning/wtp/datalibrary/Modes/milestraveled.htm.
[13] "I-90 Center Roadway Study," WSDOT Projects, Washington State Department of Transportation, July 2006, at www.wsdot.wa.gov/projects/i90/study.
[14] "Part IV: Light Rail and Interstate 90, Sound Transit's Proposal to Place Light Rail Across I-90 will Increase Traffic Congestion," by Michael Ennis, Policy Brief, Washington Policy Center, 2007, at www.washingtonpolicy.org/Centers/transportation/policynote/07_ennis_partiv.html.
[15] "Competition, Not Monopolies, Can Improve Public Transit," by Wendell Cox, Urban Issues, The Heritage Foundation, Washington, D.C., August 2000, at http://www.heritage.org/Research/UrbanIssues/BG1389es.cfm.
[16] According to the United States Census Bureau and the Federal Highway Administration, in 1980 public transit accounted for 6.4 percent of daily commutes. By 1990, that number had fallen to 5.3%, and by 2000 had fallen to 4.7 percent.
[17] "Government Failure in Urban Transportation," by Clifford Winston, American Enterprise Institute-Brookings Joint Center for Regulatory Studies, Washington, D.C., November 2000, page 2, at www.heartland.org.
[18] "Transit Service Contracting in the United States," by Thomas R. Menzies , Jr. and Daniel Boyle, *Transportation Research News*, Number 217, November – December 2001, available through the Transportation Research Board at www.trb.org.
[19] Ibid.

20 "Competition, Not Monopolies, Can Improve Public Transit," by Wendell Cox, Urban Issues, The Heritage Foundation, Washington, D.C., August 2000, at http://www.heritage.org/Research/UrbanIssues/BG1389es.cfm.

21 The Washington Utilities and Transportation Commission licenses companies to provide auto transportation, excursion passenger services, and charter passenger services, see www.wutc.wa.gov.

22 "Contracting for Bus and Demand-Responsive Transit Services: A Survey of U.S. Practice and Experience," Transportation Research Board of the National Research Council, 2001, pages 132-33, at www.onlinepubs.trb.org/onlinepubs/sr/sr258.pdf.

23 "New FTA rules may halt Metro's shuttle service," by Susan Gilmore, *The Seattle Times*, May 10, 2008.

24 Michigan Senate Bill 281, Appropriations: 2005 – 2006 Transportation Budget, Public Act 158 of 2005, Section 710, at www.michiganvotes.org/Legislation.aspx?ID=36568.

25 See "Competing for Highway Maintenance: Lessons for Washington State," Parts I and II, published by Washington Policy Center, September 1998 and January 1999, available at www.washingtonpolicy.org.

26 "Department of Transportation Highways and Rail Programs Performance Audit," prepared for the Joint Legislative Audit Review Committee (JLARC) by Cambridge Systematics, Inc., March 13, 1998.

27 More examples and details are discussed in "Competing for Highway Maintenance: Lessons for Washington State," by Dennis Lisk, January 1999, and, "Competitive Contracting for Highway Maintenance: Lessons Learned from National Experience," by Eric Montague and Geoffrey Segal, January 2004, available at www.washingtonpolicy.org.

28 "Sound Move, Year 8, Review of Progress Toward Achieving a Regional High Capacity Transportation System," Sound Transit Citizens Oversight Panel Report, April 7, 2005, page i, at www.soundtransit.org/pdf/working/cc/COPSoundMoveYear8.pdf.

29 "Citizens' Year-End 2005 Performance Report of Sound Transit," Sound Transit Citizen Oversight Panel, January 19, 2006, at www.soundtransit.org/pdf/working/cc/Year-End_Report_2005.pdf.

30 "Performance Audit Report, Sound Transit Link Light Rail Project," October, 2007, Washington State Auditor's Office, at www.sao.wa.gov/reports/auditreports/auditreportfiles/ar1000005.pdf.

31 "Sound Move – The 10 Year Regional Transit System Plan," as adopted by Sound Transit, May 1996.

32 "University Link Financial Plan," Sound Transit, June 2006.

33 "Citizens' Year-End 2005 Performance Report on Sound Transit," Citizen Oversight Panel, January 19 2006, at www.soundtransit.org/pdf/working/cc/Year-End_Report_2005.pdf.

34 "Sound Move, Year 8, Review of Progress Toward Achieving a Regional High Capacity Transportation System," Sound Transit Citizens Oversight Panel Report, April 7, 2005, page vi, at www.soundtransit.org/pdf/working/cc/COPSoundMoveYear8.pdf.

35 "Quarterly Financial Report, Fourth Quarter, 2007," Sound Transit, December 31, 2007, at www.soundtransit.org/Documents/pdf/about/financial/2007/Q4_2007_Financial_Report.pdf.

36 "Sound Move, Paying for the System," Sound Transit, May 1996.

[37] "2007 Washington Policy Center Traffic Congestion Poll," available at www.washingtonpolicy.org.

[38] "Sound Move, The 10-Year Regional Transit System Plan," Sound Transit, May 1996.

[39] "University Link Financial Plan," Sound Transit, June 2006.

POLICY GUIDE

Michael Ennis is director of the Center for Transportation at Washington Policy Center. Before joining Washington Policy Center, Michael worked for the Washington state Senate and House of Representatives and was formerly a staff assistant for U.S. Senator Slade Gorton. Michael served in the U.S. Army with the 2nd Ranger Battalion and has been active in local government affairs. He earned his Bachelor's Degree from the  University of Washington where he studied Political Science. He also earned his Master's of Public Administration degree from the Daniel J. Evans School of Public Affairs at the University of Washington.

Liv Finne is director of the Center for Education at Washington Policy Center. Liv served as an adjunct scholar for WPC over the last few years. She holds a law degree from Boston University School of Law and a Bachelor's Degree in English and Biology from Wellesley College. She retired from civil litigation practice to raise two children and work as business partner for a small business she owns with her husband. Liv is passionate about improving Washington's education system. 

Carl Gipson is director of the Center for Small Business at Washington Policy Center. Carl also directs technology and telecommunications policy research at WPC. He was formerly director of communications and operations for WPC. Carl holds a Bachelor's Degree in Political Science from Western Washington University. 

Paul Guppy is vice president for research at Washington Policy Center. He is a graduate in Liberal Arts of Seattle University and holds a Master's Degree in American Government and Public Policy from Claremont Graduate University, and a Master's Degree in Political Science from the London School of Economics. He completed higher education programs at the Sorbonne, Paris and at Gonzaga University in Florence, Italy. He served for 12 years in Washington D.C., most of that time as a Legislative Director and Chief of Staff in the United States Congress, before joining WPC in 1998 as vice president for research.

Brandon Houskeeper is a policy analyst with Washington Policy Center and director of WashingtonVotes.org, WPC's legislative information website. Before joining the WPC, Brandon served as the Government Affairs Director for a professional home builders association, bringing with him over six years of experience and understanding of the legislative process at the state and local level. Brandon earned his Bachelor's Degree in Political Science from the University of Washington.

Jason Mercier is director of the Center for Government Reform at Washington Policy Center. Prior to joining WPC, Jason served as Director of Evergreen Freedom Foundation's Economic Policy Center. He is a voting member on the American Legislative Exchange Council's Tax and Fiscal Policy Task Force and is a contributing editor of the Heartland Institute's Budget & Tax News. Jason also serves as Treasurer on the board of the Washington Coalition for Open Government and was an advisor to the 2002 Washington State Tax Structure Committee. He received a Bachelor's Degree in Political Science from Washington State University.

Todd Myers is director of the Center for the Environment at Washington Policy Center. Previously he served as communications director for the Washington State Department of Natural Resources, director of public relations for the Seattle SuperSonics and director of public affairs for the Seattle Mariners. Todd holds a Master's Degree in Russian and International Studies.

Roger Stark, MD, is a health care policy analyst with Washington Policy Center. Dr. Stark graduated from the University of Nebraska College of Medicine and completed his general surgery residency in Seattle and his cardiothoracic residency at the University of Utah. After practicing in Tacoma, he was one of the co-founders of the open-heart surgery program at Overlake Hospital. He retired from private practice in 2001 and served as Board Chair and Executive Director of the Overlake Hospital Foundation. Dr. Stark has been a member of many local and national professional societies. He currently serves on the board of the Washington Liability Reform Coalition, the governing board of Overlake Hospital, and is an active member of the Woodinville Rotary.

Washington Policy Center would also like to thank the following for helping produce *Policy Guide for Washington State, 3rd Edition*:

Justin Bryant and **Lisa Lennick** provided research assistance to Washington Policy Center analysts as part of WPC's Doug and Janet True Internship program during the Spring 2008 academic term.

Kimberly Hendrickson assisted with proofreading and editing.

John Barnes, Communications Director at Washington Policy Center, formatted the book and coordinated its printing and publication.

Our leaders are the region's leaders.

Make a difference, invest in ideas.

Washington Policy Center believes that good ideas, supported by sound research and promoted through publications, public forums, and the media, over time, create an environment in which sound public policy decisions are made.

WPC continues to provide policymakers with innovative, market-based solutions through our research centers:

- *Center for Small Business*
- *Center for the Environment*
- *Center for Transportation*
- *Center for Health Care*

- *Center for Education*
- *Center for Government Reform*
- *WashingtonVotes.org – WPC's free legislative information website*

Policymakers are increasingly looking to the work of WPC for the development of public policy. National and local leaders alike praise the Policy Center's innovative ideas.

As a supporter you will receive high-quality studies, our weekly email updates, and invitations to events, conferences and forums, featuring both national and local public policy experts. For more information, please contact us at 206-937-9691, or visit us at www.washingtonpolicy.org.

Levels of Support

☐	$5,000 Presidents Club	Name: ___________________________
☐	$2,500 Benefactor	Address: _________________________
☐	$1,000 Leadership Council	City: _________ State ______ Zip ______
☐	$500 Patron	Phone: __________________________
☐	$100 Research Circle	Fax/Email: _______________________
☐	$50 Associate	

Please make checks payable to Washington Policy Center or provide credit card here:
Charge my: ☐ Visa ☐ Master Card ☐ AmEx #_____________________
Exp. _________ Signature: _________________________________

Please send to: PO Box 3643, Seattle, WA 98124-3643, fax 206-624-8038
Or visit www.washingtonpolicy.org to join online on our secure website.
Washington Policy Center is a 501(c)(3) non-profit, tax-exempt organization.
(T.I.N. 91-1752769)